Für [illegible]

Danke für Einsatz und Passion

[illegible]

BERND SIEFERT

SWEET
Gold

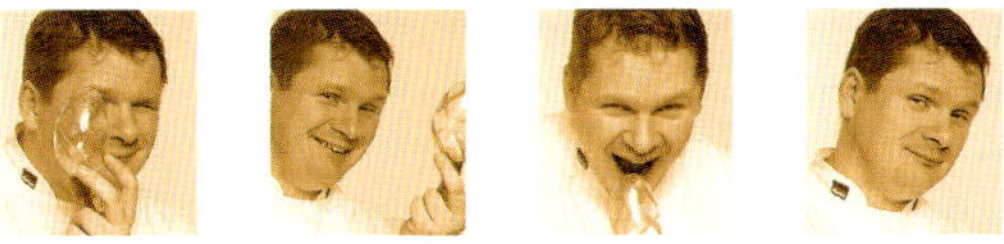

TORTEN / CAKES

DESSERTS

ZUCKER / SUGAR

1

MATTHAES VERLAG GMBH

FOREWORD

Books are my real passion although I had never intended to write one myself. Again and again people asked me to do it and then the publisher Matthaes Verlag approached me with an invitation to write this book. After thinking it over I agreed.

The purpose of this book is to transmit the art of this wonderfully creative craft. If this book succeeds in opening a new chapter in the story of patisserie, I will have achieved my aim. Because it is my wish that our marvellous profession should regain the status it deserves.

Originally we had planned to produce one volume, but over time we discovered that one book was not enough to accommodate in detail the whole spectrum of patisserie and to achieve my aim. Therefore the first volume of this short series contains ideas, recipes, variations and techniques on the subject of cakes, desserts and sugar. I am particularly interested in presenting realisable new creations for professional patissiers and pastry cooks.

The next volume, which I am already working on and which will be published next year, will tell you a lot about marzipan, pralines, ice cream ...

There are two things I would like to point out: Even the best recipes are worth nothing without high-quality ingredients. And secondly: It won't work without a little practice! I had a lot of practice when I was preparing for the World Championship together with my team colleague Manfred Bacher. Our joint victory made the effort worth it.

If you want to know how I arrive at my ideas, I can't give you an answer that will explain everything. But there is one thing: On my travels around the world I try to absorb everything in order to create something new later on, after sifting through the ideas. I have honed this process to a fine art during my time with the "Young Wild Ones".

I have been given the chance to create something new and to add a new book to my extensive collection of books – my own one. I hope you will have just as much fun leafing through the book as I had putting it together.

I usually end my seminars with something my teacher always used to say: "When you go to a professional training event and take away two things and apply just one of them, it will have been worth it." I hope that you can take away a lot from this book, whether you are a pastry cook, a chef, a patissier or a hobby chef or pastry cook with a passion.

Always remember: mastery takes practice, and if you don't succeed at your first attempt, God will have given you a reason to try it again.

Yours

Bernd Siefert
Michelstadt im Odenwald

PS: Why not pay a visit to our homepage: www.cafesiefert.de

VORWORT

Bücher sind meine große Leidenschaft, auch wenn ich selbst nie eines schreiben wollte. Ich wurde von verschiedenen Leuten immer wieder dazu gedrängt, und schließlich kam der Matthaes Verlag auch noch mit einer konkreten Anfrage auf mich zu. Nach einiger Überlegung sagte ich ja.

Ziel des Buchs war, einen Spiegel der Kunst dieses wunderschönen kreativen Handwerks zu vermitteln. Sollte es damit gelingen, ein neues Kapitel im großen Buch der Konditorei aufzuschlagen, so ist mein Ziel erreicht, denn ich wünsche mir, dass dieser wunderschöne Beruf wieder das Ansehen bekommt, das er verdient.

Wenn Sie wissen möchten, wie ich zu meinen Ideen komme, kann ich Ihnen keine umfassende Antwort geben. Nur eines: Auf meinen Reisen in die ganze Welt versuche ich alles aufzunehmen, um es dann später zu filtern und daraus etwas Neues zu schaffen. Dieses Fähigkeit habe ich bei meinen Jungs von den „Jungen Wilden" vervollkommnet.

Ich habe die Chance bekommen, etwas Neues zu schaffen und meiner umfangreichen Büchersammlung ein neues Buch hinzuzufügen – mein eigenes. Ich hoffe, dass es Ihnen genau so viel Spaß macht, in dem Buch zu blättern, wie es mir gemacht hat, es zu erarbeiten.

Wir wollten ursprünglich einen Band machen, aber im Laufe der Zeit hat sich herausgestellt, dass ein Buch nicht ausreicht, um das ganzes Konditoreispektrum in seiner Ausführlichkeit unterzubringen und mein Ziel zu erreichen. So enthält der erste Band dieser kleinen Reihe Ideen, Rezepte, Variationen und Techniken zum Thema Torten, Desserts und Zucker. Es ist mir ein großes Anliegen, realisierbare neue Kreationen für den Profibereich der Konditorei und Patisserie vorzustellen.

Im nächsten Band, an dem ich bereits arbeite und der im nächsten Jahr erscheint, erfahren Sie vieles zum Thema Marzipan, Pralinen, Eis ...

Zwei Dinge möchte ich hervorheben: Ohne hochwertige Zutaten sind auch die besten Rezepte nichts wert. Und ohne etwas Übung geht es nicht! Viel Übung bekam ich, als ich zusammen mit meinem Teamkollegen Manfred Bacher die Weltmeisterschaft vorbereitete. Unser gemeinsamer Sieg hat die Mühe gelohnt.

Ich beende meine Seminare immer mit einem Satz, den einer meiner Lehrer stets sagte: „Wenn du auf eine Fortbildung gehst und zwei Dinge mitnimmst und davon eines umsetzt, hat es sich schon bezahlt gemacht." Ich hoffe, dass Sie vieles aus diesem Buch mitnehmen können, ob Sie nun Konditor, Koch, Patissier oder auch passionierter Hobbykoch oder Hobbykonditor sind.

Denken Sie daran, es ist noch nie ein Meister von Himmel gefallen, und wenn es beim ersten Versuch nicht gelingt, hat der Herrgott Ihnen einen Grund gegeben, es nochmals zu probieren.

Ihr

BERND SIEFERT

Michelstadt im Odenwald

PS: Schauen Sie doch mal auf unsere Homepage: www.cafesiefert.de

GRUSSWORTE

GREETINGS

Ein Vorwort für ein Buch zu schreiben ist so was, wie Pate stehen für ein neues Werk.

Es gibt verschiedene Wege, in den Olymp eines Berufs zu kommen. Einer ist, Weltmeister oder Ähnliches zu werden. Der andere ist, ein erfolgreiches Buch zu schreiben, welches die Fachleute interessiert. Du hast nun beide Lorbeerkränze erkämpft, und du bist jetzt im Olymp oder der Hall of Fame.

Das tönt nach Lebensziel erreicht – mitnichten.

Du hast dich aus dem Fenster gelehnt, bist sehr erfolgreich. Die Verehrer und Neider mehren sich. Du bist ein Vorbild und auch Hoffnung für eine Branche, vor allem aber für unseren Nachwuchs. Eben warst du noch bei den „Jungen Wilden", und nun wartet diese Verantwortung, Idol unter dem Brennglas zu sein. Ich weiß, dass du das gut meistern wirst, weil ich dich als geerdeten, guten Freund kennen gelernt habe.

Beeindruckend waren deine Äußerungen, wie du erzähltest, dass du in Paris vor dieser Konditorei standest, welche diese sensationellen Glace herstellt, und du dich dort entschieden hast, da zu arbeiten und diese Kunst zu erlernen. Egal was es kostet. Diesen Wissensdurst und Leidenschaft, nebst dem Willen, sich einer anderen Sprache und Mentalität auszusetzen, um zu lernen, haben aus dir das gemacht, für das du heute stehst. Du hältst das Wissen aber nicht für dich, sondern teilst es in deinen Seminaren und jetzt mit diesem wunderschönen Buch.

Ich wünsche dir allen Erfolg und Glück mit „Sweet Gold".

Franz Ziegler

Konditormeister und Buchautor, Schweiz

Writing a foreword for a book is like being the godfather of a new piece of art.

There are different ways of reaching the pinnacle of one's profession. One of them is to become world champion or something similar. Another one is to write a successful book that is of interest to the experts. You have now achieved both of these and have reached the top or the hall of fame.

One might think that you are now content to rest on your laurels – but that is not so.

You have pushed the boat out and are very successful. There are more and more people who admire you or who are jealous of you. But whatever people think, you are an example to the trade and give it hope, especially for our young blood. It is not long ago that you were a "Young Wild One" yourself and now you have the responsibility of being an idol and the focus of attention. I know that you will handle that well because I have got to know you as a good and grounded friend.

I was very impressed when you told me of the time when you were in Paris and found yourself standing in front of a patisserie that produces these sensational Glaces, and you spontaneously decided to work there and learn their craft. At any cost. This thirst for knowledge and the passion, as well as the willingness to expose yourself to another language and mentality in order to learn, have made you into what you are today. You don't keep your knowledge to yourself but share it with others in your seminars and workshops and now also in this beautiful book.

I wish you every success and good luck with "Sweet Gold".

Franz Ziegler

Master pastry cook and writer, Switzerland

GRUSSWORTE

GREETINGS

For Bernd confectionary is a passion which has always fascinated him, a kind of familiar atavism. His passion and his destiny could be sensed as soon as he started with Fauchon, just as his teamwork skill and his interest in learning and understanding techniques and taste.

His career, his sensitivity and his creativity made him the great and recognized expert he is today. The book he presents today reflects what he is, what he does and what he would like to convey to his peers. This book will be a valuable and comprehensive support for those engaged in the field of cooking and backing and will take them effortlessly and with incomparable dexterity through all facets of the trade.

Pierre Hermé

Patissier and pastry cook of international reputation, Paris, France

Für Bernd ist die Patisserie eine Leidenschaft, die ihn seit jeher gefangen hält, sozusagen ein familiärer Atavismus. Seine Leidenschaft und seine Bestimmung waren bereits bei seinem Eintritt bei Fauchon zu spüren, ebenso seine Teamfähigkeit und sein Interesse, Techniken und Geschmacksrichtungen zu erlernen und zu verstehen.

Sein Werdegang, seine Sensibilität und seine Kreativität machten ihn zu dem großen und anerkannten Fachmann, der er heute ist. Das Buch, das er hier vorstellt, spiegelt das wider, was er ist, was er macht und was er Seinesgleichen vermitteln möchte. Dieses Werk wird für all diejenigen, die im Bereich des Koch- und Backhandwerks tätig sind, eine wertvolle und umfassende Unterstützung sein und sie mit Leichtigkeit und unvergleichlicher Fingerfertigkeit durch alle Abteilungen des Gewerbes führen.

Pierre Hermé

Patissier und Konditor mit Weltruf, Paris, Frankreich

Bernd Siefert – he is a sweet seducer whose creations you simply can't resist.

I wish him all the best from the depth of my heart!

Johann Lafer

Michelin Star and television chef, Germany

Bernd Siefert – er ist einfach ein süßer Verführer, wer kann seinen Kreationen schon widerstehen?

Von ganzem Herzen wünsche ich ihm weiterhin alles Gute!

Johann Lafer

Sterne- und Fernsehkoch, Deutschland

GRUSSWORTE

GREETINGS

In jungen Jahren hatte ich Gelegenheit, den wissbegierigen und ehrgeizigen Bernd Siefert auf der INTERKONDICA in Wiesbaden bei seinen ersten Zuckerdemos kennen zu lernen.

Mit Bewunderung verfolgte ich seither seine internationalen Erfolge in Berufswettbewerben und vor allem sein innovatives und unermüdliches Engagement für unseren Beruf und dessen Image. Es freut mich besonders, dass Bernd mit dieser Präsentation sein Wissen und seine Kreativität einem noch breiteren Publikum vorstellen kann.

Ich wünsche dir den verdienten Erfolg.

Ewald Notter
Notter School of Pastry Arts, L.L.C.
Orlando, Florida

Years ago I had the opportunity of getting to know Bernd Siefert as an ambitious young man who was eager to learn while he was giving his first sugar demonstrations at INTERKONDICA in Wiesbaden in Germany.

Since then I have followed his international success in professional competitions and – above all – his untiring and innovative commitment to our profession and its public image. I am particularly pleased to see Bernd presenting his knowledge and creativity to an even wider public with this publication.

I wish you every success – you have deserved it!

Ewald Notter
Notter School of Pastry Arts, L.L.C.
Orlando, Florida

Wenn man Bernd Siefert kennen lernt, bemerkt man schnell, dass man vor einer sehr leidenschaftlichen Person steht. Es ist phantastisch, wie er ein solch umfassendes und hervorragend bebildertes Buch zustande bringen konnte, in dem so viele filigrane Zuckerschaustücke, Desserts für die Patisserie sowie Kuchen oder Torten in exzellenter Eleganz enthalten sind. So etwas kann nur Bernd Siefert vollbringen – ganz ohne Zweifel ein Geschenk an all unsere Sinne.

Albert Adrià
Chef Patissier
El Bulli, Spanien

When you get to know Bernd Siefert, you notice very quickly that you are dealing with a very passionate person. The way he managed to compile such a comprehensive and exquisitely illustrated book is fantastic – with so many delicate sugar show pieces, desserts for patisserie as well as cakes and gateaux in excellent elegance. An achievement only Bernd Siefert can accomplish – no doubt an offering to all our senses.

Albert Adrià
Chief Patissier
El Bulli, Spain

GREETINGS

Over the last years there has been a remarkable development of skills in the field of baking and pastry and Bernd Siefert has certainly contributed to that. The renowned master pastry chef is considered to be one of the most innovative craftsmen in his field. His artistic touch with sugar and chocolate has impressed colleagues and judges all over the world as well as his clients in Michelstadt. The hallmark of his success is based on his talent, dedication and true passion for his craft. "Sweet Gold" is an inspiring collection of recipes and ideas – an invitation to experience Bernd Siefert's personal philosophy of pastry-making.

Ferdinand Metz
President
World Association of Cooks Societies (WACS)

Während der letzten Jahre gab es auf dem Gebiet der Konditorei und Patisserie eine bemerkenswerte Entwicklung, und Bernd Siefert hat ohne Zweifel seinen Teil dazu beigetragen. Der berühmte Meisterpatissier wird als einer der Innovativsten seines Fachs bezeichnet. Seine Kunstwerke aus Zucker und Schokolade haben nicht nur seine Kunden in Michelstadt beeindruckt, sondern auch seine Kollegen und Preisrichter auf der ganzen Welt. Sein Erfolg beruht auf seinem Talent, seiner Hingabe und seiner echten Leidenschaft für sein Handwerk. „Sweet Gold" ist eine inspirierende Sammlung von Rezepten und Ideen – eine Einladung, in Bernd Sieferts persönliche Philosophie einzutauchen.

Ferdinand Metz
Präsident
Weltverband der Köche (WACS)

He has mastered the traditional, such as Black Forest Gateau, as well as avantgarde recipes such as Rosmary-Honey Parfait with Apricot and Cucumber Salad, and always delights us with his new sweet creations. Since Bernd Siefert won the title of World Champion in 1997, the man from the Odenwald region in Germany has demonstrated that he belongs to the international "Champions League" of pastry cooks. With his excellent craftsmanship he uses chocolate, sugar and fruit to make true pieces of art which are a delight to all experts in the field of patissery and confectionery. We are very fortunate that such a master in his field shares his profound knowledge with us and lets us participate in his creative ideas and innovations.

Reinhold Metz
President
Association of German Chefs (VKD)

Er beherrscht eine traditionelle „Schwarzwälder Kirsch" ebenso wie ein Rosmarinhonigparfait mit Aprikosen-Gurken-Salat und begeistert mit immer wieder neuen süßen Kreationen. Spätestens seit seinem Weltmeistertitel 1997 ist der Odenwälder Bernd Siefert in die internationale Konditoren-„Champions-League" aufgestiegen. Seine handwerklich exzellenten Kunstwerke aus Schokolade, Zucker und Früchten erfreuen jeden Fachmann, der sich der gehobenen Patisserie und Confiserie verschrieben hat. Gut, dass ein solcher Meister seines Fachs sein profundes Wissen teilt und andere an seinen kreativen Ideen und Innovationen teilhaben lässt.

Reinhold Metz
Präsident
Verband der Köche Deutschlands e. V. (VKD)

GRUSSWORTE

GREETINGS

Ein Buch ist etwas, das denjenigen unsterblich macht, der es geschrieben hat. Was also soll man noch über Bernd Siefert sagen, diesen Giganten der Konditoreikunst von Weltruf, der mit seiner außergewöhnlichen Ruhe und seinem Temperament die Schwelle der unvergänglichen Erinnerung überschreitet.

Ein großer Konditor, ein großer Mann, ein großes Buch.

Auf Wiedersehen und bis bald,

Stefano Laghi
Fachlehrer und Buchautor, Italien

A book is something that makes the person who has written it immortal. What else can be said about Bernd Siefert, this giant of the patisserie craft with a worldwide reputation, who with his exceptionally calm disposition and his temperament is stepping across the threshold of immortal remembrance.

A great pastry cook, a great man, a great book.

See you again soon,

Stefano Laghi
Instructor and writer, Italy

„Sweet Gold" reflektiert auf einzigartige Weise Bernds Talent, seinen Enthusiasmus sowie seine Leidenschaft für unseren Beruf.

Patisseriekunst und perfektes handwerkliches Können, verbunden mit einer Vielzahl überaus inspirierender und praktischer Tipps, sind in diesem Buch auf eindrucksvolle Weise zusammengefasst.

Auch die erfrischend anderen Fotos heben seine künstlerischen Fähigkeiten noch hervor.

Dein Freund

Gottfried Schützenberger
Chef Patissier
Hotel Hyatt, Singapur

"Sweet Gold" reflects a unique blend of Bernd's talent, enthusiasm and obsession regarding our profession.

Culinary art and perfect craftsmanship, with plenty of very inspiring yet practical tips, are combined into one impressive and useful compendium.

The photographs, too, take a fresh new look and portray his artistic skills.

Your friend

Gottfried Schützenberger
Chief Patissier
Hotel Hyatt, Singapore

GREETINGS

Bernd Siefert: a creative mind with the courage to try the unusual. The many impressions he has collected on his worldwide travels are expressed in his compositions.

His first book "Sweet Gold" is not only a masterpiece, it is a symphony of form, material and colour.

Otto Kemmer
Chairman of the German Association of Pastry Cooks

Bernd Siefert, ein schöpferischer Geist mit dem Mut zum Außergewöhnlichen. Die vielfältigen Eindrücke, welche er auf seinen Reisen weltweit gesammelt hat, finden in seinen Kompositionen ihr Forum.

Sein erstes Buch „Sweet Gold" ist nicht nur ein Meisterwerk, es ist eine Sinfonie von Form, Material und Farbe.

Otto Kemmer
Vorsitzender des Deutschen Konditorenbundes

Dear Reader

The book you are holding in your hands is vivid proof of the fact that our profession is alive. This is a prime example of the creativity and wealth of imagination we now find on the increase again with some of our colleagues. For some years now, I have seen Bernd Siefert in action at events that are important for our profession, and thus have been able to follow his development. He has succeeded in creating a specialist book of national and international importance. It shows our successors the whole spectrum covered by our profession. Experienced colleagues, too, will enjoy using this book as a reference source. I really would like to say how lucky German pastry cooks are to have Bernd Siefert's inspiration. Bernd Siefert is a new, fresh spirit who will advance the world of patisserie/confiserie. I hope for him that the flow of his ideas never diminishes. I wish him every success for the future.

Günther Koerffer
President of UIPCG
International Union of Confectioners, Pastry Cooks
and Ice Cream Makers

Lieber Leser,

das vor Ihnen liegende Buch ist ein strahlender Beweis, dass unser Beruf lebt. Es ist ein Paradebeispiel für die Kreativität und den Erfindungsreichtum, der bei einigen unserer Kollegen jetzt wieder wächst. Ich habe Bernd Siefert seit einigen Jahren auf Events, die für unseren Beruf wichtig sind, in Aktion sehen und so auch seine Entwicklung verfolgen können. Es ist ihm gelungen, ein Fachbuch zu schaffen, das von nationaler und internationaler Bedeutung ist. Es zeigt unserem Nachwuchs, wie breit die Palette unseres Berufs ist. Auch erfahrene Kollegen werden dieses Werk gerne zum Nachschlagen nutzen. Ich kann den deutschen Konditoren an dieser Stelle nur gratulieren. Bernd Siefert ist ein neuer, frischer Geist, der die Patisserie/Confiserie weiterbringen wird. Ich hoffe für ihn, dass seine Ideen nicht weniger werden. Für die Zukunft wünsche ich ihm viel Erfolg.

Günther Koerffer
Präsident der UIPCG
Weltverband der Konditoren, Patissiers, Confiseure
und Eishersteller

GRUSSWORTE

GREETINGS

Ich traf Bernd Siefert zum ersten Mal 1988 in Wiesbaden. Er war damals noch Lehrling, und ich stellte meine Bücher „Compagnon du Tour de France" in Deutschland vor. Inzwischen hat er schon mehrere Beiträge für meine Zeitschrift geliefert, und es war jedes Mal ein Vergnügen, seine Kreationen zu genießen. Es ist mir eine besondere Freude, ihm zu seinem ersten Fachbuch zu gratulieren. Ich wünsche Ihnen, liebe Leser, viel Vergnügen bei seinen exzellenten Kreationen.

Yves Thuries

Buchautor „Compagnon du Tour de France", Frankreich

I met Bernd Siefert for the first time in 1988 in Wiesbaden. At that time he was still an apprentice and I was introducing my books Compagnon du Tour de France in Germany. He has already provided several contributions to my magazine, and each time we took great pleasure in his novel recipes. I am particularly pleased to have this chance to congratulate him on his first book on this specialist subject. To the reader: I wish you much enjoyment from Bernd's excellent creations.

Yves Thuries

Writer of the series, Compagnon du Tour de France, France

Es ist mir eine große Freude, ein Grußwort zum ersten Buch meines Freundes Bernd Siefert schreiben zu dürfen.

Unsere beruflichen Wege haben sich bei Anlässen wie dem U.I.P.C.G.-Wettbewerb (Union Internationale de la Pâtisserie-Confiserie-Glacierie) sowie bei Fachmessen und in Fachschulen gekreuzt. Aus diesem Grunde darf ich sagen, dass ich Bernd Siefert gut kenne. Er gehört zu den privilegierten und glücklichen Menschen, die vom Feuer der Leidenschaft zum Beruf befallen sind.

Die Bereitschaft, seine Kunstfertigkeit sowie sein Wissen in einem Fachbuch weiterzugeben und mit anderen Menschen zu teilen, ist lobenswert, und ich möchte ihm dafür danken. Ein Künstler, der seine Geheimnisse teilt, ist großzügig – so ist Bernd Siefert. Sein Buch ist ein Meilenstein der Konditorei und wird die europäische Zunft bereichern.

Elisio Tonti

Fachlehrer und Buchautor, Italien

It is a great pleasure for me to be asked to write a word of greeting for the first book of my friend Bernd Siefert.

Our professional paths have crossed on such occasions as the U.I.P.C.G. competition (International Union of Confectioners, Pastry Cooks and Ice Cream Makers) as well as at trade fairs and in training institutions. For this reason I can rightfully say that I know Bernd Siefert well. He is one of the privileged and happy people with a real passion for his chosen profession.

It is very laudable of him that he is prepared to pass on his skills and knowledge and share them with other people, and I would like to thank him for that. An artist who shares his secrets is generous – and so is Bernd Siefert. His book is a milestone in the craft of patisserie and will enrich our future in Europe.

Elisio Tonti

Instructor and writer, Italy

GRUSSWORTE

GREETINGS

What a wonderful book – generous in knowledge and beautifully composed, it excites and stimulates both the novice and the master. Its author is a true gentleman and one of the world's most talented pastry artists. I have known Bernd for 15 years, first as a competitor, then a colleague, mentor and teacher, and he has constantly evolved. He is not one to rest on his many laurels, he persistently develops his extraordinary skills and unique style, reaching the very pinnacle of pastry art.

I hope you are inspired as much as I am with his original desserts and entremets, and his stunning sugar work. The blown sugar stork is perfection itself, a masterpiece of the kind that is rare to find these days.

I highly recommend this valuable resource to all serious and dedicated pastry professionals, and I am sure you will gain enormous benefit from the wealth of Bernd's knowledge, creative insight and international experience.

Brendan Hill

Team Manager
Australian National Pastry Team

Was für ein wundervolles Buch – aufgrund der großzügigen Weitergabe von Fachwissen und wunderschön zusammengestellten Rezepten verzaubert und stimuliert es sowohl Anfänger als auch Meister. Der Autor ist ein wahrer Gentleman und einer der talentiertesten Patisseriekünstler der Welt. Ich lernte Bernd vor 15 Jahren als Konkurrenten kennen, später dann als Kollegen, Mentor und Lehrer, der sich ständig weiterentwickelte. Er gehört nicht zu denen, die sich auf ihren zahlreichen Lorbeeren ausruhen – vielmehr arbeitet er ständig an seinen außergewöhnlichen Fähigkeiten sowie seinem einzigartigen Stil, um irgendwann in den Olymp der Patisseriekunst einzugehen. Ich hoffe, dass Sie von seinen originellen Desserts und Süßspeisen sowie seinen phantastischen Zuckerkreationen genauso fasziniert sind wie ich. Der geblasene Zuckerstorch ist Perfektion pur, ein Meisterwerk, das heutzutage seinesgleichen sucht.

Ich kann diese wertvolle Quelle an Wissen nur wärmstens allen ernsthaften und ambitionierten Konditoren empfehlen, und ich bin sicher, dass Sie von dem Reichtum von Bernds Wissen, seiner Kreativität und seiner internationalen Erfahrung nur profitieren können.

Brendan Hill

Teamleiter
Australisches Nationalteam der Konditoren

INHALT

CONTENT

TORTEN

CAKES

Schwarzwälder Classixxx

Schwarzwälder Classixxx

Natürlich kommt man um das Thema „Schwarzwälder Kirsch“ in Deutschland nicht herum. Aber was vor 70 Jahren noch eine Buttercreme war, kann heute auch etwas ganz anderes sein. Die Mischung eines klassischen Geschmacks, nämlich Kirschwasser mit hochwertiger Schokolade, ist eine der besten Mischungen, die ich kenne.

No German pastry cookbook would be complete without “Black Forest Gateaux”. But where you would have been talking strictly butter cream 70 years ago, these days we have moved on. The combination of these classic tastes (kirsch with high-quality chocolate) is one of the best I know.

Ingredients

- Chocolate sponge mixture without flour, with cocoa nibs
- Tanzania dark chocolate mousse
- Kirsch filling
- Kirsch/Bavarian cream with cocoa butter powder
- Noir chocolate icing
- Chocolate lattice
- Gelatinised morello cherries
- Chocolate curls
- Cocoa powder

4 Cakes, Ø 20 cm
2 Cakes, Ø 28 cm

Zusammensetzung

- Schokoladenbiskuit ohne Mehl mit Kakaonibs
- Bitterschokoladenmousse Tansania
- Kirschfüllung
- Kirschwasser-Bayerische-Creme mit pulverisierter Kakaobutter
- Schokoladenglasur Noir
- Schokoladengitter
- Gelierte Sauerkirschen
- Schokaldencurls
- Kakaopulver

4 Torten, Ø 20 cm
2 Torten, Ø 28 cm

Schokoladenbiskuit ohne Mehl mit Kakaonibs

315 g	*Marzipan*
315 g	*Eigelb*
520 g	*Eiweiß*
520 g	*Zucker*
165 g	*Kakaopulver*
225 g	*Kakaonibs*

Marzipan mit Eigelb schaumig schlagen, Eiweiß mit Zucker zu Schnee schlagen. Eischnee und Kakaopulver im Wechsel unter die Marzipanmasse heben. Mit einer 8er-Lochtülle auf eine Backmatte dressieren, mit Kakaonibs bestreuen und bei 180 °C etwa 15 Minuten backen.

Chocolate sponge mixture without flour, with cocoa nibs

315 g	*marzipan*
315 g	*egg yolk*
520 g	*egg white*
520 g	*sugar*
165 g	*cocoa powder*
225 g	*cocoa nibs*

Beat the marzipan with the egg yolk until frothy; add sugar to the egg white and beat until stiff. Fold in the beaten egg white and the cocoa powder, in turns, into the marzipan mixture. Pipe the mixture onto a baking mat; sprinkle cocoa nibs across the top and bake for about 15 minutes at 180 °C.

Bitterschokoladenmousse Tansania

125 g	*Milch*
125 g	*Sahne*
65 g	*Eigelb*
35 g	*Zucker*
390 g	*Bitterkuvertüre, 75 %*
530 g	*geschlagene Sahne*

Milch mit Sahne aufkochen. Eigelb mit Zucker schaumig schlagen. Milchsahne einarbeiten. Die Masse im Wasserbad auf 85 °C erhitzen. Gehackte Bitterkuvertüre einrühren. Wenn die Masse eine glatte Konsistenz hat, die Sahne unterheben.

Tanzania dark chocolate mousse

125 g	*milk*
125 g	*cream*
65 g	*egg yolk*
35 g	*sugar*
390 g	*dark couverture, 75 %*
530 g	*whipped cream*

Boil the milk with the cream. Beat the egg yolk with sugar until frothy. Work in the milk/cream mixture. Heat the mixture in a bowl in hot water up to 85 °C. Stir in the chopped up dark couverture. When the mixture is smooth, fold in the cream.

1

2

3

4

5

Untemperierte Kuvertüre auf gefrorene Marmorplatte gießen

Pour the untempered couverture onto a frozen marble slab

Sofort mit Winkelpalette verstreichen

Spread out immediately using an angled spatula

Mit einem Messer in gewünschte Form schneiden

Use a knife to cut to the required shape

Sofort zu Locken biegen

Immediately bend to make the curly shape

Entweder direkt auf der Torte platzieren oder kühl lagern

Either place directly onto the cake or store in a cool place

Kirsch filling

1,000 g	*deep-frozen morello cherries*
200 g	*sugar*
120 g	*wheat powder*
50 g	*kirsch*

Defrost the morello cherries, drain the juice into a pan and heat up, mix the sugar with wheat powder and stir into the juice, fold in the drained cherries. Allow the mixture to cool down and then stir in the kirsch.

Kirschfüllung

1000 g	*Sauerkirschen, tiefgekühlt*
200 g	*Zucker*
120 g	*Weizenpuder*
50 g	*Kirschwasser*

Sauerkirschen auftauen, Kirschsaft abgießen und erhitzen, Zucker mit Weizenpuder mischen und Saft damit abbinden, abgetropfte Kirschen unterheben. Masse kalt werden lassen, dann Kirschwasser einrühren.

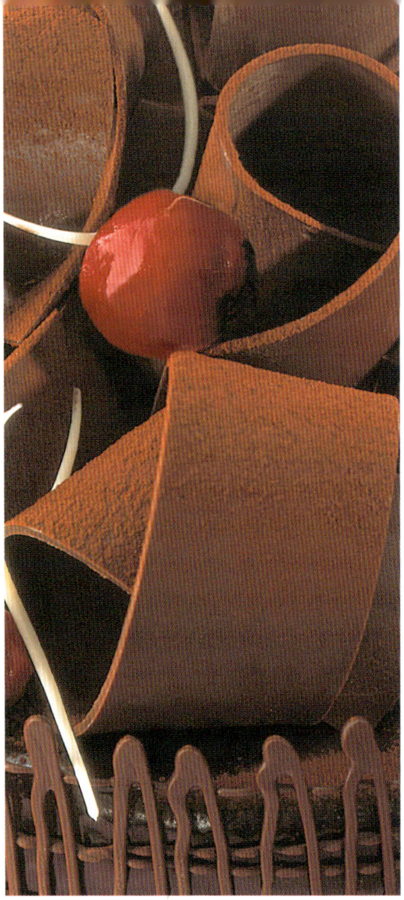

Basisrezept Bayerische Creme

280 g	*Milch*
85 g	*Eigelb*
55 g	*Zucker*

Milch aufkochen. Eigelb und Zucker schaumig schlagen und kochende Milch unterrühren. Masse im Wasserbad bei 85 °C pasteurisieren, dann so schnell wie möglich auf 4 °C herunterkühlen.

Basic recipe for Bavarian cream

280 g	*milk*
85 g	*egg yolk*
55 g	*sugar*

Boil the milk. Beat the egg yolk and sugar until frothy and stir into boiling milk. Pasteurise the mixture by heating it in a bowl in hot water up to 85 °C, then cool down to 4 °C as fast as possible.

Kirsch/Bavarian cream with cocoa butter powder

420 g	*basic recipe for Bavarian cream*
100 g	*cocoa butter powder*
490 g	*white couverture*
840 g	*whipped cream*
150 g	*kirsch*

Heat up the basic recipe, stir in the cocoa butter powder and work in the finely chopped couverture. Fold in the cream and finally the kirsch.

Kirschwasser-Bayerische-Creme mit pulverisierter Kakaobutter

420 g	*Basisrezept Bayerische Creme*
100 g	*pulverisierte Kakaobutter*
490 g	*weiße Kuvertüre*
840 g	*geschlagene Sahne*
150 g	*Kirschwasser*

Basisrezeptur erhitzen, pulverisierte Kakaobutter einrühren, fein gehackte Kuvertüre einarbeiten. Dann die Sahne und zum Schluss das Kirschwasser unterheben.

Putting it all together

Place the chocolate sponge in the baking ring, add the kirsch filling, add the dark chocolate mousse, put on the second layer of chocolate sponge, leave it all for a little while and then cover with the kirsch/ Bavarian cream. Put into the deep-freeze until frozen, then take the cake out of the ring and cover with Noir chocolate icing and decorate.

Zusammensetzung Torte

Schokoladenbiskuit in Ring einlegen, Kirschfüllung aufbringen, Bitterschokoladenmousse einfüllen, zweiten Schokoladenbiskuit auflegen, leicht anziehen lassen und mit Kirschwasser-Bayerische-Creme abdecken. Tiefgefrieren, ausformen, mit Schokoladenglasur Noir überziehen und dekorieren.

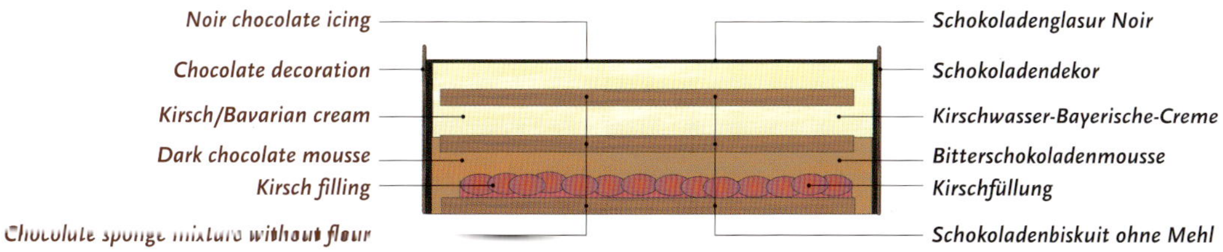

Südengland

Southern England

Ich liebe Schottland. Aber da gehören nun mal Orangenmarmelade und Whisky hin. Zu Südengland passen feine Geschmacksnuancen wie Ingwer, Tee und Vollmilchschokolade.

I love the Scottish Highlands. Everyone knows this is the country for orange marmalade and whisky. I associate subtle nuances of taste with southern England, such as ginger, tea and milk chocolate.

Ingredients

- Decorative sponge with cornflowers
- Ginger sponge
- Milk chocolate mousse
- Bavarian black tea cream
- Spray couverture
- Chocolate spiral
- Dried slices of orange
- Fresh fruit
- Chocolate curls

4 Cakes, Ø 20 cm

2 Cakes, Ø 28 cm

Zusammensetzung

- Dekorbiskuit mit Kornblumen
- Ingwerbiskuit
- Vollmilch-schokoladenmousse
- Bayerische Creme vom schwarzen Tee
- Sprühkuvertüre
- Schokoladenspirale
- Getrocknete Orangenscheiben
- Frische Früchte
- Schokoladencurls

4 Torten, Ø 20 cm

2 Torten, Ø 28 cm

Ingwerbiskuit

175 g	*Zucker*
200 g	*Eigelb*
300 g	*Eiweiß*
150 g	*Zucker*
125 g	*Weizenpuder*
75 g	*Mandelgrieß*
125 g	*Mehl*
100 g	*Ingwer*

Zucker mit Eigelb schaumig rühren. Eiweiß mit Zucker zu Schnee schlagen. Weizenpuder, Mandelgrieß und Mehl mischen und im Wechsel mit dem Eischnee unter die Eimasse melieren. Mit einer 8er-Lochtülle auf eine Backmatte dressieren und fein gehackten, kandierten Ingwer aufstreuen. Biskuit bei 180 °C etwa 15 Minuten backen.

Ginger sponge

175 g	*sugar*
200 g	*egg yolk*
300 g	*egg white*
150 g	*sugar*
125 g	*wheat powder*
75 g	*grated almonds*
125 g	*flour*
100 g	*ginger*

Stir the sugar with egg yolk until frothy. Add sugar to the egg white and beat until stiff. Mix the wheat powder with grated almonds and flour together, add the mixture and the beaten egg white, in turn, into the egg mixture. Pipe the mixture onto a baking mat; sprinkle the finely chopped candied ginger over it. Bake the sponge cake at 180 °C for 15 minutes.

Vollmilch-Schokoladenmousse

2	*Blatt Gelatine*
95 g	*Zucker*
55 g	*Wasser*
50 g	*Vollei*
120 g	*Eigelb*
400 g	*Vollmilchkuvertüre*
400 g	*geschlagene Sahne*

Gelatine in kaltem Wasser einweichen. Zucker mit Wasser zum Kettenflug kochen. Ei und Eigelb schaumig schlagen und den kochenden Zucker hineinlaufen lassen. Masse kalt schlagen, dann ausgepresste und in der Mikrowelle aufgelöste Gelatine zugeben. Vollmilchkuvertüre in der Mikrowelle auflösen und einarbeiten. Die Sahne unterziehen und sofort abfüllen.

Milk chocolate mousse

2	*sheets of gelatine*
95 g	*sugar*
55 g	*water*
50 g	*whole egg*
120 g	*egg yolk*
400 g	*milk chocolate couverture*
400 g	*whipped cream*

Soak the gelatine in cold water. Boil the sugar in water up to 117 °C. Beat the egg and egg yolk until frothy and then let the boiling sugar run into it. Beat the mixture until cold, then add the gelatine which has been pressed out and dissolved. Dissolve the milk chocolate couverture and work into the mixture. Fold in the cream and immediately put into the chosen containers.

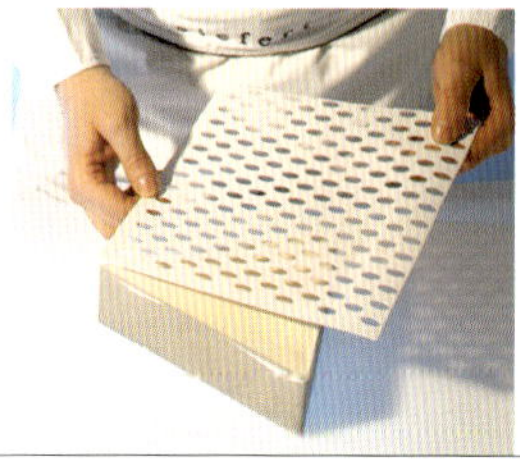

1

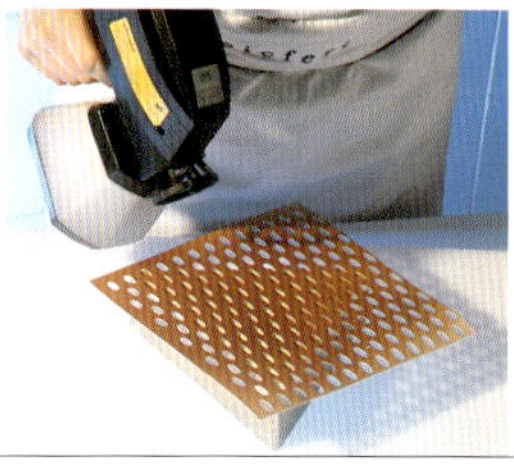

2

3

Schablone auf die gefrostete Torte legen

Place the template onto the frozen cake

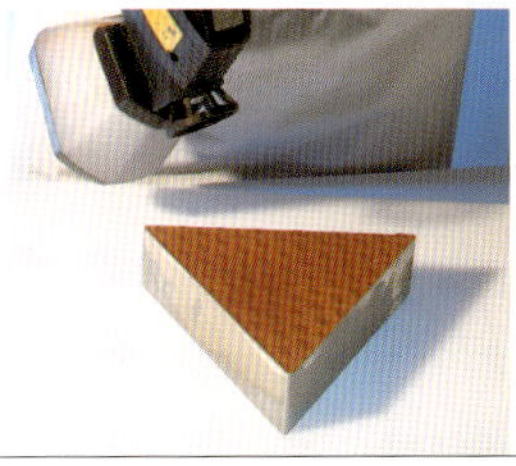

Nochmals mit Sprühkuvertüre absprühen

Again, spray with spray couverture

4

Mit Sprühkuvertüre absprühen

Spray it with spray couverture

Form vorsichtig erwärmen

Carefully heat up the mould

5

Schablone abnehmen

Remove the template

Form abziehen

Remove the mould

6

Bayerische Creme vom schwarzen Tee

7	*Blatt Gelatine*
500 g	*Vollmilch*
50 g	*Tee*
160 g	*Eigelb*
180 g	*Zucker*
450 g	*geschlagene Sahne*

Gelatine in kaltem Wasser einweichen. Milch aufkochen, über den Tee gießen und mindestens 5 Minuten ziehen lassen. Dann absieben oder, besser, mit einem Passiertuch abpressen. Eigelb mit Zucker schaumig schlagen, die Teemilch zugießen und bei 85 °C pasteurisieren. Die Gelatine auspressen und zugeben. Masse im Eiswasserbad abkühlen, sobald die Masse zu gelieren beginnt, die Sahne unterziehen.

Bavarian black tea cream

7	*sheets of gelatine*
500 g	*milk chocolate*
50 g	*tea*
160 g	*egg yolk*
180 g	*sugar*
450 g	*whipped cream*

Soak the gelatine in cold water. Bring the milk to boil, pour onto the tea and leave to steep for at least 5 minutes. Then pour through a strainer, or better, strain through a muslin cloth. Beat the egg yolk with sugar until frothy, add the tea milk and pasteurise at 85 °C. Press out the gelatine and add to the mixture. Cool the mixture in ice-cold water and when it starts to gelatinate, fold in the cream.

Spray couverture

100 g	*dark couverture, 70 %*
	cocoa butter

Dissolve the dark couverture and add the cocoa butter (max. 50 g, depending on the couverture).

Sprühkuvertüre

100 g	*Bitterkuvertüre, 70 %*
	Kakaobutter

Bitterkuvertüre auflösen und Kakaobutter zugeben (max. 50 g, je nach Kuvertüre).

Putting it all together

Line a baking ring with décor sponge, add ginger sponge and then spread the milk chocolate mousse over it. Add a second ginger sponge and fill up with Bavarian black tea cream. All other stages see above.

Zusammensetzung Torte

Einen Ring mit Dekorbiskuit auslegen, Ingwerbiskuit einlegen, darauf die Vollmilchschokoladenmousse geben, einen zweiten Ingwerbiskuit einlegen und mit Bayerischer Creme vom schwarzen Tee auffüllen. Alle weiteren Schritte siehe Stepps.

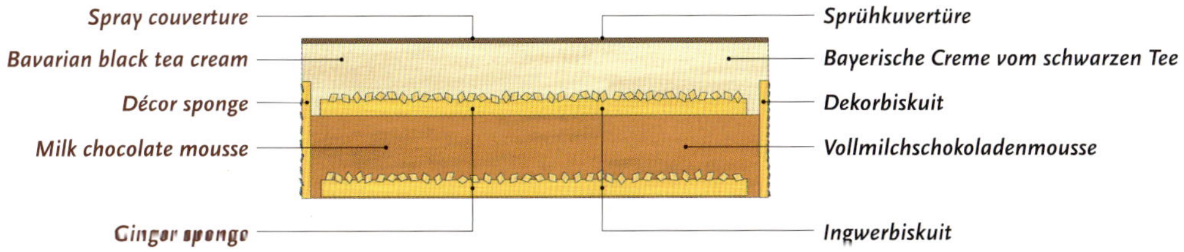

PANNA COTTA WALDBEERE

WILD BERRY PANNA COTTA

Bella Italia lässt grüssen: Sizialianische Pistazien, Frutti de Bosco, verheissungsvolle Vanille und ein Hauch exotischer Zimtblüten – einfach der leckerste Klassiker Italiens.

A touch of Bella Italia: Sicilian pistachios, frutti de bosco, enticing vanilla and a touch of exotic cinnamon flowers – simply the most delicious classic from Italy.

Ingredients

- Pistachio sponge
- Panna Cotta wild berry jelly filling
- Panna Cotta Bavarian cream
- Jelly icing with vanilla flavour
- Couverture spaghetti with green colouring
- Two marbled couverture spirals
- Wild berries
- Pistachios

4 Cakes, Ø 20 cm
2 Cakes, Ø 28 cm

Zusammensetzung

- Pistazienbiskuit
- Waldbeer-Panna-Cotta-Gelee-Einlage
- Panna-Cotta-Bayerische-Creme
- Vanilliertes Kaltgelee
- Grün gefärbte Kuvertürespaghetti
- Zwei marmorierte Kuvertürespiralen
- Waldbeeren
- Pistazien

4 Torten, Ø 20 cm
2 Torten, Ø 28 cm

Pistazienbiskuit

- 225 g *Eigelb*
- 175 g *Zucker*
- 330 g *Eiweiß*
- 75 g *Zucker*
- 200 g *Mehl*
- 50 g *Weizenpuder*
- 50 g *Pistazien, fein gerieben*

Eigelb und Zucker schaumig rühren. Eiweiß mit Zucker zu Schnee schlagen. Mehl, Weizenpuder und Pistazien mischen und im Wechsel mit dem Eischnee unter die Eigelbmasse melieren. Mit einer 8er-Lochtülle auf eine Backmatte dressieren und bei 180 °C etwa 15 Minuten backen.

Pistachio sponge

- 225 g *egg yolk*
- 175 g *sugar*
- 330 g *egg white*
- 75 g *sugar*
- 200 g *flour*
- 50 g *wheat powder*
- 50 g *pistachios, finely ground*

Beat the egg yolk with sugar until frothy. Add sugar to the egg white and beat until stiff. Mix the flour, wheat powder and pistachios together and then add the mixture and the beaten egg white, in turn, into the egg mixture. Pipe the mixture onto a baking mat. Bake the sponge cake at 180 °C for about 15 minutes.

Waldbeer-Panna-Cotta-Gelee-Einlage

- 10 *Blatt Gelatine*
- 250 g *Sahne*
- 300 g *Waldbeerpüree*
- 100 g *Zucker*

Gelatine einweichen. Sahne mit Waldbeerpüree und Zucker erhitzen. Ausgedrückte Gelatine in der heißen Masse auflösen. In passende Silikonformen gießen und tiefgefrieren.

Panna Cotta wild berry jelly filling

- 10 *sheets of gelatine*
- 250 g *cream*
- 300 g *puree of wild berries*
- 100 g *sugar*

Soak the gelatine. Heat the cream with the wild berry puree and sugar. Dissolve the squeezed gelatine in the hot mixture. Pour into suitable silicon moulds and deep-freeze.

1

2

3

4

5

Weiße Kuvertüre mit dunkler Kuvertüre bespinnen

Add a fine lattice layer of dark couverture onto white couverture

Mit einer Winkelpalette kleine Mengen herausnehmen

Use an angled spatula to take out small quantities

Kuvertüre auf einen tiefgefrorenen Stein aufstreichen

Spread the couverture onto a deep-frozen stone slab

Dekore sobald erkaltet, abheben

Once the décors have cooled down, lift them off

Dekore sofort verwenden oder aufbewahren

You can use the décors immediately or keep them for later

Panna Cotta Bavarian cream

14	*sheets of gelatine*
1,000 g	*cream*
2	*vanilla pods*
10 g	*cinnamon flowers*
200 g	*sugar*
200 g	*egg yolk*
900 g	*whipped cream*

Soak the gelatine. Powder the cinnamon flowers with a mortar and pestle and add to the cream together with the vanilla pods. Bring to boil. Beat the sugar with the egg yolk until frothy and then stir into the cream; pasteurise at 85 °C, dissolve the squeezed-out gelatine into the hot mixture, leave it to cool down to jelling point and then fold in the cream.

Panna-Cotta-Bayerische-Creme

14	*Blatt Gelatine*
1000 g	*Sahne*
2	*Vanilleschoten*
10 g	*Zimtblüten*
200 g	*Zucker*
200 g	*Eigelb*
900 g	*geschlagene Sahne*

Gelatine einweichen. Sahne mit Vanilleschoten und gemörserten Zimtblüten aufkochen. Zucker mit Eigelb schaumig schlagen, kochende Sahne einrühren, auf 85 °C pasteurisieren und ausgedrückte Gelatine in der heißen Masse auflösen. Bis zum Gelierpunkt abkühlen lassen, dann die Sahne unterziehen.

Putting it all together

Place the pistachio sponge into a baking ring, add the wild berry Panna Cotta, fill in Bavarian cream and then put the second pistachio sponge on top. Add another layer of Bavarian Cream, deep-freeze, turn out of the ring, cover with jelly icing and then decorate with couverture décors and fruits.

Zusammensetzung Torte

Pistazienbiskuit in einen Ring einlegen Waldbeer-Panna-Cotta einlegen, Bayerische Creme einfüllen und einen zweiten Boden auflegen. Mit Bayerischer Creme auffüllen, tiefkühlen, ausformen, mit Kaltgelee überziehen und mit Kuvertüredekoren sowie Früchten ausgarnieren.

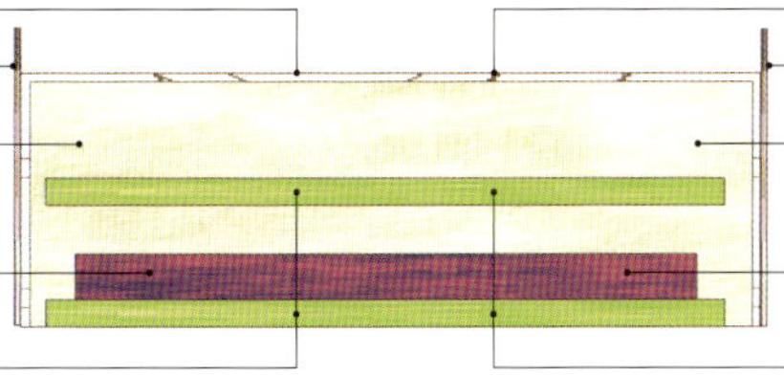

SPANISCHER ERDBEER-RHABARBER

SPANISH STRAWBERRY RHUBARB

Warum Spanien? Ich habe diese Art von Torte, aber mit anderen Zutaten, zum ersten Mal in Spanien gesehen. Eine Torte, bei der einfach drei separate Elemente hergestellt werden. Meine Idee war es nun, diese Elemente zu vervielfältigen, also drei Biskuits, drei mittlere und drei obere Teile – drei mal drei ... Die Möglichkeiten zu variieren sind immens, natürlich nur, wenn es zusammenpasst.

Why Spain? I saw this type of cake for the first time in Spain, although with different ingredients. To make it, you simply prepare three separate elements. My idea was to multiply these elements, i.e. three sponges, three middle layers and three top layers – three times three. There are many variations, but of course the parts have to go together.

Ingredients	**Zusammensetzung**
Almond dacquoise	Mandeldacquoise
White chocolate rhubarb mousse	Weisse Schokoladen-Rhabarber-Mousse
Strawberry mousse	Erdbeermousse
Flamed meringue	Geflämmter Baiser
Strawberry jelly icing	Erdbeerkaltgelee
Chocolate décor	Schokoladendekor
Fresh strawberries and rhubarb	Frische Erdbeeren und Rhabarber
4 Cakes, Ø 20 cm	4 Torten, Ø 20 cm
2 Cakes, Ø 28 cm	2 Torten, Ø 28 cm

Mandeldacquoise

225 g	*Eiweiß*
75 g	*Zucker*
190 g	*Mandelgrieß*
190 g	*Puderzucker*

Eiweiß mit Zucker zu Schnee schlagen, Mandelgrieß und Puderzucker mischen und unter den Eischnee melieren. Madeldacquoise mit einer 12er-Lochtülle auf ein 20 cm großes Backpapier aufdressieren. Bei 160 °C etwa 20 Minuten backen.

Almond dacquoise

225 g	*egg white*
75 g	*sugar*
190 g	*grated almonds*
190 g	*icing sugar*

Beat the egg white with sugar until stiff, mix the grated almonds with the icing sugar and turn into the beaten egg white. Use a round no. 12 nozzle to arrange the almond dacquoise onto baking paper 20 × 20 cm, and bake the almond dacquoise at 160 °C for about 20 minutes.

1

2

3

4

Weisse Schokoladen-Rhabarber-Mousse

400 g	*Rhabarberpüree*
40 g	*Zucker*
40 g	*Cremepulver*
100 g	*Eigelb*
	Mark von 2 Vanilleschoten
260 g	*weiße Kuvertüre*
20 g	*pulverisierte Kakaobutter*
600 g	*geschlagene Sahne*

Rhabarberpüree, Zucker, Cremepulver, Eigelb und das Mark der Vanilleschoten mischen und zu Creme kochen. Weiße Kuvertüre und die Kakaobutter unter die heiße Creme mischen. Masse leicht abkühlen lassen, dann die Sahne unterziehen. In Silikonformen füllen und tiefkühlen.

White chocolate rhubarb mousse

400 g	*rhubarb puree*
40 g	*sugar*
40 g	*cream powder*
100 g	*egg yolk*
	pith of 2 vanilla pods
260 g	*white couverture*
20 g	*cocoa butter powder*
600 g	*whipped cream*

Mix the rhubarb puree, sugar, cream powder, egg yolk and the pith of the vanilla pods and cook into a cream. Turn the white couverture and the cocoa butter into the hot cream. Leave the mixture to cool down slightly and then fold in the cream. Fill into silicon moulds and deep-freeze.

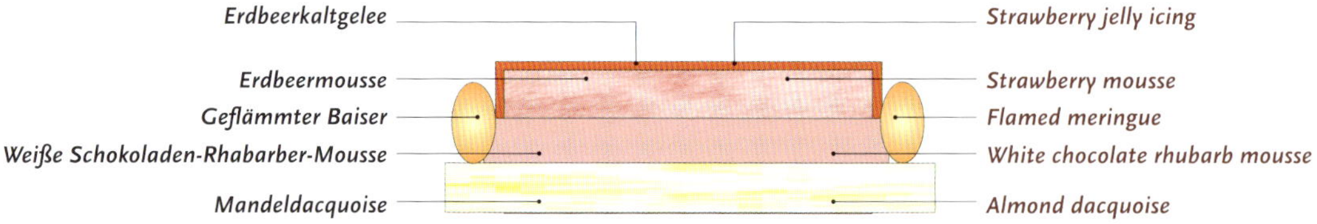

Kuvertüre auf eine gefrorene Marmorplatte geben

Spread the couverture onto a frozen marble slab

Mit einer Winkelpalette verstreichen, bis sie anzieht

Use an angled spatula to spread it out until it starts to set

Mit einem runden Ausstecher Rollen abschaben

Use a round cutting shape to scrape off the curls

Fertiges Schokoladendekor

Finished chocolate décor

Strawberry mousse

200 g	*strawberry puree*
100 g	*sugar*
15 g	*lemon juice*
50 g	*cocoa butter powder*
450 g	*whipped cream*

Mix and warm up the strawberry puree, sugar and lemon juice and stir in the cocoa butter until it has dissolved. Leave the mixture to cool and then fold in the cream.

Line the silicon mould with corrugated plastic film, fill in the strawberry mousse, put in the deep-freezer and turn out when required.

Erdbeermousse

200 g	*Erdbeerpüree*
100 g	*Zucker*
15 g	*Zitronensaft*
50 g	*pulverisierte Kakaobutter*
450 g	*geschlagene Sahne*

Erdbeerpüree, Zucker und Zitronensaft mischen und erwärmen. Die Kakaobutter unterrühren, bis sie aufgelöst ist. Masse abkühlen, dann die Sahne unterziehen.

Silikonform mit gewellter Plastikfolie auslegen, Erdbeermousse einfüllen, tiefgefrieren und bei Bedarf ausformen.

Meringue

150 g	*sugar*
10 g	*egg white powder*
125 g	*egg white, pasteurised*

Mix 50 g of the sugar with the egg white powder and beat together with the egg white until stiff. Work in the remaining sugar and then use a triangular piping nozzle to pipe the mixture along the edge of the cake; flame off with a cooking torch.

Baiser

150 g	*Zucker*
10 g	*Eiweißpulver*
125 g	*Eiweiß, pasteurisiert*

50 g Zucker mit Eiweißpulver mischen und mit dem Eiweiß zu einem stabilen Schnee schlagen. Restlichen Zucker einarbeiten und mit einer dreieckigen Lochtülle auf den Rand der Torte spritzen und abflämmen

Putting it all together

Spread the rhubarb mousse over the dacquoise. Cover the strawberry mousse with jelly icing and place on top of the rhubarb mousse. Dress the dacquoise with the meringues and flame off with a cooking torch. Decorate to taste.

Zusammensetzung Torte

Dacquoise mit Rhabarbermousse belegen. Erdbeermousse mit Kaltgelee überziehen, auf die Rhabarbermousse auflegen. Baiser auf die Dacquoise dressieren und mit einem Gasbrenner abflämmen. Dekorieren.

Andalusien

Andalucia

Was hat ein chinesisches Schriftzeichen auf einer spanischen Torte zu tun? In diesem Fall ist es mein Name, aber Orangen kommen ja bekanntlich auch aus China. Der Schwung des Schokoladentuchs symbolisiert das Temperament des Flamencos.

Why is there a Chinese letter on a Spanish cake? In this case it is my name but, of course, oranges also come from China. The sweep of the chocolate cloth symbolises the flamenco temperament.

Ingredients

- Almond brittle sponge
- Orange cream filling
- Chocolate praline mousse
- Noir chocolate icing
- Metallic jelly icing
- Couverture décor
- Orange wedges
- Fresh lavender flowers

- 4 Cakes, Ø 20 cm
- 2 Cakes, Ø 28 cm

Zusammensetzung

- Mandelkrokantbiskuit
- Orangencremeeinlage
- Schokoladenpralinémousse
- Schokoladenglasur Noir
- Metallic-Kaltgelee
- Kuvertüredekor
- Orangenspalten
- Frische Lavendelblüten

- 4 Torten, Ø 20 cm
- 2 Torten, Ø 28 cm

Mandelkrokantbiskuit

200 g	*Eigelb*
380 g	*Eiweiß*
130 g	*Zucker*
100 g	*Zucker*
150 g	*Mehl*
150 g	*zerlassene Butter*
120 g	*Krokant*

Eigelb und Eiweiß jeweils getrennt mit dem jeweiligen Zucker stabil aufschlagen, beide Massen abwechselnd mit dem Mehl vorsichtig melieren, die Butter am Ende leicht angleichen und unterziehen. Mit einem Dressierbeutel und 8er-Lochtülle in gewünschter Form auf Backpapier aufdressieren und gehackten Krokant aufstreuen. Bei 200 °C etwa 12 Minuten backen.

Almond brittle sponge

200 g	*egg yolk*
380 g	*egg white*
130 g	*sugar*
100 g	*sugar*
150 g	*flour*
150 g	*melted butter*
120 g	*almond brittle*

Beat the egg yolk and the egg white separately with the respective quantities of sugar. Carefully mix in the flour, each mixture in turn. Finally soften the butter and then fold it into the mixture. Use a piping bag with a no. 8 nozzle to pipe an appropriate shape onto the baking paper and then sprinkle the almond brittle over it. Bake at 200 °C for about 12 minutes.

Orangencremeeinlage

3	*Blatt Gelatine*
225 g	*Vollei*
225 g	*Zucker*
200 g	*Orangensaft*
14 g	*Orangenschale*
270 g	*Butter*

Gelatine in kaltem Wasser einweichen, Ei mit Zucker aufschlagen, Orangensaft mit der Schale aufkochen und unter die Eier laufen lassen, Masse bei 85 °C pasteurisieren. Gelatine ausgepresst in der Masse auflösen und kalte Butter Stück für Stück untermixen. Masse in Silikonformen füllen, einfrieren und ausformen.

Orange cream filling

3	*sheets of gelatine*
225 g	*whole egg*
225 g	*sugar*
200 g	*orange juice*
14 g	*orange peel*
270 g	*butter*

Soak the gelatine in cold water, beat the egg with sugar, boil up the orange juice with the peel and let it run into the egg, then pasteurise the mixture at 85 °C. Squeeze out the gelatine and let it dissolve in the mixture, then blend in the cold butter bit by bit. Fill the mixture into silicon moulds, freeze and then turn out.

1

2

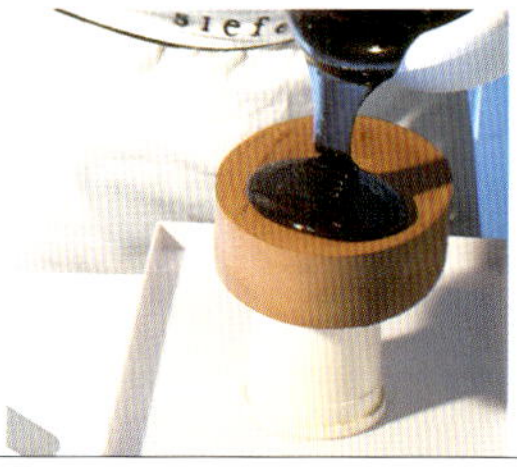
3

4

5

Metallicpulver in ein Schälchen geben und mit Kaltgelee mischen

Put the metallic powder in a little bowl and mix with jelly icing

Metallic-Kaltgelee in ein Garniertütchen füllen

Put the metallic jelly icing into a piping bag

Torte mit Schokaladenglasur überziehen

Spread the cake with the chocolate icing

Metallic-Kaltgelee mit dem Garniertütchen aufbringen

Apply the metallic jelly icing with the piping bag

Mit einer Palette verstreichen

Use a spatula to spread the icing

Chocolate praline mousse

6	*sheets of gelatine*
60 g	*sugar*
300 g	*milk*
300 g	*cream*
120 g	*egg yolk*
360 g	*praline mixture, 60 %*
360 g	*dark couverture, 70 %*
1,080 g	*whipped cream*

Soak the gelatine in cold water. Pasteurise the sugar, milk, cream and egg yolk at 85 °C, work in the squeezed-out gelatine, praline mixture and couverture until it turns into a ganache. Then fold in the cream.

Schokoladenpralinémousse

6	*Blatt Gelatine*
60 g	*Zucker*
300 g	*Milch*
300 g	*Sahne*
120 g	*Eigelb*
360 g	*Pralinémasse, 60 %*
360 g	*Bitterkuvertüre, 70 %*
1080 g	*geschlagene Sahne*

Gelatine in kaltem Wasser einweichen. Zucker, Milch, Sahne und Eigelb bei 85 °C pasteurisieren, ausgepresste Gelatine, Pralinémasse und Kuvertüre einarbeiten, bis eine Ganache entsteht. Dann die Sahne unterziehen.

Putting it all together

Place one almond brittle sponge on baking paper in each 20 cm ring, spread the deep-frozen orange cream filling on the sponge and then fill in chocolate praline mousse. Add a second sponge and top up with chocolate praline mousse. Smooth the surface, deep-freeze, then turn out of the ring and cover with Noir chocolate icing and finally decorate with metallic jelly icing.

Zusammensetzung Torte

Jeweils einen Mandelkrokantbiskuit auf Backpapier in 20er-Ring absetzen, tiefgekühlte Orangencremeeinlage auf Biskuit auflegen, Schokoladenpralinémousse einfüllen, zweiten Biskuit einlegen und mit Schokoladenpralinémousse auffüllen. Glatt streichen, tiefkühlen, aus dem Ring ausformen und mit Schokoladenglasur Noir überziehen und mit Metallic-Kaltgelee dekorieren.

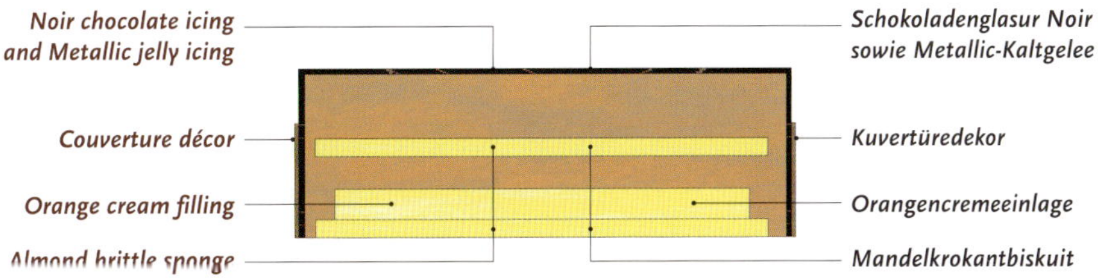

ÖSTERREICHISCHE APFELMOUSSETORTE

AUSTRIAN APPLE MOUSSE CAKE

Geklaut ist geklaut: Eigentlich ist es ja die Torte meiner Frau Isabel, die damit zur „Konditorin des Jahres“ gewählt wurde. Hier nun meine Version.

The truth will out: I have to confess that I pinched this one from my wife Isabel, who won the title “Pastry Cook of the Year” with this recipe. Here is my version.

Ingredients	Zusammensetzung
Décor sponge	Dekorbiskuit
Puff pastry cases	Blätterteigböden
Apple jelly with caramelised apples	Apfelgelee mit karamellisierten Äpfeln
Apple mousse	Apfelmousse
Walnut dacquoise	Walnussdacquoise
Crème brûlée filling	Crème-brûlée-Einlage
Apple jelly icing	Apfelkaltgelee
Filo pastry	Filoteig
Vanilla	Vanille
Chocolate décor	Schokoladendekor
Fresh fruit	Frische Früchte
4 Cakes, Ø 20 cm	4 Torten, Ø 20 cm
2 Cakes, Ø 28 cm	2 Torten, Ø 28 cm

Blätterteigböden

750 g	*Butter*
300 g	*Mehl*
700 g	*Mehl*
30 g	*Salz*
225 g	*Butter*
300 g	*Wasser*
5 g	*Essig*

Aus 750 g Butter und 300 g Mehl einen Teig herstellen, zu einem flachen Quadrat formen und mit Folie abgedeckt 1 Stunde kalt stellen.

Restliche Zutaten zu einem geschmeidigen Teig arbeiten. Zu einem Rechteck formen und in Folie eingewickelt 1 Stunde ruhen lassen. Teig in die Butter-Mehl-Mischung legen. Achtung: Beide Mischungen müssen identische Konsistenzen haben. Zur einfachen Tour zusammenschlagen. Im Abstand von 2 Stunden 2-mal in doppelter Tour zusammenschlagen, wobei der Teig nach jeder Tour kalt gestellt wird. Vor dem Zuschneiden nochmals in einfacher Tour zusammenschlagen. Der in doppelter Tour zusammengeschlagene Blätterteig kann mehrere Tage aufbewahrt werden. Böden mit der Ausrollmaschine auf Stufe 1,5 bis 2 ausrollen und bei 180 °C etwa 30 Minuten backen.

Puff pastry cases

750 g	*butter*
300 g	*flour*
700 g	*flour*
30 g	*salt*
225 g	*butter*
300 g	*water*
5 g	*vinegar*

Use 750 g butter and 300 g flour to make a pastry, shape into a shallow square, cover with foil and cool for 1 hour.

Work the remainder of the ingredients into a smooth pastry. Form into a rectangular shape, wrap up in foil and leave to rest for 1 hour. Place the pastry into the butter/flour mixture. Important: the two mixtures must be of the same consistency. Give it a single turn of rolling, folding and turning. Give it another 2 double turns, with an interval of 2 hours between mixes, placing the pastry into the refrigerator after each mixing. Before cutting, give the mixture once again a single turn. Once the puff pastry has been prepared like this, it can be stored for several days. Roll out the cases with the pastry roller on 1.5 or 2 and bake at 180 °C for about 30 minutes.

1

2

3

4

Chinesisches Schriftzeichen als Steinsiegel

Chinese character in the form of a stone seal

Kuvertüretupfen auf eine gefrorene Marmorplatte dressieren

Arrange dabs of couverture onto a frozen marble slab

Kuvertüre mit tiefgefrorenem Schriftzeichen siegeln

Apply the deep-frozen seal to the couverture

Kuvertüresiegel mit Goldpuder abstäuben

Dust some gold powder over the couverture seal

Apple jelly with caramelised apples

10	*sheets of gelatine*
200 g	*sugar*
800 g	*coarsely diced apples*
100 g	*sugar*
15 g	*pectin*
500 g	*naturally cloudy apple juice*
2 g	*crystalline citric acid*
50 g	*Rum raisins*

Soak the gelatine in cold water. Let the sugar caramelise in a frying pan, turn in the diced apples, leave to cool and then drain off.

Mix the sugar with the pectin, stir into the apple juice and boil for 3 minutes. Then mix the citric acid with 1 teaspoon of water and add to the boiling apple juice. Bring back to boil. Stir in the squeezed-out gelatine and leave to cool. Fold in the caramelised apples and rum raisins.

Apfelgelee mit karamellisierten Äpfeln

10	*Blatt Gelatine*
200 g	*Zucker*
800 g	*grob gewürfelte Äpfel*
100 g	*Zucker*
15 g	*Pektin*
500 g	*naturtrüber Apfelsaft*
2 g	*kristalline Zitronensäure*
50 g	*Rumrosinen*

Gelatine in kaltem Wasser einweichen. Zucker in einer Pfanne karamellisieren lassen, Apfelwürfel unterschwenken, abkühlen lassen und absieben.

Zucker und Pektin mischen, in den Apfelsaft einrühren und 3 Minuten aufkochen. Dann Zitronensäure mit 1 Teelöffel Wasser mischen und in den kochenden Apfelsaft geben. Dann nochmals aufkochen lassen. Ausgedrückte Gelatine einrühren und abkühlen lassen. Karamellisierte Äpfel und Rumrosinen unterheben.

Apfelmousse

15	*Blatt Gelatine*
800 g	*pürierte Äpfel*
2 g	*Ascorbinsäure*
50 g	*Zucker*
270 g	*Zucker*
180 g	*Eiweiß*
630 g	*geschlagene Sahne*

Gelatine einweichen. Pürierte Äpfel mit Ascorbinsäure und 50 g Zucker verrühren, eingeweichte und ausgedrückte Gelatine auflösen und Apfelpüree unterrühren. Erst den mit 270 g Zucker geschlagenen Eischnee unterheben, dann die Sahne unterziehen.

Apple mousse

15	*sheets of gelatine*
800 g	*pureed apples*
2 g	*ascorbic acid*
50 g	*sugar*
270 g	*sugar*
180 g	*egg white*
630 g	*whipped cream*

Soak the gelatine. Add the ascorbic acid and 50 g sugar to the pureed apples and stir well, dissolve the soaked and squeezed-out gelatine and stir into the apple puree. Beat the egg white with 270 g sugar and fold into the apple puree, followed by the cream.

Walnussdacquoise

150 g	*Eiweiß*
125 g	*Zucker*
115 g	*Mandelstaub*
115 g	*Puderzucker*
50 g	*Mehl*
50 g	*Eiweiß*
25 g	*Sahne*
50 g	*gehackte Walnüsse*

150 g Eiweiß mit Zucker zu Schnee schlagen. Mandelstaub, Puderzucker und Mehl mischen, die 50 g Eiweiß und die Sahne flüssig einarbeiten, dann vorsichtig den Eischnee unterheben. Mit einer 8er-Lochtülle in gewünschter Form auf Backpapier dressieren und die Walnüsse aufstreuen. Bei 160 °C etwa 15 Minuten backen.

Walnut dacquoise

150 g	*egg white*
125 g	*sugar*
115 g	*almond dust*
115 g	*icing sugar*
50 g	*flour*
50 g	*egg white*
25 g	*cream*
50 g	*chopped walnuts*

Beat 150 g egg white with sugar until stiff. Mix the almond dust, icing sugar and flour, work in the 50 g of egg white and cream liquid and then carefully fold in the beaten egg white. Use a round nozzle size 8 to arrange the desired shapes onto baking paper and sprinkle on the walnuts. Bake at 160 °C for about 15 minutes.

Crème brûlée filling

5	*sheets of gelatine*
400 g	*cream*
160 g	*honey*
1	*vanilla pod*
100 g	*egg yolk, pasteurized*

Soak the gelatine. Add the honey, scraped-out vanilla pith and the vanilla pod to the cream and bring to boil. Take out the vanilla pod. Stir the hot mixture into the egg yolk and add the soaked and squeezed and dissolved gelatine. Fill into silicon moulds and deep-freeze.

Crème-brûlée-Einlage

5	*Blatt Gelatine*
400 g	*Sahne*
160 g	*Honig*
1	*Vanilleschote*
100 g	*Eigelb, pasteurisiert*

Gelatine einweichen. Sahne mit Honig, ausgestrichenem Vanillemark sowie Vanilleschote aufkochen. Vanilleschote entnehmen. Heiße Masse unter das Eigelb rühren, die eingeweichte, ausgedrückte und aufgelöste Gelatine zugeben. In Silikonformen füllen und tiefkühlen.

Putting it all together

Place the décor sponge and thin puff pastry case into a mould, followed by the walnut dacquoise and the apple jelly with caramelised apples, then put on the deep-frozen crème brûlée, top up with apple mousse and put in the deep-freeze. Cover with jelly icing, turn out and decorate.

Zusammensetzung Torte

Dekorbiskuit und dünnen Blätterteigboden in eine Form einlegen, Walnussdacquoise einlegen, Apfelgelee mit karamellisierten Äpfeln einfüllen, tiefgefrorene Crème brûlée aufsetzen, mit Apfelmousse auffüllen und tiefkühlen. Mit Kaltgelee abglänzen, ausformen und dekorieren.

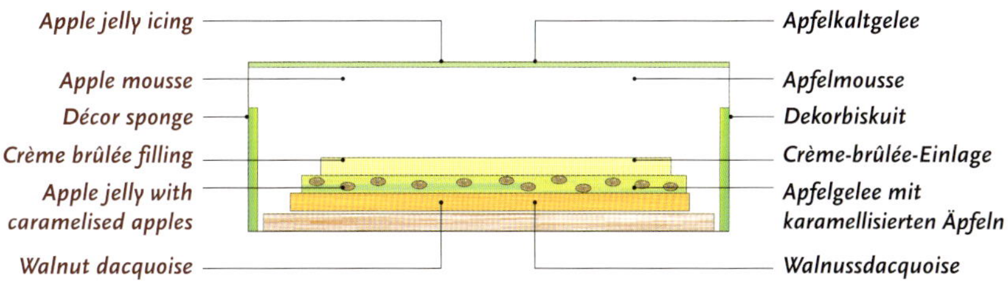

Wiener Hofburg

Viennese Castle

Da ich ja nichts stehen lassen kann, wie es ist, habe ich auch die gute alte Sachertorte vergewaltigt. Hier ist die Version, wie ich mir heute eine Sachertorte vorstelle. Übrigens: Wir fliegen unsere Sachertorte, die Wiener Hofburg, mittlerweile schon nach Wien ein.

As I am notorious for changing things, I have even come up with a variation on the good old Sacher cake. Here is my contemporary version of this renowned cake. By the way: we now export our Viennese Castle, our version of the Sacher cake, by plane to Vienna.

Ingredients	Zusammensetzung
Rum cream	Rumsahne
Chocolate caramel mousse	Schokoladen-karamellmousse
Raspberries in rum	Himbeeren in Rum
Sacher sponge	Sacherbiskuit
White spray couverture	Weisse Sprühkuvertüre
Noir chocolate icing	Schokoladenglasur Noir
Chocolate décor	Schokoladendekor
Raspberries	Himbeeren
4 Cakes, Ø 20 cm	4 Torten, Ø 20 cm
2 Cakes, Ø 28 cm	2 Torten, Ø 28 cm

1

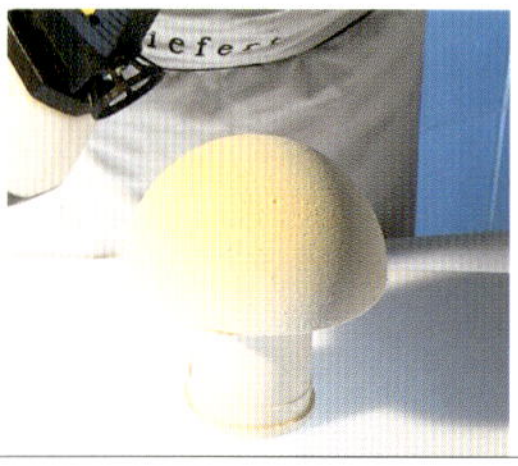

2

3

4

5

Rumsahne

8,5	Blatt Gelatine
1000 g	Sahne
135 g	Zucker
200 g	Rum

Gelatine in kaltem Wasser einweichen. Sahne mit Zucker steif schlagen. Gelatine auflösen und Rum einrühren. Sahne in die Rumgelatine unterziehen.

Rum cream

8.5	sheets of gelatine
1,000 g	cream
135 g	sugar
200 g	rum

Soak the gelatine in cold water. Whip the cream with the sugar until stiff. Dissolve the gelatine and stir in the rum. Fold the cream into the rum gelatine.

Schokoladenkaramellmousse

100 g	Zucker
200 g	Sahne
50 g	Eigelb
250 g	Bitterkuvertüre, 66 %
600 g	geschlagene Sahne

Zucker karamellisieren, mit 200 g Sahne ablöschen. Eigelb zugeben und Masse im Wasserbad bei 85 °C pasteurisieren. Die fein gehackte Kuvertüre zugeben und die 600 g Sahne unterheben.

Chocolate caramel mousse

100 g	sugar
200 g	cream
50 g	egg yolk
250 g	dark couverture, 66 %
600 g	whipped cream

Caramelise the sugar and then add 200 g of cream. Add the egg yolk and then pasteurise the mixture by heating it in a bowl in hot water up to 85 °C. Add the finely chopped couverture and fold in the 600 g of cream.

Himbeeren in Rum

100 g	Rum
50 g	Zucker
500 g	Himbeeren

Rum mit Zucker mischen und Himbeeren darin einlegen, wenn möglich mehrere Tage.

Raspberries in rum

100 g	rum
50 g	sugar
500 g	raspberries

Mix the rum with sugar and soak the raspberries in the mixture, if possible for several days.

Tiefgefrorene Torte ausformen

Turn out the deep-frozen cake

Mit weißer Sprühkuvertüre absprühen

Spray with white spray couverture

Mit einer Garniertüte Schokoladenglasur Noir aufdekorieren

Use a decorating bag to pipe on the Noir chocolate icing

Einen Tropfen Schokoladenglasur auf die Schokoladenplättchen geben

Put a dab of chocolate icing onto the chocolate leaves

Plättchen an die Torte anlegen

Arrange the leaves around the cake

Sacher sponge

50 g	water
600 g	whole egg
280 g	sugar
200 g	flour
100 g	wheat powder
100 g	grated almonds
1/2	lemon peel
2 g	salt
2 g	clove powder
4 g	cinnamon powder
100 g	liquid couverture, 99 %
100 g	liquid butter

Beat the egg with sugar, first warm and then cold. Mix the remaining dry ingredients and stir into the egg mixture. Mix the couverture with the butter and fold into the mixture. Fill a suitable baking tin with about 3 cm of the mixture and then bake at 180 °C for about 20 minutes.

Sacherbiskuit

50 g	Wasser
600 g	Vollei
280 g	Zucker
200 g	Mehl
100 g	Weizenpuder
100 g	Mandelgrieß
1/2	Zitronenschale
2 g	Salz
2 g	Nelkenpulver
4 g	Zimtpulver
100 g	flüssige Kuvertüre, 99 %
100 g	flüssige Butter

Wasser mit Ei und Zucker erst warm, dann kalt schlagen. Die restlichen trockenen Zutaten mischen und unter die Eimasse melieren. Die Kuvertüre und die Butter mischen und unter die Masse ziehen. In einer passenden Form 3 cm hoch einfüllen und bei 180 °C etwa 20 Minuten backen.

Putting it all together

Line a semi-spheric mould with rum cream. Fill in the chocolate caramel mousse. Add the rum raspberries and cover with Sacher sponge. Deep-freeze and turn out. Apply decorations (see stages).

Zusammensetzung Torte

Halbkugelform mit Rumsahne auschemisieren. Schokoladenkaramellmousse einfüllen. Rumhimbeeren einlegen und mit Sacherbiskuit abdecken. Tiefgefrieren und ausformen. Torte garnieren (siehe Stepps).

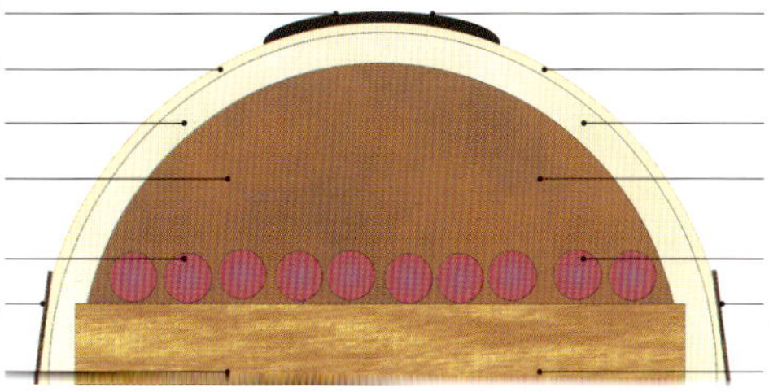

MANGO-CHILI-SAHNE

MANGO CHILLI CREAM

Die Grundidee für diese Torte ist einer meiner Klassiker: Das Mexiko-Dessert. Als wir ein bisschen Masse übrig hatten, sagte meine Schwester Astrid: „Lass uns doch mal eine Sahnetorte machen.“ Und siehe da: Das war die erste Sahnetorte, die wir an diesem Tag verkauften. Mut wird belohnt.

The basic idea for this cake is one of my classics: the Mexico dessert. When we had a little mixture left over, my sister Astrid once said: “Let’s make a cream gateau”. And lo and behold: that was the first cream gateau we sold that day. Who dares wins.

Ingredients	**Zusammensetzung**
Décor sponge	Dekorbiskuit
Almond banana sponge	Mandel-Bananen-Biskuit
Mango mousse	Mangomousse
Chilli cheese cream	Chili-Käsesahne
Chilli jelly icing	Chili-Kaltgelee
Chocolate décor	Schokoladendekor
Candied chilli pod	Kandierte Chilischote
Mango and mango sauce	Mango und Mangosauce
4 Cakes, Ø 20 cm	4 Torten, Ø 20 cm
2 Cakes, Ø 28 cm	2 Torten, Ø 28 cm

Zigarettenmasse für den Dekorbiskuit

100 g	*Butter*
100 g	*Puderzucker*
100 g	*flüssiges Eiweiß*
100 g	*Mehl*
	Lebensmittelfarbe

Butter mit Puderzucker glatt rühren, Eiweiß und Mehl abwechselnd unterrühren. Mit Lebensmittelfarbe einfärben. Masse mit einer Winkelpalette in Silikonreliefform einstreichen.

Cigarette mixture for the décor sponge

100 g	*butter*
100 g	*icing sugar*
100 g	*liquid egg white*
100 g	*flour*
	food colouring

Stir the butter with icing sugar until smooth, then blend in the egg white and flour alternately. Apply the food colouring. Use an angled spatula to spread the mixture into a silicon relief mould.

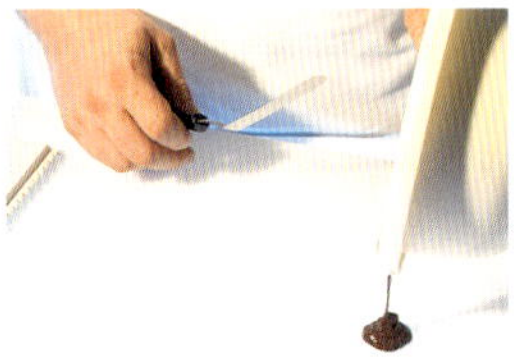

1

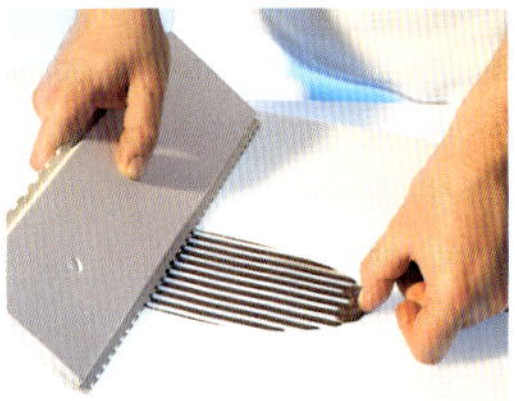

2

Dekorbiskuit

500 g	*Vollei*
375 g	*Mandelgrieß*
375 g	*Puderzucker*
100 g	*Mehl*
325 g	*Eiweiß*
75 g	*Zucker*
75 g	*zerlassene Butter*

Ei mit Mandelgrieß, Puderzucker und Mehl schaumig rühren. Eiweiß mit Zucker zu Schnee schlagen und unter die Eimasse heben. Zuletzt die Butter unterziehen. Den Biskuit in die vorbereitete Silikonreliefform einfüllen und bei 220 °C etwa 10 Minuten backen. Wenn die Reliefmatte aus dem Ofen kommt, sofort mit Zucker bestreuen, damit die Feuchtigkeit im Biskuit bleibt.

Décor sponge

500 g	*whole egg*
375 g	*grated almonds*
375 g	*icing sugar*
100 g	*flour*
325 g	*egg white*
75 g	*sugar*
75 g	*melted butter*

Stir the egg with ground almonds, icing sugar and flour until frothy. Add sugar to the egg white and beat until stiff; then fold into the egg mixture. Finally fold in the butter. Fill the sponge mixture into the prepared silicon relief mould and bake at 220 °C for about 10 minutes. When taking the relief mould from the oven, sprinkle on the sugar immediately so that the moisture remains in the sponge.

Temperierte Kuvertüre auf Folie geben

Spread the tempered couverture onto foil

3

Sobald die Kuvertüre anzieht, verdrehen

When the couverture begins to set, twist it

Mit einem Dekorkamm abziehen

Draw a decorating comb across it

4

Wenn sich die Folie lösen lässt, abziehen

Pull the foil off as soon as this is possible

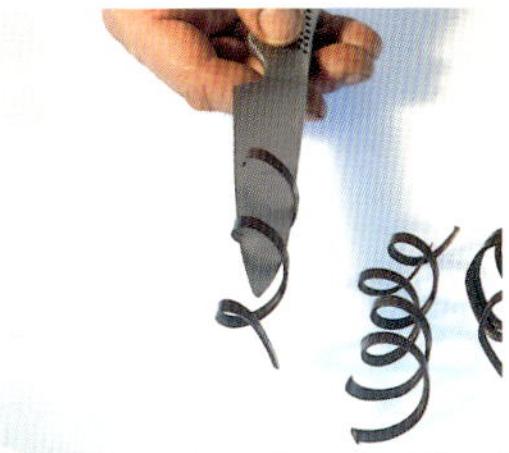

5

Fertiger Schokoladendekor

Finished chocolate décor

Almond banana sponge

200 g	egg yolk
130 g	sugar
360 g	egg white
100 g	sugar
150 g	flour
150 g	melted butter
100 g	chopped almonds
100 g	chopped banana chips

Beat 130 g sugar with the egg yolk until frothy; add 100 g sugar to the egg white and beat until stiff. Fold in the flour. Finally fold in the butter. Use a round piping nozzle size 8 to dress on the mixture in the shape required and then sprinkle on the almonds and banana chips. Bake at 180 °C for about 15 minutes.

Mandel-Bananen-Biskuit

200 g	Eigelb
130 g	Zucker
360 g	Eiweiß
100 g	Zucker
150 g	Mehl
150 g	zerlassene Butter
100 g	gehackte Mandeln
100 g	gehackte Bananenchips

Eigelb mit 130 g Zucker schaumig rühren und Eiweiß mit 100 g Zucker zu Schnee schlagen. Mehl unterheben. Zuletzt die Butter unterziehen. Masse mit einer 8er-Lochtülle in gewünschter Form aufdressieren und Mandeln sowie Bananenchips aufstreuen. Bei 180 °C etwa 15 Minuten backen.

Mangomousse

8	*Blatt Gelatine*
560 g	*Mangopüree*
130 g	*Eiweiß*
150 g	*Zucker*
420 g	*geschlagene Sahne*

Gelatine einweichen. Das Mangopüree unter die ausgedrückte, aufgelöste Gelatine rühren. Eiweiß mit Zucker steif schlagen und unterheben, dann die Sahne unterziehen.

Mango mousse

8	*sheets of gelatine*
560 g	*mango puree*
130 g	*egg white*
150 g	*sugar*
420 g	*whipped cream*

Soak the gelatine. Stir the mango puree into the squeezed-out and dissolved gelatine. Add the sugar to the egg white and beat until stiff; then fold into the mixture, followed by the cream.

Chilli cheese cream

7	sheets of gelatine
105 g	whole egg
40 g	egg yolk
105 g	sugar
140 g	curd cheese (quark)
1/4	lemon, juice and grated rind
	Tabasco to taste
630 g	whipped cream

Soak the gelatine. Beat the egg yolk with sugar until frothy and pasteurise at 85 °C. Stir in the curd cheese, lemon juice and grated rind as well as the Tabasco. Add the squeezed-out and dissolved gelatine and finally fold in the cream.

Chili-Käsesahne

7	Blatt Gelatine
105 g	Vollei
40 g	Eigelb
105 g	Zucker
140 g	Quark
1/4	Zitrone, Saft und Abrieb
	Tabasco nach Geschmack
630 g	geschlagene Sahne

Gelatine einweichen. Ei, Eigelb und Zucker schaumig rühren und bei 85 °C pasteurisieren. Quark, Zitronensaft und -abrieb sowie Tabasco einrühren. Masse unter die ausgedrückte und aufgelöste Gelatine montieren, zuletzt die Sahne unterheben.

Putting it all together

First place the decorative edge and almond/banana sponge into the ring. Fill in the mango mousse, add a second sponge and top up with chilli cheese cream. Leave in a cool spot, cover with mango puree and chilli jelly icing and then decorate.

Zusammensetzung Torte

Zuerst Dekorrand und Mandel-Bananen-Biskuit in den Ring einlegen. Die Mangomousse einfüllen, einen zweiten Biskuit einlegen und mit Chili-Käsesahne auffüllen. Kühl stellen, mit Mangopüree und Chili-Kaltgelee abgelieren und dekorieren.

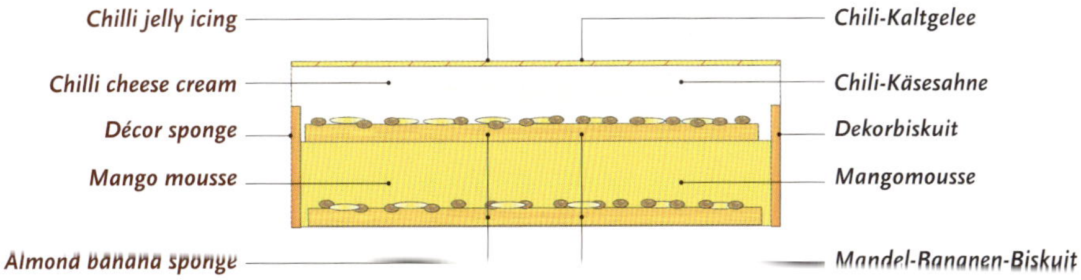

Friesensahne

Frisian Cream

East meets West.

Ein Klassiker im Nordwesten: Vanillesahne mit Pflaumenmus und Blätterteig. Hier kombiniert mit einer Zutat, die man eher im Osten der Republik bekommt: Sanddorn. Als Mousse unschlagbar.

East meets West.

A classic from northwest Germany: vanilla cream with plum preserve and puff pastry. Combined here with an ingredient more readily found in eastern Germany: sea buckthorn. As a mousse you can't beat it.

Ingredients	**Zusammensetzung**
Puff pastry	Blätterteig
Vanilla cream	Vanillesahne
Plum preserve	Pflaumenmus
Sea buckthorn mousse	Sanddornmousse
Spray couverture	Sprühkuvertüre
Chocolate décor	Schokoladendekor
Fruit	Früchte
Vanilla pod	Vanilleschote
4 Cakes, Ø 20 cm	4 Torten, Ø 20 cm
2 Cakes, Ø 28 cm	2 Torten, Ø 28 cm

Blätterteigböden

800 g	*Butter*
80 g	*Mehl*
1000 g	*Mehl*
500 g	*Wasser*
15 g	*Salz*
10 g	*Essig*
100 g	*Butter*

Aus 800 g Butter und 80 g Mehl einen Teig herstellen, zu einem flachen Quadrat formen und in Folie eingewickelt 1 Stunde kalt stellen.

Restliche Zutaten zu einem geschmeidigen Teig arbeiten. Zu einem Rechteck formen und in Folie eingewickelt 1 Stunde ruhen lassen. Den Teig in die Butter-Mehl-Mischung legen, dabei müssen beide Mischungen identische Konsistenzen haben, und in einer einfachen Tour zusammenschlagen. Im Abstand von 2 Stunden 2-mal in doppelter Tour zusammenschlagen, wobei der Teig nach jeder Tour kalt gestellt wird. Vor dem Zuschneiden nochmals in einfacher Tour zusammenschlagen. Der in doppelter Tour geschlagene Blätterteig kann mehrere Tage aufbewahrt werden. Böden mit der Ausrollmaschine auf Stufe 2,5 ausrollen, ausschneiden, stippen, ruhen lassen und dann bei 200 °C etwa 30 Minuten backen.

Puff pastry cases

800 g	*butter*
80 g	*flour*
1,000 g	*flour*
500 g	*water*
15 g	*salt*
10 g	*vinegar*
100 g	*butter*

Use 800 g butter and 80 g flour to make a pastry, shape into a shallow square, wrap up in foil and leave in a cool place for 1 hour.

Work the remainder of the ingredients into a smooth pastry. Form into a rectangular shape, wrap up in foil and leave to rest for 1 hour. Place the pastry into the butter/flour mixture: the two mixtures must be of the same consistency and given a single turn of rolling, folding and turning. Give the pastry another 2 double turns with an interval of 2 hours between mixes, placing the pastry into the refrigerator after each mixing. Before cutting, give the mixture another single turn. Once the puff pastry has been prepared like this, it can be stored for several days. Roll out the pastry with the pastry roller set to 2.5, then cut out, prick, and let rest; bake at 200 °C for about 30 minutes.

1

2

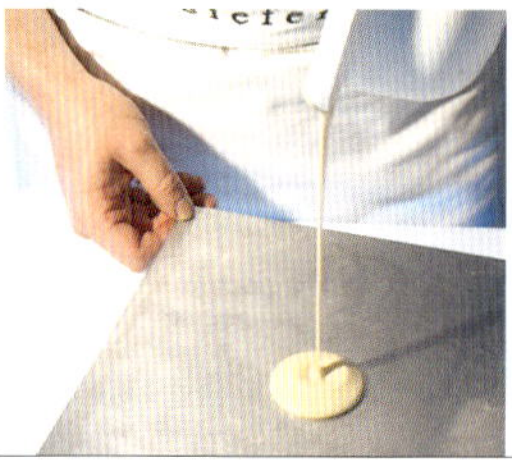
3

5 % Pflanzenöl in aufgelöste Kuvertüre gießen

Pour 5 % oil into the dissolved couverture

4

Mit einer Winkelpalette verstreichen und tiefgefrieren

Use an angled spatula to spread it out and then deep-freeze

Öl unterrühren

Stir in the oil

5

Sobald die Kuvertüre gefroren ist, Blech auf Zimmertemperatur kommen lassen. Mit einem flexiblen Messer Kuvertüre zu sich ziehen und gezackte Fächer herstellen

Once the couverture has frozen, bring back to room temperature. Use a flexible knife to drag couverture towards you and make jagged fans

---

Kuvertüre auf ein heißes Blech gießen

Pour the couverture onto a hot baking sheet

6

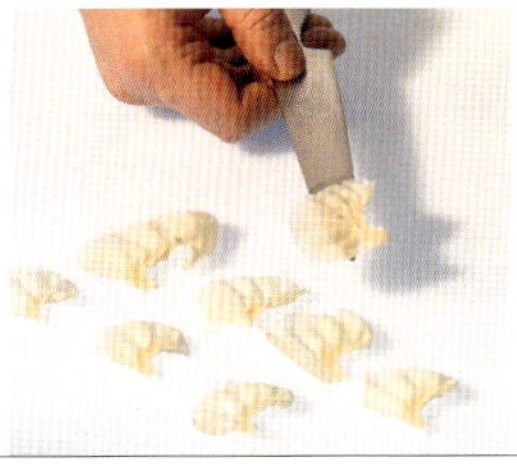

Glatte Fächer erhält man, wenn man eine Spachtel von sich wegschiebt

To make fans with smooth edges use a spatula in a movement away from you

---

Vanillesahne

10	*Blatt Gelatine*
200 g	*Sahne*
240 g	*Zucker*
60 g	*Vanillezucker*
2	*Vanilleschoten*
800 g	*geschlagene Sahne*

Gelatine einweichen. Sahne mit Zucker, Vanillezucker und Vanilleschoten aufkochen. Vanilleschoten entnehmen, ausgedrückte Gelatine in der Masse auflösen. Etwas abkühlen lassen, dann die Sahne unterheben.

Vanilla cream

10	*sheets of gelatine*
200 g	*cream*
240 g	*sugar*
60 g	*vanilla sugar*
2	*vanilla pods*
800 g	*whipped cream*

Soak the gelatine. Add the sugar, vanilla sugar and vanilla pods to the cream and bring to boil. Remove the vanilla pods and dissolve the squeezed-out gelatine in the mixture. Leave to cool down a bit and then fold in the cream.

Sanddornmousse

7	*Blatt Gelatine*
125 g	*Blutorangen, Saft und Schale*
375 g	*Sanddornpüree*
130 g	*Zucker*
60 g	*Eiweiß, pasteurisiert*
300 g	*geschlagene Sahne*
25 g	*Rum*

Gelatine in kaltem Wasser einweichen. Blutorangensaft und Abrieb der Schale kurz aufkochen, ausgedrückte Gelatine darin auflösen. Masse durch ein Sieb in das Sanddornpüree gießen. Zucker und Eiweiß zu Schnee schlagen und unter das Fruchtpüree ziehen. Danach die Sahne unterheben. Zum Schluss den Rum einrühren.

Sea buckthorn mousse

7	*sheets of gelatine*
125 g	*blood oranges, juice and zest*
375 g	*sea buckthorn puree*
130 g	*sugar*
60 g	*egg white, pasteurised*
300 g	*whipped cream*
25 g	*rum*

Soak the gelatine in cold water. Bring the juice and grated rind of the blood orange to boil and dissolve the squeezed-out gelatine. Pour the mixture through a strainer into the sea buckthorn puree. Add sugar to the egg white and beat until stiff and fold into the fruit puree. Then fold in the cream. Finally stir in the rum.

Putting it all together

Spread plum preserve over the puff pastry. Spread on the sea buckthorn mousse. Pipe on the vanilla cream, using a special nozzle. Add a second pastry case after spreading plum preserve over it and then decorate with vanilla cream. Leave in a cool place. Cover the cake lightly with spray couverture, apply a dusting of décor icing sugar to the side of the cake and apply finishing touches.

Zusammensetzung Torte

Blätterteig mit Pflaumenmus bestreichen. Sanddornmousse aufstreichen. Vanillesahne mit einer Spezialtülle aufdressieren. Zweiten, mit Pflaumenmus bestrichenen Boden auflegen und mit Vanillesahne dekorieren. Kühl stellen. Torte mit Sprühkuvertüre leicht absprühen, Rand mit Dekorpuderzucker bestäuben und ausgarnieren.

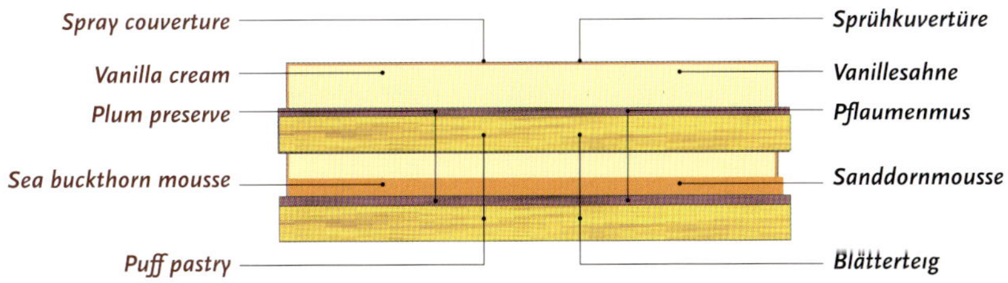

Walnuss-Zitronen-Torte

Walnut Lemon Gateau

Buttercreme ist tot? Kann ich eigentlich nicht sagen. Wir haben einen guten Absatz mit Buttercremetorten, und ich glaube, wenn man auf Qualität setzt und Kreativität in der Ausführung hat, hat Buttercreme eine Zukunft. Lang lebe der König.

Is butter cream passé? I wouldn't really say that it is. We sell a lot of butter cream gateaux and I believe that with quality and creative designs butter cream has a future. Long live the king.

Ingredients	**Zusammensetzung**
Décor sponge	Dekorbiskuit
Walnut sponge	Walnussbiskuit
French butter cream with walnuts	Französische Buttercreme mit Walnuss
Lemon cremeux	Zitronencremeux
Jelly icing	Kaltgelee
Spray couverture	Sprühkuvertüre
Fruit	Früchte
Chocolate décor	Schokoladendekor
4 Cakes, Ø 20 cm	4 Torten, Ø 20 cm
2 Cakes, Ø 28 cm	2 Torten, Ø 28 cm

Zigarettenmasse für Dekorbiskuit

100 g	*Butter*
100 g	*Puderzucker*
100 g	*Eiweiß*
100 g	*Mehl*
	Lebensmittelfarbe
	Kakaopulver

Butter und Puderzucker glatt rühren. Eiweiß und Mehl abwechselnd unterrühren, Einen Teil mit Lebensmittelfarbe, den anderen Teil mit Kakaopulver einfärben. Verarbeitung siehe Stepps.

Cigarette mixture for décor sponge

100 g	*butter*
100 g	*icing sugar*
100 g	*egg white*
100 g	*flour*
	food colouring
	cocoa powder

Blend the icing sugar with the butter until smooth. Fold in the egg white and the flour in turns and colour one part with food colouring and the other part with cocoa powder. For further processing see stages.

Dekorbiskuit

500 g	*Vollei*
375 g	*Mandelgrieß*
375 g	*Puderzucker*
100 g	*Mehl*
325 g	*Eiweiß*
75 g	*Zucker*
75 g	*Butter*

Ei, Mandelgrieß, Puderzucker und Mehl schaumig schlagen, Eiweiß und Zucker zu Schnee schlagen, Eischnee unter die Mandelmasse heben, Butter angleichen und unterziehen. Verarbeitung siehe Stepps. Für eine 60 × 40 cm große Backmatte werden etwa 600 g Masse benötigt. 10 Minuten bei 220 °C backen, dann sofort mit Zucker bestreuen und in die gewünschte Form schneiden. Reste können gut eingefroren werden.

Décor sponge

500 g	*whole egg*
375 g	*grated almonds*
375 g	*icing sugar*
100 g	*flour*
325 g	*egg white*
75 g	*sugar*
75 g	*butter*

Beat the egg, grated almonds, icing sugar and flour until frothy, beat the egg white with sugar until stiff, fold the beaten egg into the almond mixture, soften the butter and fold in. For further processing see stages. For a baking mat measuring 60 × 40 cm you need about 600 g of mixture. Bake for 10 minutes at 220 °C; then sprinkle on the sugar immediately and cut to the desired shape. Any off-cuts can be frozen for later use.

1

2

3

4

Zigarettenmasse mit hitzebeständiger Lebensmittelfarbe einfärben

Apply heat resistant food colouring to the cigarette mixture

5

Linien mit einer Winkelpalette verstreichen

Use an angled spatula to spread out the lines

Mischen

Mix thoroughly

6

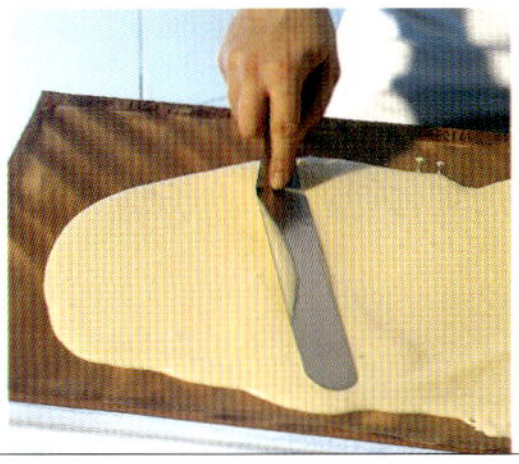

Dekorbiskuit aufstreichen

Spread on the décor sponge

Mit einem Dressiersack Linien auf eine Backmatte dressieren

Use a piping bag to dress lines onto a baking mat

7

Nach dem Backen Backmatte abziehen und Dekorbiskuit zuckern

After baking, pull off the baking mat and add a sprinkling of sugar to the décor sponge

Mit Kakao eingefärbte Zigarettenmasse daneben dressieren

Colour the cigarette mixture with cocoa and pipe next to the lines

8

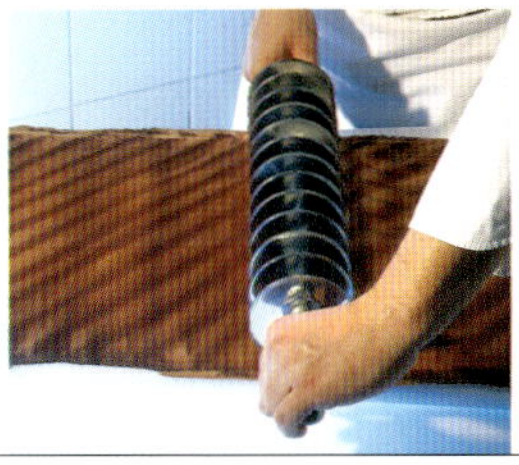

Mit einer Schneiderolle gewünschte Größe schneiden

Use a cutting wheel to cut to the required size

Walnussbiskuit

	Abrieb von 2 Orangen
270 g	*Eigelb*
170 g	*Zucker*
480 g	*Eiweiß*
210 g	*Zucker*
180 g	*Mehl*
130 g	*Walnusskrokant*
180 g	*flüssige Butter*

Abrieb von 2 Orangen, Eigelb und 170 g Zucker schaumig schlagen. Das Eiweiß mit 210 g Zucker zu Schnee schlagen. Eischnee unterziehen, Mehl und Walnusskrokant untermelieren. Zum Schluss Butter angleichen und unterziehen. Masse mit einer Lochtülle auf Backpapier dressieren und bei 180 °C etwa 15 Minuten backen.

Walnut sponge

	grated rind from 2 oranges
270 g	*egg yolk*
170 g	*sugar*
480 g	*egg white*
210 g	*sugar*
180 g	*flour*
130 g	*walnut brittle*
180 g	*liquid butter*

Beat the egg yolk together with the orange rind and 170 g of sugar until frothy. Beat egg white with 210 g of sugar until stiff. Fold in the beaten egg and then blend in the flour and walnut brittle. Finally soften the butter and fold in. Use a round nozzle to pipe the mixture onto baking paper and bake at 180 °C for about 15 minutes.

Französische Buttercreme mit Walnuss

300 g	*Vollei*
250 g	*Zucker*
750 g	*Butter*
70 g	*Walnusspaste*

Ei mit Zucker auf 85 °C pasteurisieren, kalt schlagen. Butter mit Walnusspaste schaumig rühren. Eimischung unter die Butter ziehen.

French butter cream with walnuts

300 g	*whole egg*
250 g	*sugar*
750 g	*butter*
70 g	*walnut paste*

Pasteurise the egg with sugar at 85 °C and beat cold. Beat the butter with the walnut paste until frothy. Fold the egg mixture into the butter.

Lemon cremeux

6	*sheets of gelatine*
250 g	*lemon juice*
	grated rind from 6 lemons
300 g	*sugar*
300 g	*whole egg*
380 g	*butter*

Soak the gelatine. Pasteurise the lemon juice, lemon rind, sugar and egg at 85 °C. Stir in the squeezed-out gelatine, pass through a fine strainer and blend in the cold butter. Pour into prepared moulds on printed foil, deep-freeze and then pull off the foil with a sharp tug.

Zitronencremeux

6	*Blatt Gelatine*
250 g	*Zitronensaft*
	Abrieb von 6 Zitronen
300 g	*Zucker*
300 g	*Vollei*
380 g	*Butter*

Gelatine einweichen. Zitronensaft, Zitronenabrieb, Zucker und Ei bei 85 °C pasteurisieren. Ausgedrückte Gelatine unterrühren, durch ein feines Sieb passieren und kalte Butter untermixen. In vorbereitete Formen auf bedruckte Folie gießen, tiefgefrieren, dann Folie in einem Ruck abreißen.

Putting it all together

Insert the décor into the mould. Then put on the walnut sponge. Spread on a layer of walnut butter cream, insert the sponge, place the lemon cremeux, another sponge layer and finish off with the walnut butter cream. Slightly freeze and then spray with spray couverture. Finish the cake off with the lemon cremeux and jelly icing. Decorate to taste.

Zusammensetzung Torte

Dekorbiskuit in Form einlegen. Walnussbiskuit einsetzen. Eine Schicht Walnussbuttercreme einfüllen, Biskuit aufsetzen, Zitronencremeux einlegen, wieder Biskuit, mit Walnussbuttercreme abschließen. Kurz anfrosten, dann mit Sprühkuvertüre absprühen. Mit Kaltgelee abgeliertes Zitronencremeux auflegen. Dekorieren.

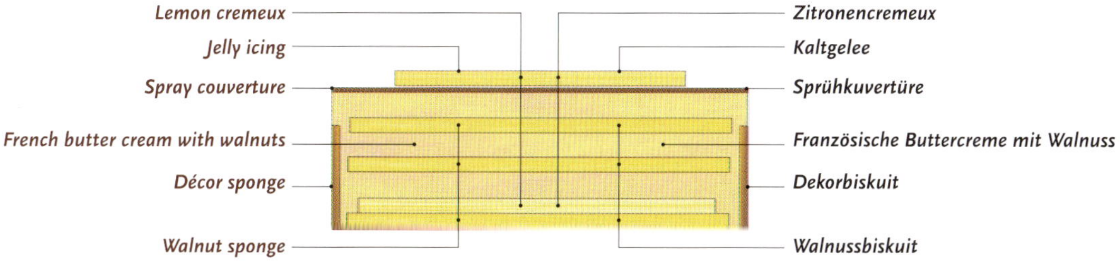

CAROLA

Baumkuchen ist, wie wir Deutschen immer meinen, der deutsche Kuchen schlechthin. Natürlich gibt es baumkuchenähnliche Gebäcke auch in Spanien, Österreich und in den ehemaligen Ostblockländern. Aber nicht in dieser Qualität und Vielfalt wie bei uns. Carola ist die spezielle Form des Baumkuchens als Tortenring. Leider benötigt man eine Baumkuchenmaschine zur Herstellung.

Germans generally believe that Baumkuchen (also translated as "tree cake") is the classic German cake. Of course, similar types of cakes exist in other countries, such as Spain, Austria and the former Iron Curtain countries. But not of the same quality and in so many different varieties as in Germany. Carola is a special form of Baumkuchen made in a cake ring. You will need a Baumkuchen machine to make these cakes.

Ingredients	Zusammensetzung
Carola Baumkuchen, 12 cake rings	Carolabaumkuchen, 12 Tortenringe
Gingerbread vermicelli with potato sponge	Lebkuchenstreusel mit Kartoffelbiskuit
Wild berry mousse	Waldbeermousse
Jellied mulled wine cream	Gelierte Glühweincreme
Mulled wine jelly icing	Glühweinkaltgelee
Chocolate décor	Schokoladendekor
Fruits and spices	Früchte und Gewürze
4 Cakes, Ø 20 cm	4 Torten, Ø 20 cm
2 Cakes, Ø 28 cm	2 Torten, Ø 28 cm

1

2

3

Gelierte Glühweincreme

2	*Blatt Gelatine*
150 g	*Zucker*
150 g	*Eigelb*
125 g	*Rotwein*
1	*Orange, Abrieb und Saft*
1	*Zimtstange*
1	*Nelke*
190 g	*Butter*
20 g	*Rum*

Gelatine in kaltem Wasser einweichen. Zucker und Eigelb schaumig schlagen. Rotwein, Orangenabrieb und Saft mit Zimt und Nelke aufkochen. Flüssigkeit durch ein Sieb in die Eigelbmasse gießen und bei 85 °C pasteurisieren. Gelatine auspressen und in der Masse auflösen. Die Butter flöckchenweise untermixen. Zum Schluss den Rum einrühren. In Silikonform tiefgefrieren.

Jellied mulled wine cream

2	*sheets of gelatine*
150 g	*sugar*
150 g	*egg yolk*
125 g	*red wine*
1	*orange, zest and juice*
1	*cinnamon stick*
1	*clove*
190 g	*butter*
20 g	*rum*

Soak the gelatine in cold water. Beat the egg yolk and sugar until frothy. Bring the red wine to boil together with the orange zest and juice as well as the cinnamon and clove. Pour the liquid through a strainer into the egg yolk mixture and pasteurise at 85 °C. Squeeze out the gelatine and dissolve into the mixture. Cut the butter into flakes and blend in. Finally stir in the rum. Deep-freeze in a silicon mould.

Gefrostete Metallhalbkugel mit temperierter Kuvertüre bespinnen

Pipe tempered couverture onto a frozen metallic hemisphere

Sobald die Kuvertüre angezogen hat, vorsichtig abformen

Carefully remove the couverture as soon as it sets

Den Dekor in die umgedrehte Halbkugel setzen und ganz fest werden lassen (mindestens 30 Minuten)

Place the décor into the turned over hemisphere and leave until firmly set (at least 30 minutes)

Wild berry mousse

6	*sheets of gelatine*
350 g	*puree of wild berries*
5 g	*lemon juice*
1	*vanilla pod*
85 g	*egg white*
115 g	*sugar*
250 g	*whipped cream*

Soak the gelatine in cold water. Stir the wild berry puree together with the lemon juice and the vanilla pith. Add sugar to the egg white and beat until stiff. Dissolve the gelatine. Add the wild berry puree to the gelatine. Fold in the beaten egg white. Finally fold in the cream.

Tip: Prepare the wild berry puree yourself. Then you can determine the mixture of berries yourself, giving the wild berry puree your own individual flavour.

Waldbeermousse

6	*Blatt Gelatine*
350 g	*Waldbeerpüree*
5 g	*Zitronensaft*
1	*Vanilleschote*
85 g	*Eiweiß*
115 g	*Zucker*
250 g	*geschlagene Sahne*

Gelatine in kaltem Wasser einweichen. Das Waldbeerpüree mit Zitronensaft und Vanillemark verrühren. Eiweiß mit Zucker zu Schnee schlagen. Gelatine auflösen. Waldbeerpüree zu der Gelatine geben. Eischnee unterheben. Zum Schluss die Sahne unterziehen.

Tipp: Machen Sie das Waldbeerpüree selbst. Dann können Sie das Mischungsverhältnis der Beeren selbst festlegen und geben dem Waldbeerpüree Ihre eigene Note.

Carolabaumkuchen, 12 Tortenringe

200 g	*Marzipanrohmasse*
400 g	*Eigelb*
380 g	*Butter*
15 g	*Zitronenabrieb*
1	*Vanilleschote*
4 g	*Salz*
200 g	*Weizenpuder*
380 g	*Zucker*
700 g	*Eiweiß*
200 g	*Mehl*

Marzipanrohmasse mit Eigelb glatt arbeiten. Butter und Gewürze zugeben und schaumig schlagen. Weizenpuder mit Zucker mischen, Eiweiß beigeben und zu Schnee schlagen. Buttermasse abwechselnd mit Eischnee und Mehl vermischen. Mit der Baumkuchenmaschine und der Carolawalze mindestens 6 Lagen Baumkuchenmasse backen. Aprikotieren und mit Fondant glasieren.

Wer keine Baumkuchenmaschine hat, backt den Baumkuchen nur mit Oberhitze im Ofen und benutzt ihn dann, in dünne Scheiben geschnitten, als Rand.

Carola Baumkuchen, 12 cake rings

200 g	*marzipan paste*
400 g	*egg yolk*
380 g	*butter*
15 g	*lemon peel*
1	*vanilla pod*
4 g	*salt*
200 g	*wheat powder*
380 g	*sugar*
700 g	*egg white*
200 g	*flour*

Blend the marzipan paste with egg yolk until smooth. Add the butter and spices and whisk until frothy. Mix the wheat powder with the sugar, add the egg white and whisk until stiff. Alternately blend the beaten egg white and flour into the butter mixture. Use the Baumkuchen machine and the Carola roller to bake at least 6 layers of the cake mixture. Cover with apricot jam and glaze it with Fondant.

If you do not have a Baumkuchen machine, bake it in the oven with only the top heating element on; then cut it into thin slices and use as edging.

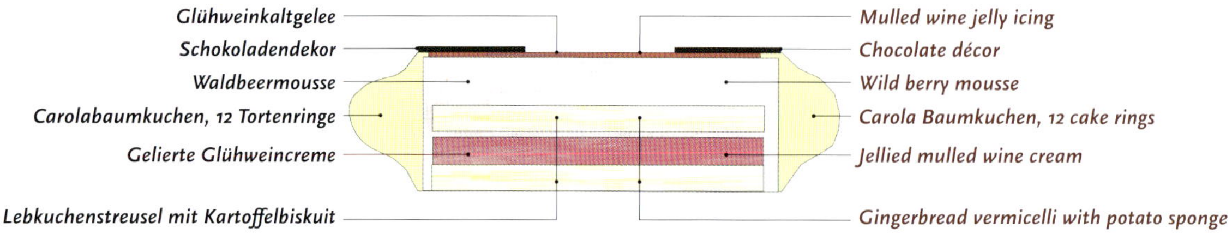

Gingerbread vermicelli with potato sponge

150 g	*flour*
5 g	*gingerbread spice*
12 g	*sugar*
30 g	*honey in powder*
125 g	*melted butter*

Mix the dry ingredients. Stir in the butter with a cooking spoon.

80 g	*egg yolk*
	grated rind from 1 Lemon
45 g	*sugar*
250 g	*boiled, floury potatoes*
120 g	*egg white*
80 g	*sugar*
10 g	*semolina*
25 g	*grounded almonds*

Whisk the egg yolk, grated rind from the lemon, 45 g sugar and potatoes until frothy. Beat the egg white with 80 g sugar until stiff. Stir into the egg yolk mixture, alternately incorporating the semolina and almonds. Pipe the mixture onto baking paper, cover with vermicelli and bake at 180 °C for about 20 minutes.

Putting it all together

Place the gingerbread vermicelli into the cake ring for the Baumkuchen. Add the jellied mulled wine cream. Fill in the wild berry mousse and place second pastry layer on top. Use wild berry mousse to make a smooth surface. Keep refrigerated. As soon as the wild berry mousse has become rigid, spread the mulled wine jelly icing over it.

Lebkuchenstreusel mit Kartoffelbiskuit

150 g	*Mehl*
5 g	*Lebkuchengewürz*
12 g	*Zucker*
30 g	*Honig in Pulver*
125 g	*zerlassene Butter*

Trockene Zutaten mischen. Die Butter unterrühren, so dass Streusel entstehen.

80 g	*Eigelb*
	Abrieb von 1 Zitrone
45 g	*Zucker*
250 g	*gekochte, mehlige Kartoffeln*
120 g	*Eiweiß*
80 g	*Zucker*
10 g	*Weizengrieß*
25 g	*geriebene Mandeln*

Eigelb, Zitronenabrieb, 45 g Zucker und gekochte Kartoffeln schaumig schlagen. Eiweiß und 80 g Zucker zu Schnee schlagen. Abwechselnd mit Weizengrieß und Mandeln unter die Eigelbmasse rühren. Masse mit einer Lochtülle auf Backpapier aufdressieren, mit Streuseln bestreuen und bei 180 °C etwa 20 Minuten backen.

Zusammensetzung Torte

Lebkuchenstreusel in Carolabaumkuchenring einlegen. Gelierte Glühweincreme einlegen. Die Waldbeermousse einfüllen, zweiten Boden einlegen. Mit Waldbeermousse glatt streichen. Kalt stellen. Sobald die Waldbeermousse stabil ist, mit Glühweinkaltgelee gelieren. Dekorieren.

MASCARPONE ARMAGNAC

MASCARPONE ARMAGNAC

Europäisches Multi-Kulti: Mascarpone aus Italien, Armagnac aus Frankreich, Caro-Kaffee aus Deutschland und Zwetschgen aus meiner Heimat, dem Odenwald. Good Old Europe lässt grüssen.

Greetings from South, West and Central Europe: Mascarpone from Italy, Armagnac from France, Chicory coffee from Germany and plums from the Odenwald region, where I come from. A homage to European unity.

Ingredients

- Chocolate sponge
- Prunes and chocolate mousse with Armagnac
- Mascarpone mousse/ Chicory coffee
- Chocolate icing Blanc and Noir
- Chocolate décor
- Spices and prunes

4 Cakes, Ø 20 cm

2 Cakes, Ø 28 cm

Zusammensetzung

- Schokoladenbiskuit
- Trockenpflaumen-Schokoladenmousse mit Armagnac
- Mascarponemousse-Caro-Kaffee
- Schokoladenglasur Blanc und Noir
- Schokoladendekor
- Gewürze und Trockenpflaumen

4 Torten, Ø 20 cm

2 Torten, Ø 28 cm

Schokoladenbiskuit

210 g	*Marzipan*
210 g	*Eigelb*
345 g	*Eiweiß*
345 g	*Zucker*
110 g	*Kakaopulver*

Marzipan mit Eigelb glatt rühren, Eiweiß mit Zucker zu Schnee schlagen. Eischnee unter die Marzipanmasse ziehen, zuletzt das Kakaopulver einarbeiten. Bei 180 °C etwa 25 Minuten backen.

Mascarponemousse-Caro-Kaffee Kaffeemix

35 g	*Zucker*
35 g	*Caro-Kaffee*
150 g	*Wasser*
105 g	*Armagnac*

Zucker und Caro-Kaffee (Getreidekaffee) mischen, mit heißem Wasser aufgießen. Sobald die Flüssigkeit kalt ist, Armagnac unterrühren.

9	*Blatt Gelatine*
225 g	*Kaffeemix*
100 g	*Zucker*
100 g	*Vanillecreme*
50 g	*Eigelb*
375 g	*Mascarpone*
750 g	*geschlagene Sahne*

Gelatine einweichen. Kaffeemix, Zucker, Vanillecreme, Eigelb und Mascarpone vorsichtig verrühren. Masse unter die ausgedrückte Gelatine ziehen. Zuletzt Sahne unterziehen.

Chocolate sponge

210 g	*marzipan*
210 g	*egg yolk*
345 g	*egg white*
345 g	*sugar*
110 g	*cocoa powder*

Beat the marzipan with the egg yolk until smooth; add sugar to the egg white and beat until stiff. Fold the beaten egg into the marzipan mixture and then work in the cocoa powder. Bake at 180 °C for about 25 minutes.

Mascarpone mousse/ Chicory coffee mix

35 g	*sugar*
35 g	*Chicory coffee*
150 g	*water*
105 g	*Armagnac*

Mix the sugar and Chicory coffee together and pour hot water over it. Once the liquid has cooled down, stir in the Armagnac.

9	*sheets of gelatine*
225 g	*coffee mix*
100 g	*sugar*
100 g	*vanilla cream*
50 g	*egg yolk*
375 g	*Mascarpone cheese*
750 g	*whipped cream*

Soak the gelatine. Then mix the coffee mix, sugar, vanilla cream, egg yolk and Mascarpone carefully together. Fold the mixture into the squeezed-out gelatine. Finally fold in the cream.

1

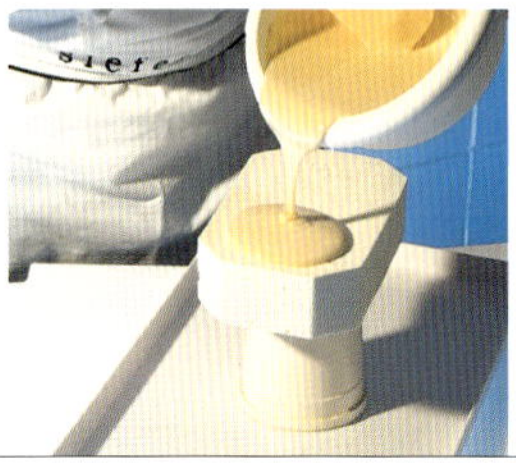

2

3

4

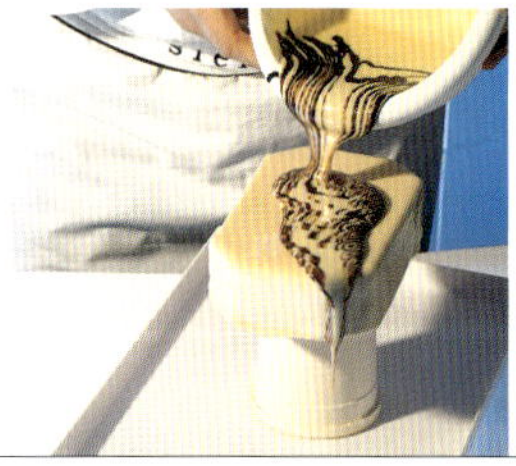

5

Tiefgefrorene Tortenform mit einem Gasbrenner erwärmen und ausformen

Use a gas torch to heat up the deep-frozen cake mould and turn out the cake

Mit Schokoladenglasur Blanc übergießen

Pour the Blanc chocolate icing over it

Mit einer Winkelpalette abziehen

Smooth with an angled spatula

Weiße Glasur mit Schokoladenglasur Noir bespinnen

Pipe the Noir chocolate icing over the white icing

Torte diagonal übergießen

Pour a diagonal pattern across the cake

Prunes and Chocolate Mousse with Armagnac

100 g	cream
130 g	prunes
25 g	butter
50 g	egg yolk, pasteurised
50 g	sugar
250 g	dark couverture, 60 %
500 g	whipped cream
100 g	Armagnac

Boil the prunes in the cream and butter until soft. Stir the egg yolk and sugar together and then blend with the prune cream. Work the chopped-up dark couverture into the hot mixture and then fold in the cream and finally the Armagnac.

Putting it all together

Put the prune/chocolate mousse into a silicon form and deep-freeze. Place the sponge layer into a mould, add the prune/chocolate mousse and cover with Mascarpone mousse, then add a second layer of sponge base, top up with Mascarpone mousse, smooth the top and put into the deep-freeze. For decorations see stages.

Trockenpflaumen-Schokoladenmousse mit Armagnac

100 g	Sahne
130 g	Trockenpflaumen
25 g	Butter
50 g	Eigelb, pasteurisiert
50 g	Zucker
250 g	Bitterkuvertüre, 60 %
500 g	geschlagene Sahne
100 g	Armagnac

Sahne, Trockenpflaumen und Butter weich kochen. Eigelb und Zucker verrühren und unter die Pflaumensahne rühren. Die gehackte Bitterkuvertüre unter die heiße Masse einarbeiten, dann die Sahne und zum Schluss den Armagnac unterziehen.

Zusammensetzung Torte

Trockenpflaumen-Schokoladenmousse in eine Silikonform füllen und tiefgefrieren. Biskuitboden in eine Form einlegen, Trockenpflaumen-Schokoladenmousse aufsetzen, mit Mascarponemousse bedecken, einen zweiten Boden auflegen, mit Mascarponemousse auffüllen, glatt streichen und tiefgefrieren. Dekor siehe Stepps.

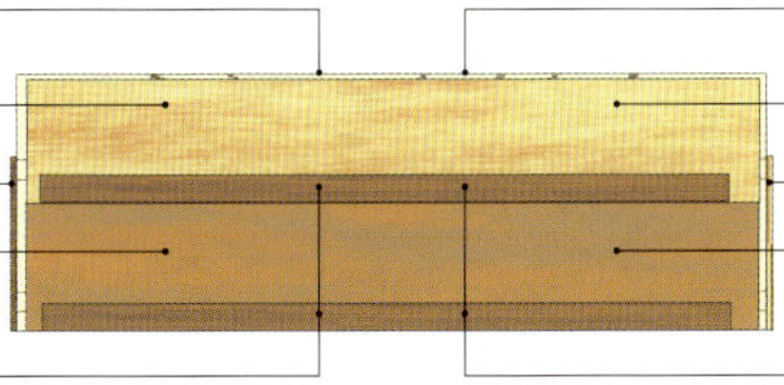

Pistazien-Kirsch

Pistachio-Cherry

Ein Stück Toskana, auch wenn die Pistazien aus Sizilien stammen und der Safran aus den Abruzzen kommt. Das Konzept bei diesen Mousse-tartes mag ich sehr gerne, da man viel variieren kann und das Verhältnis der Sahne zum Gebackenem dem Zeitgeist entspricht.

Here is a piece of Toscanny, even though the pistachios are from Sicily and the saffron from the Abruzzo. I really like the concept of this mousse tart, because it allows a lot of variations and the proportion of cream to pastry fits in with modern trends.

Ingredients	Zusammensetzung
Pistachio mousse "Sicily"	Pistazienmousse Sizilia
Pistachio cherry tart	Pistazienkirschtarte
Chocolate décor	Schokoladendekor
Green spray couverture	Grüne Sprühkuvertüre
Cherries	Kirschen
Saffron jelly icing	Safrankaltgelee
Cherry jelly filling	Kirschgeleeeinlage
4 Cakes, Ø 20 cm	4 Torten, Ø 20 cm
2 Cakes, Ø 28 cm	2 Torten, Ø 28 cm

Kirschgelee-Einlage

8	*Blatt Gelatine*
500 g	*Sauerkirschpüree*
100 g	*Zucker*

Gelatine einweichen. Sauerkirschpüree mit Zucker vermischen. Ausgedrückte Gelatine auflösen und Fruchtpüree unterrühren. In Silikonförmchen einfüllen und tiefkühlen.

Cherry jelly filling

8	*sheets of gelatine*
500 g	*morello cherry puree*
100 g	*sugar*

Soak the gelatine. Then mix the sugar into the morello cherry puree. Dissolve the squeezed-out gelatine and stir in the fruit puree. Fill into small silicon moulds and deep-freeze.

Pistazienmousse Sizilia

7	*Blatt Gelatine*
120 g	*Eigelb*
120 g	*Zucker*
75 g	*Milch*
150 g	*Pistazienmark*
750 g	*geschlagene Sahne*

Gelatine einweichen. Eigelb, Zucker und Milch verrühren und pasteurisieren. Ausgedrückte Gelatine in der Masse auflösen und Pistazienmark einrühren. Sobald die Masse leicht abgekühlt ist, die Sahne unterziehen. Ausgeformtes tiefgefrorenes Kirschgelee in einen größeren Metallring einlegen, mit Pistazienmousse auffüllen, glatt streichen und tiefgefrieren.

Pistachio mousse "Sicily"

7	*sheets of gelatine*
120 g	*egg yolk*
120 g	*sugar*
75 g	*milk*
150 g	*pistachio paste*
750 g	*whipped cream*

Soak the gelatine. Stir the egg yolk, sugar and milk together and pasteurise. Dissolve the squeezed-out gelatine in the mixture and stir in the pistachio paste. As soon as the mixture has cooled down slightly, fold in the cream. Turn out the deep-frozen cherry jelly and place into a larger baking ring, top up with pistachio mousse, smoothe with a pallet knife and put into the deep-freeze.

1

2

3

4

5

6

7

Gelb gefärbte Kakaobutter auf Plastikfolie sprenkeln

Dye the cocoa butter yellow and sprinkle over the plastic foil

Grün gefärbte Kakaobutter dazusprenkeln

Then add the green-coloured cocoa butter

Mit einer Winkelpalette verstreichen

Use an angled spatula to spread out

Folie in Streifen schneiden

Cut the foil into strips

Messer in temperierte Kuvertüre tauchen

Dip the knife into tempered couverture

Kuvertüre auf Folienstreifen streichen

Spread the couverture onto the foil strips

Fertiges Dekor

Finished décor

Pistachio cherry tart

200 g	butter
200 g	icing sugar
200 g	grated almonds
50 g	grated pistachios
25 g	wheat powder
25 g	rum
150 g	whole egg
400 g	yoghurt
70 g	pistachio paste
300 g	morello cherries

Stir all ingredients together until smooth, except the morello cherries. Pour into the previously baked shortcrust case. Spread loosely onto the morello cherries. Bake at 180 °C for about 20 minutes.

Pistazienkirschtarte

200 g	Butter
200 g	Puderzucker
200 g	Mandelgrieß
50 g	Pistaziengrieß
25 g	Weizenpuder
25 g	Rum
150 g	Vollei
400 g	Joghurt
70 g	Pistazienpaste
300 g	Sauerkirschen

Alle Zutaten, außer Sauerkirschen, miteinander glatt rühren. In vorgebackene Mürbeteigform einfüllen. Sauerkirschen lose aufstreuen. Bei 180 °C etwa 20 Minuten backen.

Putting it all together

Turn out the pistachio mousse and spray with the green-coloured white spray couverture while deep-frozen. Then place onto the cold pistachio cherry tart. Decorate the tart with chocolate décor, cherries with their stems and saffron jelly icing.

Zusammensetzung Torte

Die Pistazienmousse ausformen und mit grün gefärbter weißer Sprühkuvertüre tiefgefroren absprühen und auf die kalte Pistazienkirschtarte auflegen. Torte mit Schokoladendekor, Stielkirschen und Safrankaltgelee dekorieren.

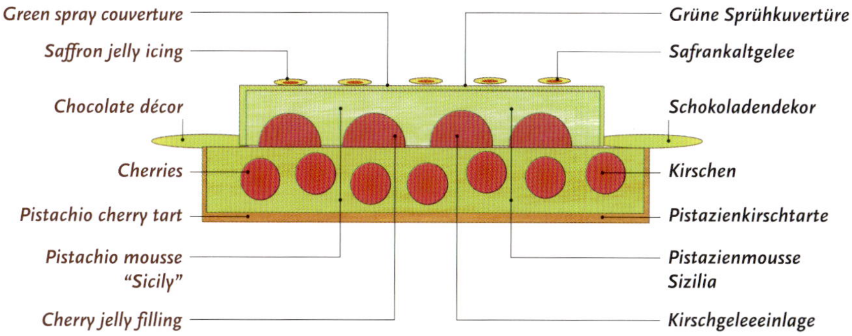

TOLSTOIS PREISELBEERGARTEN

TOLSTOY'S CRANBERRY GARDEN

Flockensahne lieben alle! Und meine Frau Isabel ist eine Spezialistin im Herstellen der Flockensahne. Eigentlich sollte die Torte einen anderen Namen tragen. Aber Matthias Hoffmann, der Fotograf des Buchs, meinte, sie erinnere ihn an „Tolstois Kirschgarten“. Hier meine Variante mit Preiselbeeren und Haselnüssen.

Everybody loves flaky fresh cream cake, and my dear wife Isabel is an expert at making this delicacy. I had originally planned a different name for this cake, but Matthias Hoffmann, the photographer for this book, thought that it reminded him of Tolstoy's "Cherry Garden". Here is my version with cranberries and hazelnuts.

Ingredients	Zusammensetzung
Choux pastry base	Streuselbrandteigboden
Hazelnut cream	Haselnusssahne
Cranberries	Preiselbeeren
Rum cream	Rumsahne
Caramelised hazelnuts	Karamellisierte Haselnüsse
Chocolate décor	Schokoladendekor
White spray couverture	Weisse Sprühkuvertüre
4 Cakes, Ø 20 cm	4 Torten, Ø 20 cm
2 Cakes, Ø 28 cm	2 Torten, Ø 28 cm

Haselnussstreusel

40 g	*geröstete Haselnüsse*
90 g	*Zucker*
200 g	*Mehl*
	Salz
	Abrieb von 1 Zitrone
110 g	*Butter*

Die Haselnüsse mahlen, dann mit Zucker, Mehl, Salz und Abrieb von 1 Zitronenschale vermischen. Butter zerlassen und mit dem Rührlöffel unterrühren.

Hazelnut vermicelli

40 g	*roasted hazelnuts*
90 g	*sugar*
200 g	*flour*
	salt
	grated rind from 1 lemon
110 g	*butter*

Grind the hazelnuts and then mix with the sugar, flour, salt and grated rind from 1 lemon. Melt the butter and stir in using a cooking spoon.

1

2

3

Streuselbrandteigboden

300 g	*Wasser*
140 g	*Milch*
90 g	*Butter*
	Salz
200 g	*Mehl*
300 g	*Vollei*
80 g	*Eigelb*

Wasser, Milch, Butter und Salz aufkochen, Mehl zugeben, abrösten und auskühlen lassen. Vollei und Eigelb nach und nach zugeben. Brandteig mit einer Winkelpalette dünn in eine Schablone auf einer Backmatte aufstreichen. Haselnussstreusel auf 4 Böden (Ø 20 cm) bzw. auf 2 Böden (Ø 28 cm) aufstreuen. Bei 200 °C etwa 20 Minuten backen.

Choux pastry base

300 g	*water*
140 g	*milk*
90 g	*butter*
	salt
200 g	*flour*
300 g	*whole egg*
80 g	*egg yolk*

Bring the water, milk, butter and salt to boil, add flour, roast and leave to cool. Add the whole egg and egg yolk in small increments. Use an angled spatula to spread the choux pastry thinly on a template onto a baking mat. Sprinkle the hazelnut vermicelli either on 4 crusts (Ø 20 cm) or on 2 crusts (Ø 28 cm). Bake at 200 °C for about 20 minutes.

Weiße Kuvertüre im engen Zickzack auf eine Marmorplatte spritzen

Pipe the white couverture onto a marble slab in a close zigzag pattern.

4

Am Rand der Marmorplatte abschneiden

Cut off at the edge of the marble slab

Erste Reihe quer aufspritzen

Pipe the first row horizontally

5

Fertiger Zaun

Finished fence

Zaun fertig stellen

Complete the fence

Hazelnut cream

12	*sheets of gelatine*
80 g	*egg yolk*
100 g	*whole egg*
80 g	*sugar*
100 g	*hazelnut paste*
800 g	*whipped cream*
40 g	*chopped hazelnut brittle*
20 g	*hazelnut brandy*

Soak the gelatine in cold water. Pasteurise the egg yolk, whole egg and sugar at 85 °C. Squeeze the gelatine and dissolve in the egg mixture. Add the hazelnut paste, leave to cool down a little and then fold in the cream. Finally fold in the hazelnut brittle and brandy.

Haselnusssahne

12	*Blatt Gelatine*
80 g	*Eigelb*
100 g	*Vollei*
80 g	*Zucker*
100 g	*Haselnusspaste*
800 g	*geschlagene Sahne*
40 g	*Haselnusskrokant, gehackt*
20 g	*Haselnussbrand*

Gelatine in kaltem Wasser einweichen. Eigelb, Vollei und Zucker bei 85 °C pasteurisieren. Ausgepresste Gelatine darin auflösen. Haselnusspaste zugeben, leicht abkühlen lassen, dann Sahne unterziehen. Zuletzt den Haselnusskrokant und -brand unterheben.

Preiselbeeren

250 g	*Zucker*
25 g	*Pektin*
500 g	*Preiselbeeren*
50 g	*Rotwein*

50 g Zucker mit Pektin mischen. Preiselbeeren und Rotwein erhitzen, Petktin-Zucker-Gemisch zugeben, aufkochen. Restlichen Zucker einrieseln lassen und nochmals aufkochen, dann abkühlen lassen.

Cranberries

250 g	*sugar*
25 g	*pectin*
500 g	*cranberries*
50 g	*red wine*

Mix 50 g sugar with the pectin. Heat the cranberries and red wine, add the sugar with the pectin and bring to boil. Let the remainder of the sugar run into the mixture and bring back to boil, then leave to cool.

Rum cream

12	*sheets of gelatine*
80 g	*egg yolk*
80 g	*sugar*
200 g	*milk*
800 g	*whipped cream*
160 g	*rum*

Soak the gelatine in cold water. Pasteurise the egg yolk, sugar and milk at 85 °C. Squeeze out the gelatine and dissolve in the egg mixture. Leave the mixture to cool down to jelling point and then fold in the cream and the rum. Deep-freeze in a silicon mould.

Rumsahne

12	*Blatt Gelatine*
80 g	*Eigelb*
80 g	*Zucker*
200 g	*Milch*
800 g	*geschlagene Sahne*
160 g	*Rum*

Gelatine in kaltem Wasser einweichen. Eigelb, Zucker und Milch bei 85 °C pasteurisieren. Ausgedrückte Gelatine darin auflösen. Masse abkühlen, bis zum Gelierpunkt abkühlen lassen, dann die Sahne und den Rum unterziehen. In Silikonform tiefgefrieren.

Putting it all together

Spread rum cream on the underside of the choux pastry and place on a shortcrust pastry base. Fill up with rum cream. Pipe on a cranberry jam in the shape of a spiral. Spread rum cream onto the 2nd crust and place on top of the first one. Fill up with hazelnut cream. Then put on the hazelnut vermicelly choux pastry crust and put into the deep-freeze. Spray lightly with white spray couverture and decorate.

Zusammensetzung Torte

Brandteigboden von unten mit Rumsahne bestreichen und auf einen Mürbeteigboden legen. Mit Rumsahne auffüllen. Spirale aus Preiselbeermarmelade aufdressieren. 2. Boden von unten mit Rumsahne bestreichen und auflegen. Mit Haselnusssahne auffüllen. Streuselbrandteigboden auflegen und tiefgefrieren. Mit weißer Sprühkuvertüre leicht absprühen und dekorieren.

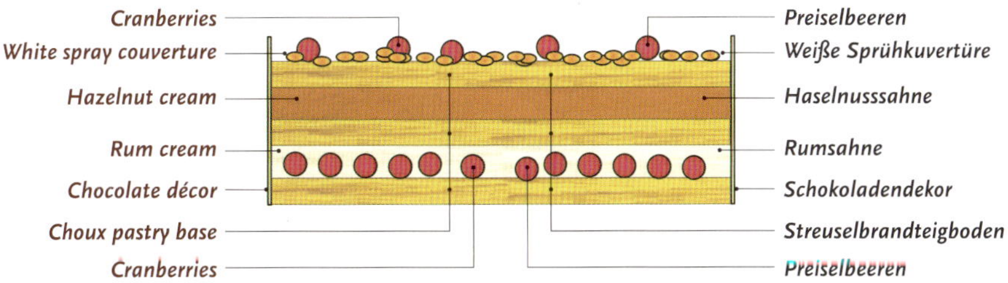

BERND

HIMBEER-LIMONEN-THYMIAN-MOUSSE

RASPBERRY-LIME-THYME MOUSSE

Meine Lieblingstorte im Sommer. Sehr erfrischend und leicht durch die Früchte und trendy durch die Zugabe des Thymians. Wem es zu jung und zu wild sein sollte, lässt das „Grünzeug“ einfach weg.

This is my favourite summer gateau. Very refreshing and light thanks to the fruit, as well as up to the minute on account of the thyme. If this turns out to be too young and wild for you, simply leave out the green stuff.

Ingredients	Zusammensetzung
Coconut dacquoise	Kokosdacquoise
Raspberry mousse	Himbeermousse
Lime mousse with thyme	Limonenmousse mit Thymian
White spray couverture	Weisse Sprühkuvertüre
Chocolate décor	Schokoladendekor
Fruits	Früchte
Twig of thyme	Thymianzweig
4 Cakes, Ø 20 cm	4 Torten, Ø 20 cm
2 Cakes, Ø 28 cm	2 Torten, Ø 28 cm

Kokosdacquoise

375 g	*Eiweiß, pasteurisiert*
125 g	*Zucker*
65 g	*Mandelgrieß*
310 g	*Puderzucker*
250 g	*Kokosraspel*
65 g	*Mehl*

Eiweiß und Zucker zu Schnee schlagen. Trockene Zutaten mischen und unter den Eischnee heben. Mit einer 8er-Lochtülle auf eine Backmatte dressieren und bei 160 °C etwa 20 Minuten backen

Coconut dacquoise

375 g	*egg white, pasteurised*
125 g	*sugar*
65 g	*grated almonds*
310 g	*icing sugar*
250 g	*grated coconut*
65 g	*flour*

Beat the egg white with the sugar until stiff. Mix the dry ingredients and fold into the beaten egg. Pipe the mixture onto a baking mat. Bake at 160°C for about 20 minutes.

Himbeermousse

11	*Blatt Gelatine*
550 g	*Himbeerpüree*
110 g	*Eiweiß*
150 g	*Zucker*
380 g	*geschlagene Sahne*

Gelatine in kaltem Wasser einweichen. Ausgedrückte Gelatine auflösen und Himbeerpüree zugeben. Eiweiß mit Zucker zu Schnee schlagen und unterziehen. Zuletzt die Sahne unterheben. Mousse in eine Silikonform füllen und einfrieren.

Raspberry mousse

11	*sheets of gelatine*
550 g	*raspberry puree*
110 g	*egg white*
150 g	*sugar*
380 g	*whipped cream*

Soak the gelatine in cold water. Dissolve the squeezed-out gelatine and stir in the raspberry puree. Beat the egg white with the sugar until stiff and then fold in. Finally fold in the cream. Pour the mousse into a silicon mould and deep-freeze.

1

2

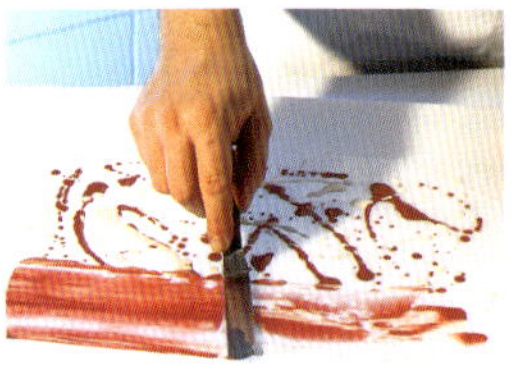

3

4

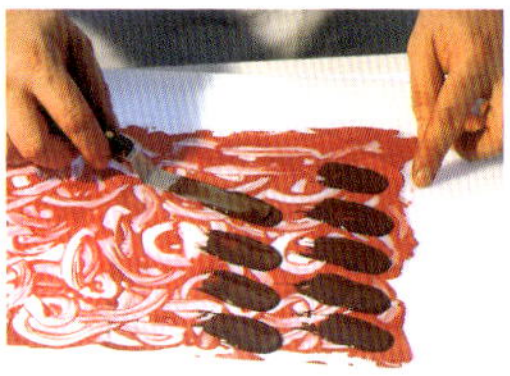

5

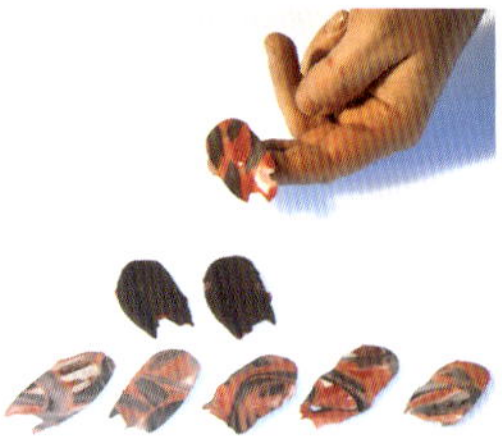

6

Rot gefärbte Kakaobutter auf Plastikfolie sprenkeln

Dye the cocoa butter red and sprinkle over the plastic foil

Weiß gefärbte Kakaobutter dazusprenkeln

Then add the white-coloured cocoa butter

Mit einer Winkelpalette verstreichen

Use an angled spatula to spread out

Mit den Fingern Muster aufzeichnen

Use your fingers to draw on patterns

Temperierte Kuvertüre mit der Winkelpalette aufstreichen

Spread on the tempered couverture with an angled spatula

Fertiges Schokoladendekor

Finished chocolate décor

Lime mousse with thyme

9	*sheets of gelatine*
275 g	*lime juice*
5	*twigs of thyme*
35 g	*sugar*
190 g	*egg white*
250 g	*sugar*
440 g	*whipped cream*

Soak the gelatine in cold water. Bring 50 g of lime juice with the thyme and 35 g sugar to boil. Add the 250 g sugar to the egg white and beat until stiff; then fold into the remaining lime juice. Finally fold in the cream.

Limonenmousse mit Thymian

9	*Blatt Gelatine*
275 g	*Limonensaft*
5	*Thymianzweige*
35 g	*Zucker*
190 g	*Eiweiß*
250 g	*Zucker*
440 g	*geschlagene Sahne*

Gelatine in kaltem Wasser einweichen. 50 g Limonensaft mit Thymian und den 35 g Zucker aufkochen. Eiweiß mit den 250 g Zucker zu Schnee schlagen und unter den restlichen Limonensaft ziehen. Zuletzt die Sahne unterheben.

Putting it all together

Place the coconut dacquoise into a baking ring. Put the raspberry mousse on top. Top up with lime mousse, place the second coconut dacquoise on top and smooth off with lime mousse. Put in the deep-freeze. Once frozen, turn out and spray with white spray couverture for a velvety finish. Use a dab of jelly to glue on the chocolate edge décor and add the finishing touches.

Zusammensetzung Torte

Kokosdacquoise in einen Ring geben. Himbeermousse einlegen. Mit Limonenmousse anfüllen, zweiten Kokosdacquoise einlegen und dann mit Limonenmousse glatt streichen. Tiefgefrieren, ausformen und mit weißer Sprühkuvertüre samtig absprühen. Den Schokoladenranddekor mit einem Geleetupfen anbringen und ausgarnieren.

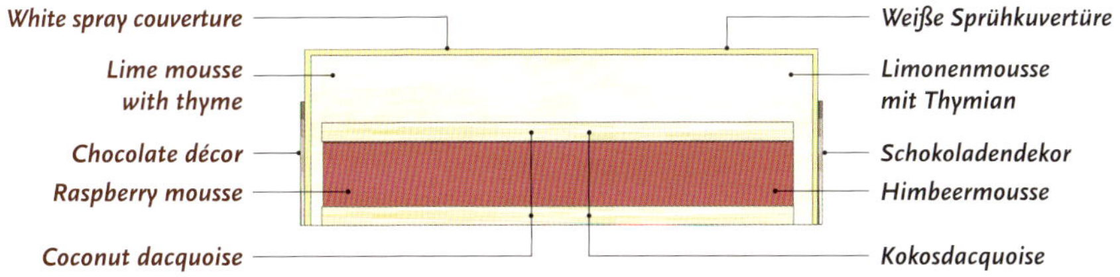

APRIKOSENFEUILLETINE

APRICOT FEUILLETINE

Der Feuilletinenugat macht süchtig. Selbst grosse Sterneköche sind bei der Aprikosenfeuilletine schon dahingeschmolzen.

Feuilletine nougat is addictive. Even famous star chefs have been known to melt when tasting an apricot feuilletine.

Ingredients	Zusammensetzung
Almond sponge	Mandelbiskuit
Bavarian cream of apricot	Bayerische Creme von der Aprikose
Preserved apricots	Eingemachte Aprikosen
Feuilletine mixture	Feuilletinemasse
Metallic apricot jelly icing	Metallic-Aprikosen-Kaltgelee
Chocolate décor	Schokoladendekor
Deep-fried rice noodles	Frittierte Reisnudeln
Flamed apricots	Geflämmte Aprikosen
4 Cakes, Ø 20 cm	4 Torten, Ø 20 cm
2 Cakes, Ø 28 cm	2 Torten, Ø 28 cm

Mandelbiskuit

175 g	Zucker
200 g	Eigelb
300 g	Eiweiß
150 g	Zucker
125 g	Mehl
125 g	Weizenpuder
75 g	Mandelgrieß

Zucker und Eigelb schaumig schlagen. Eiweiß mit den 150 g Zucker zu Schnee schlagen. Trockene Zutaten vermischen und im Wechsel mit dem Eischnee unter die Eigelbmasse heben. Biskuitmasse in gewünschter Form aufdressieren und bei 180 °C etwa 15 Minuten backen.

Bayerische Creme von der Aprikose

14	Blatt Gelatine
780 g	Milch
160 g	Zucker
2	Vanilleschoten
280 g	Eigelb
250 g	Zucker
780 g	Aprikosenpüree
780 g	geschlagene Sahne

Gelatine in kaltem Wasser einweichen. Milch, 160 g Zucker und Vanilleschoten sowie ausgestrichenes Vanillemark aufkochen. Eigelb und 250 g Zucker schaumig schlagen, Vanillemilch durch ein Sieb in die Eigelbmasse einlaufen lassen und bei 85 °C pasteurisieren. Ausgedrückte Gelatine in der heißen Masse auflösen. Sofort in das sehr kalte Aprikosenpüree einrühren. Zuletzt die Sahne unterheben.

Almond sponge

175 g	sugar
200 g	egg yolk
300 g	egg white
150 g	sugar
125 g	flour
125 g	wheat powder
75 g	grated almonds

Beat the egg yolk and sugar until frothy. Beat egg white with 150 g sugar until stiff. Mix the dry ingredients together and then add the mixture and the beaten egg white, in turn, into the egg yolk mixture. Pipe on the sponge mixture in the desired shape and bake at 180 °C for about 15 minutes.

Bavarian cream of apricot

14	sheets of gelatine
780 g	milk
160 g	sugar
2	vanilla pods
280 g	egg yolk
250 g	sugar
780 g	apricot puree
780 g	whipped cream

Soak the gelatine in cold water. Bring the milk to boil together with 160 g sugar, the vanilla pods and the scraped-out vanilla pith. Beat the egg yolk and 250 g sugar until frothy, let the vanilla milk run through a strainer into the egg yolk mixture and pasteurise at 85 °C. Dissolve the squeezed gelatine in the hot mixture. While it is still hot, stir the mixture into the apricot puree. Finally fold in the cream.

1

2

3

4

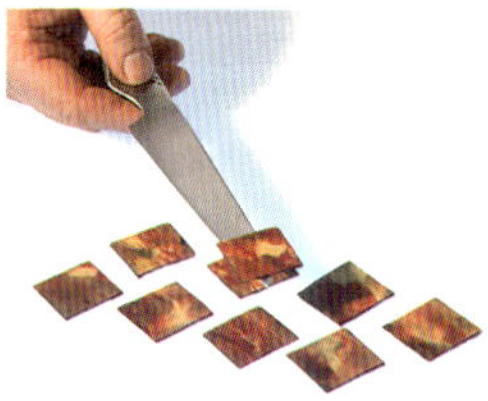

5

Gold und rot gefärbte Kakaobutter auf eine Folie sprenkeln

Sprinkle the gold- and red-coloured cocoa butter onto a sheet of foil

Mit einer Winkelpalette verstreichen

Use an angled spatula to spread out

Temperierte Kuvertüre mit einer Winkelpalette aufstreichen

Spread on the tempered couverture with an angled spatula

Sobald die Kuvertüre angezogen hat, Dekor schneiden

As soon as the couverture has set, cut the décor

Fertiges Schokoladendekor

Finished chocolate décor

Feuilletine mixture

100 g	*bitter almond nougat*
50 g	*feuilletine*

Dissolve the bitter almond nougat and stir in the feuilletine.

Feuilletinemasse

100 g	*Mandelbitternugat*
50 g	*Feuilletine*

Mandelbitternugat auflösen und Feuilletine (Waffelbruch) unterrühren.

Metallic apricot jelly icing

4	*sheets of gelatine*
500 g	*jelly icing*
200 g	*apricot puree*
1 g	*golden metallic powder*

Soak the gelatine in cold water, squeeze out, dissolve and add to the jelly icing. Stir in the apricot puree and metallic powder. Heat up a little before using.

Metallic-Aprikosen-Kaltgelee

4	*Blatt Gelatine*
500 g	*Kaltgelee*
200 g	*Aprikosenpüree*
1 g	*goldenes Metallicpulver*

Gelatine in kaltem Wasser einweichen, auspressen, auflösen und dem Kaltgelee zugeben. Aprikosenpüree und Metallicpulver unterrühren. Vor dem Gebrauch leicht erwärmen.

Putting it all together

Add half of the Bavarian cream of apricot into a hemispheric mould. Place the almond sponge on top. Fill in another layer of cream, place the drained off apricots on top, spread the feuilletine mixture on the second almond sponge before placing it on top. Deep-freeze the gateau, turn out, cover with metallic apricot jelly icing and decorate.

Zusammensetzung Torte

Bayerische Creme von der Aprikose zur Hälfte in eine Halbkugelform einfüllen. Mandelbiskuit einlegen. Nochmals Creme einfüllen, abgetropfte Aprikosen auflegen, dann den zweiten Mandelbiskuit mit Feuilletinemasse bestreichen und auflegen. Torte tiefgefrieren, ausformen, mit Metallic-Aprikosen-Kaltgelee überziehen und dekorieren.

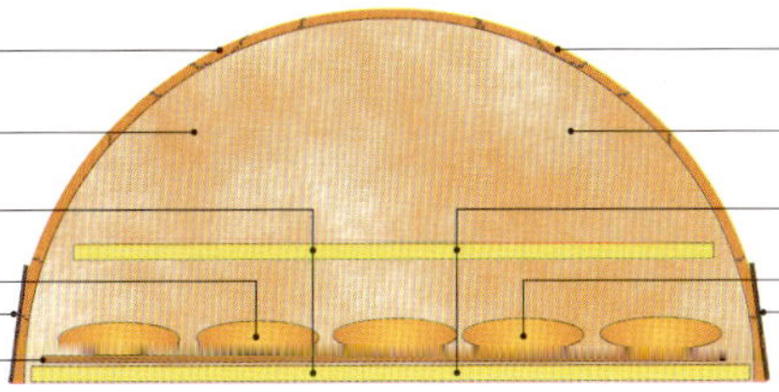

MERANER HERBST

AUTUMN IN MERANO

Südtirol im Herbst ist genauso bunt wie dieser Schokoladendekor. Maronen, Kirschwasser und Schokolade sind einfach eine herrliche Kombination.

Southern Tyrol in autumn is just as colourful as this chocolate décor. Sweet chestnuts, kirsch and chocolate are fabulous combined.

Ingredients	Zusammensetzung
Chocolate sponge	Schokoladenbiskuit
Chocolate mousse	Mousse au Chocolat
Sweet chestnut cream	Maronencreme
Amarena cherry	Amarenakirschen
Cherry jelly	Kirschgelee
Jelly icing	Kaltgelee
Noir chocolate icing	Schokoladenglasur Noir
Chocolate décor	Schokoladendekor
Fruits	Früchte
4 Cakes, Ø 20 cm	4 Torten, Ø 20 cm
2 Cakes, Ø 28 cm	2 Torten, Ø 28 cm

Schokoladenbiskuit

- 225 g *Eigelb*
- 175 g *Zucker*
- 330 g *Eiweiß*
- 75 g *Zucker*
- 200 g *Mehl*
- 50 g *Weizenpuder*
- 50 g *Kakaopulver*

Eigelb mit 175 g Zucker schaumig schlagen. Eiweiß mit 75 g Zucker zu Schnee schlagen. Trockene Zutaten mischen und im Wechsel mit dem Eischnee unter die Eigelbmasse ziehen. Biskuitmasse mit einer Spritztüte in der gewünschten Form aufdressieren und bei 180 °C etwa 15 Minuten backen.

Chocolate sponge

- 225 g *egg yolk*
- 175 g *sugar*
- 330 g *egg white*
- 75 g *sugar*
- 200 g *flour*
- 50 g *wheat powder*
- 50 g *cocoa powder*

Beat the egg yolk with 175 g sugar until frothy. Beat egg white with 75 g of sugar until stiff. Mix the dry ingredients together and then fold the mixture and the beaten egg white, in turn, into the egg yolk mixture. Use a piping bag to pipe on the sponge mixture in the desired shape and bake at 180 °C for about 15 minutes.

1

2

3

Mousse au Chocolat

- 150 g *Zucker*
- 75 g *Wasser*
- 180 g *Eigelb*
- 75 g *Vollei*
- 420 g *Bitterkuvertüre, 65 %*
- 600 g *geschlagene Sahne*

Zucker mit Wasser zum Kettenflug kochen. Eigelb mit Vollei schaumig schlagen, Zuckersud einlaufen lassen und bei 85 °C pasteurisieren. Klein gehackte Bitterkuvertüre der heißen Eimasse zugeben, zuletzt die Sahne unterheben.

Chocolate mousse

- 150 g *sugar*
- 75 g *water*
- 180 g *egg yolk*
- 75 g *whole egg*
- 420 g *dark couverture, 65 %*
- 600 g *whipped cream*

Boil the sugar in water up to 117 °C. Beat the egg yolk together with whole egg until frothy, let the sugary water run into the egg and pasteurise at 85 °C. Chop the dark couverture into small pieces and add to the hot egg mixture and finally fold in the cream.

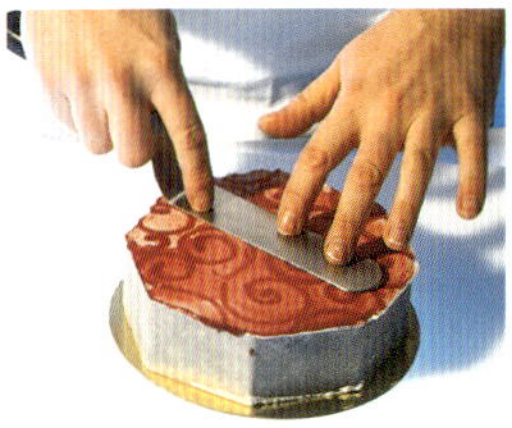

4

5

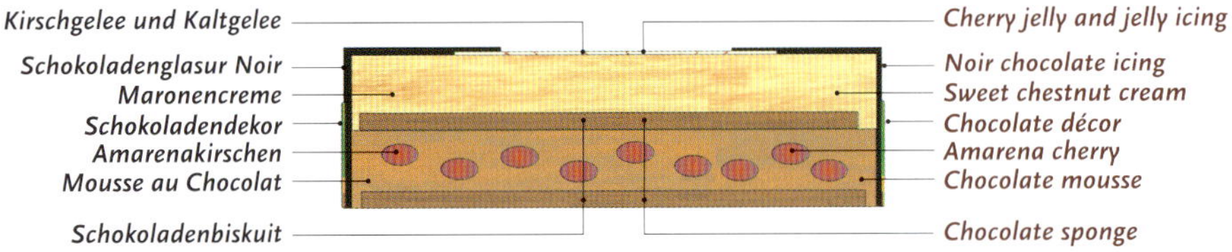

Tortenform auf Dekorfolie legen und Torte umgekehrt auf der Folie einsetzen und tiefgefrieren

Place the cake mould onto the décor foil and place the cake upside down onto the foil and then deep-freeze

Dekorfolie in einem Ruck abziehen

Pull the décor foil off with a sharp tug

Kirschgelee auf die Oberfläche geben

Put the cherry jelly on the cake

Mit einer Winkelpalette abziehen

Smooth with an angled spatula

Mit Kaltgelee abgelieren

To finish, apply jelly icing

Sweet chestnut cream

6	*sheets of gelatine*
450 g	*whole milk*
150 g	*egg yolk*
150 g	*sugar*
600 g	*sweet chestnut puree*
750 g	*whipped cream*
45 g	*kirsch*

Soak the gelatine in cold water. Pasteurise the whole milk, egg yolk and sugar at 85 °C. Dissolve the squeezed-out gelatine in the hot mixture, then stir in the sweet chestnut puree and leave to cool. Fold in the cream and finally work in the kirsch.

Maronencreme

6	*Blatt Gelatine*
450 g	*Vollmilch*
150 g	*Eigelb*
150 g	*Zucker*
600 g	*Maronenpüree*
750 g	*geschlagene Sahne*
45 g	*Kirschwasser*

Gelatine in kaltem Wasser einweichen. Vollmilch, Eigelb und Zucker bei 85 °C pasteurisieren. Ausgedrückte Gelatine in der heißen Masse auflösen, dann Maronenpüree einrühren und abkühlen lassen. Die Sahne unterheben und zum Schluss das Kirschwasser einarbeiten.

Putting it all together

Place the cake mould onto the décor foil. Pipe the sweet chestnut cream onto the cake mould, insert the chocolate sponge, spread the chocolate mousse, add 500 g Amarena cherries, cover with chocolate sponge and put into the deep-freeze. Pull off the décor foil with a sharp tug, use an angled spatula to spread on the cherry jelly so that the relief pattern remains visible, then cover with jelly icing and turn out of the mould. Allow the Noir chocolate icing to run down the sides. Use sweet chestnuts, fruit and chocolate décor to apply the finishing touches.

Zusammensetzung Torte

Tortenform auf Dekorfolie legen. Maronencreme mit dem Spritzbeutel in die Tortenform eindressieren, Schokoladenbiskuit einlegen, Mousse au Chocolat aufdressieren, 500 g Amarenakirschen auflegen, mit Schokoladenbiskuit abdecken und tiefgefrieren. Die Dekorfolie in einem Ruck abziehen, Kirschgelee mit der Winkelpalette aufstreichen, so dass das Reliefmuster sichtbar bleibt, dann mit Kaltgelee abgelieren und ausformen. Schokoladenglasur Noir am Rand herunterlaufen lassen. Die Torte mit Maronen, Früchten und Schokoladendekor ausgarnieren.

Alice im Wunderland

Alice in Wonderland

Ein Kindertraum für Gross und Klein. Käsetorte ist jedermanns Liebling. Mandarinen mit Heidelbeeren und Milchreis gab es in meiner Kindheit, und davon träume ich heute noch.

A child's dream for little ones and grown-ups alike. Cheesecake is everybody's favourite. Mandarins with blueberries and milk rice were a treat in my childhood and I still dream of them.

Ingredients	Zusammensetzung
Cheesecake sponge	Käsetortenbiskuit
Mandarin rice cream	Mandarinenreissahne
Blueberry jelly	Heidelbeergelee
Fruits	Früchte
Puff pastry	Brickteig
Décor icing sugar	Dekorpuderzucker
4 Cakes, Ø 20 cm	4 Torten, Ø 20 cm
2 Cakes, Ø 28 cm	2 Torten, Ø 28 cm

Käsetortenbiskuit

410 g	*Eiweiß*
240 g	*Zucker*
500 g	*Quark, 20 % Fett*
100 g	*saure Sahne*
200 g	*Frischkäse*
70 g	*flüssige Butter*
300 g	*Milch (ca.)*
200 g	*Eigelb*
150 g	*Mehl*
50 g	*Cremepulver*
50 g	*Zucker*

Eiweiß und Zucker zu Schnee schlagen. Restliche Zutaten mischen und schaumig rühren, dann Eischnee unterziehen. Käsetortenbiskuit in flache Silikonformen füllen und bei 180 °C etwa 20 Minuten backen.

Cheesecake sponge

410 g	*egg white*
240 g	*sugar*
500 g	*curd cheese, 20 % fat*
100 g	*sour cream*
200 g	*fromage frais*
70 g	*liquid butter*
300 g	*milk (approx.)*
200 g	*egg yolk*
150 g	*flour*
50 g	*cream powder*
50 g	*sugar*

Beat the egg white with the sugar until stiff. Mix the remaining ingredients and stir until frothy, then fold in the beaten egg white. Fill the cheesecake sponge mixture into shallow silicon moulds and bake at 180 °C for about 20 minutes.

1

2

3

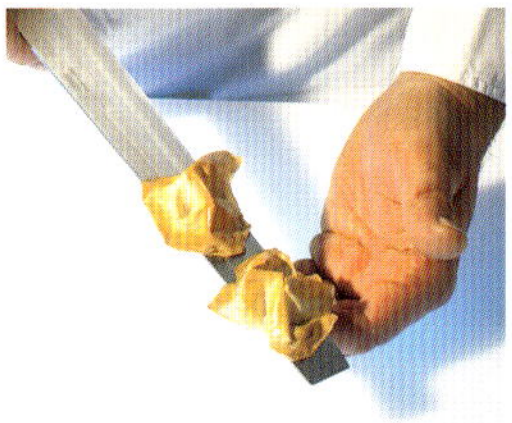

4

Heidelbeergelee

16	*Blatt Gelatine*
1000 g	*Heidelbeerpüree*
120 g	*Zucker*

Gelatine in kaltem Wasser einweichen. Fruchtpüree mit Zucker mischen und der Gelatine zugeben. Masse in Silikonformen füllen und tiefgefrieren.

Blueberry jelly

16	*sheets of gelatine*
1,000 g	*blueberry puree*
120 g	*sugar*

Soak the gelatine in cold water. Mix the fruit puree with the sugar and add to the gelatine. Fill the mixture into silicon moulds and deep-freeze.

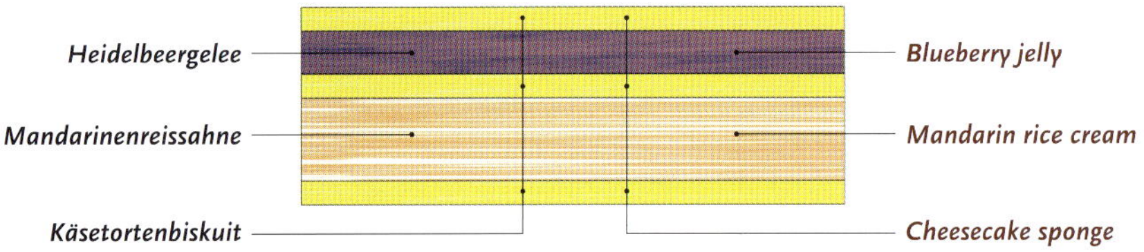

Filoteig in Form schneiden

Cut the filo pastry to the required shape

Mit Läuterzucker einstreichen

Cover with sugar syrup

Locker knüllen

Loosely bunch up together

Fertige Filoteigküchlein nach dem Backen

Finished filo pastry after baking

Mandarin rice cream

7	*sheets of gelatine*
900 g	*milk*
1	*vanilla pod*
300 g	*risotto rice*
100 g	*butter*
75 g	*egg yolk, pasteurised*
140 g	*sugar*
50 g	*yoghurt*
140 g	*mandarin juice*
	grated rind from 2 mandarins
900 g	*whipped cream*

Soak the gelatine in cold water. Boil the milk with the vanilla pith and risotto rice until creamy and then stir in the butter. Weigh 800 g of risotto, dissolve the squeezed-out gelatine in it and stir in the egg yolk, sugar, yoghurt, mandarin juice and rind. Leave the mixture to cool down slightly and then fold in the cream.

Mandarinenreissahne

7	*Blatt Gelatine*
900 g	*Milch*
1	*Vanilleschote*
300 g	*Risottoreis*
100 g	*Butter*
75 g	*Eigelb, pasteurisiert*
140 g	*Zucker*
50 g	*Joghurt*
140 g	*Mandarinensaft*
	Abrieb von 2 Mandarinen
900 g	*geschlagene Sahne*

Gelatine in kaltem Wasser einweichen. Milch und Vanillemark mit Risottoreis zu einer cremigen Masse kochen und die Butter unterrühren. 800 g Risotto abwiegen, ausgepresste Gelatine darin auflösen, Eigelb, Zucker, Joghurt, Mandarinensaft und -abrieb einrühren. Leicht erkalten lassen, dann die Sahne unterziehen.

Putting it all together

Place the first pastry base into a large frame. Spread the mandarin rice cream over the base, cover with a second pastry layer and fill this up with blueberry jelly. Place the third pastry layer on top of the jelly, put in the refrigerator, turn out and cut to the required size. Decorate with décor icing sugar, fruits, filo pastry, chocolate décor and angelica as well as mint.

Zusammensetzung Torte

Den ersten Boden in einen großen Rahmen einlegen. Mit Mandarinenreissahne auffüllen, zweiten Boden auflegen und mit Heidelbeergelee auffüllen. Den dritten Boden auflegen, kalt stellen, ausformen und in gewünschte Größe zuschneiden. Mit Dekorpuderzucker, Früchten, Filoteig, Schokoladendekor und Angelika sowie Minze dekorieren.

HERRENTORTE

GENTLEMAN'S CAKE

Es liegt ja sehr im Trend, Klassiker auseinander zu nehmen und wieder neu zusammenzusetzen. Und dieses Mal habe ich mir die Herrentorte vorgenommen. Klassiker sind wichtig, denn sie sind die Identität unserer Konditoreikultur. Aber auch die Klassiker müssen von Zeit zu Zeit neu interpretiert werden, damit sie mit der Zeit gehen.

It has become very fashionable to take classics apart and put them together again in a new way. So this time I am looking at a new way of making Herrentorte. Classics are important because they make up the identity of our patisserie culture. But even classics need to be reinterpreted from time to time if they are to survive.

Ingredients

- Pastry base for Herrentorte
- Riesling cream
- Chocolate ganache
- Couverture slabs
- Gold dust
- Chocolate décor

4 Cakes, Ø 20 cm
2 Cakes, Ø 28 cm

Zusammensetzung

- Herrentortenboden
- Rieslingcreme
- Schokoladenganache
- Kuvertüreplatten
- Goldstaub
- Schokoladendekor

4 Torten, Ø 20 cm
2 Torten, Ø 28 cm

Herrentortenböden

75 g	*Marzipanrohmasse*
225 g	*Eigelb*
125 g	*Zucker*
	Abrieb von 1 Zitrone
275 g	*Eiweiß*
1 g	*Salz*
120 g	*Zucker*
50 g	*Weizenpuder*
160 g	*Mehl*
65 g	*Weizenpuder*

Marzipanrohmasse mit Eigelb glatt arbeiten, 125 g Zucker und Zitronenabrieb zugeben und schaumig schlagen. Eiweiß mit Salz, 120 g Zucker und 50 g Weizenpuder zu Schnee schlagen, beide Massen abwechselnd mit dem Mehl und 65 g Weizenpuder melieren, mit einer Aufstreichschablone in gewünschter Höhe auf ein Backpapier aufziehen und bei 220 °C etwa 15 Minuten backen.

Pastry base for Herrentorte

75 g	*marzipan paste*
225 g	*egg yolk*
125 g	*sugar*
	grated rind from 1 lemon
275 g	*egg white*
1 g	*salt*
120 g	*sugar*
50 g	*wheat powder*
160 g	*flour*
65 g	*wheat powder*

Blend the marzipan paste with the egg yolk, add 125 g sugar and the lemon rind and beat until frothy. Beat the egg white with salt, 120 g sugar and 50 g wheat powder until stiff; blend the two mixtures together whilst also adding the flour and 65 g wheat powder in turn and then use a spreader template to spread the dough onto baking paper with the required thickness; bake at 220 °C for about 15 minutes.

Rieslingcreme

11	*Blatt Gelatine*
700 g	*Riesling*
380 g	*Zucker*
	Saft und Abrieb von 3 Zitronen
250 g	*Eigelb*
700 g	*geschlagene Sahne*

Gelatine in kaltem Wasser einweichen. Riesling, Zucker, Zitronensaft und -abrieb sowie Eigelb verrühren und auf 85 °C pasteurisieren. Gelatine ausdrücken und zugeben. Masse abkühlen lassen, dann die Sahne unterziehen, in flache Silikonformen füllen und tiefgefrieren.

Riesling cream

11	*sheets of gelatine*
700 g	*Riesling*
380 g	*sugar*
	juice and peel from 3 lemons
250 g	*egg yolk*
700 g	*whipped cream*

Soak the gelatine in cold water. Pasteurise the Riesling, sugar, lemon juice and grated rind and egg yolk at 85 °C, squeeze out the gelatine and add. Leave the mixture to cool down and then fold in the cream. Fill the Riesling cream into shallow silicon moulds and deep-freeze.

1

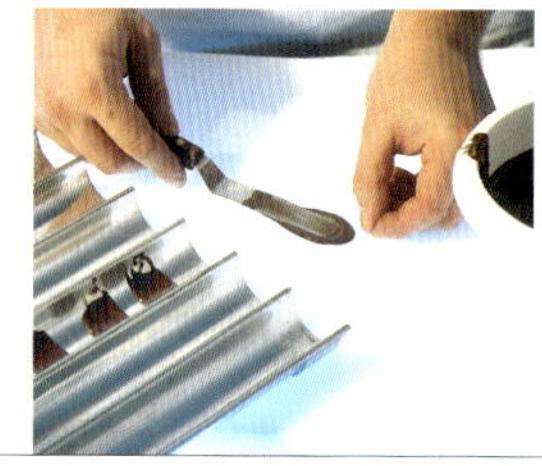
2

3

4

5

Folie in kleine Stückchen schneiden und zurechtlegen

Cut the foil into small pieces, placing them in the required order

Kuvertüre mit einer Winkelpalette auf Folie streichen und in wellenförmige Form einlegen und tiefgefrieren

Use an angled spatula to spread the couverture onto the foil, then place into a mould with a wavy shape and deep-freeze.

Dekore mit roter Kakaobutter schminken

Apply red cocoa butter to the décors

Sobald temperiert, Dekore von den Folien lösen

As soon as they are tempered, take the décors off the foil

Fertige Blütenblätter

Finished petals

Chocolate ganache

340 g	*cream*
340 g	*milk*
340 g	*glucose syrup*
1,700 g	*dark couverture, 60 %*
170 g	*butter*
170 g	*Riesling marc brandy, 40 vol. %*

Bring the cream, milk and glucose syrup to boil and pour over the finely chopped dark couverture. Stir into a homogenous mixture, fold in the butter and add Riesling marc brandy to taste. Deep-freeze the ganache in a shallow silicon mould.

Schokoladenganache

340 g	*Sahne*
340 g	*Milch*
340 g	*Glukosesirup*
1700 g	*Bitterkuvertüre, 60 %*
170 g	*Butter*
170 g	*Rieslingtresterbrand, 40 Vol.-%*

Sahne, Milch und Glukosesirup aufkochen und über die fein gehackte Bitterkuvertüre gießen. Zu einer homogenen Masse rühren, Butter unterziehen und mit Rieslingtresterbrand abschmecken. Ganache in einer flachen Silikonform tiefgefrieren.

Couverture slabs

1,000 g	*dark couverture, 70 %*
100 g	*butter fat*

Mix the tempered dark couverture with butter fat and spread very thinly on the plastic foil. Cut to the required shape.

Kuvertüreplatten

1000 g	*Bitterkuvertüre, 70 %*
100 g	*Butterfett*

Bitterkuvertüre temperiert mit Butterfett mischen und sehr dünn auf Plastikfolie aufstreichen. In gewünschte Form schneiden.

Putting it all together

Cut the pastry bases, ganache and Riesling cream to the same size. The couverture slabs should be about 2 to 3 mm larger. First place one pastry base into the mould. Follow this with a layer of couverture slab, then ganache, again couverture and then the Riesling cream. Repeat this process twice. Cover the top with couverture slabs with frayed edges. Spray on gold powder and decorate with a chocolate flower.

Zusammensetzung Torte

Herrentortenböden, Ganache und Rieslingcreme in gleicher Größe zurechtschneiden. Die Kuvertüreplatten sollten 2 bis 3 Millimeter größer sein. Zuerst einen Herrentortenboden auflegen. Dann eine Schicht Kuvertüreplatten, danach Ganache, wiederum Kuvertüre, und dann folgt die Rieslingcreme. Diesen Vorgang wiederholen. Den Abschluss bilden ausgefranste Kuvertüreplatten. Goldpuder aufsprühen und mit einer Schokoladenblüte ausdekorieren.

MANGO-GRAPEFRUIT-TORTE

MANGO-GRAPEFRUIT CAKE

Reife Mangos sind sehr süss und aromatisch. Grapefruits sind mit ihrer Säure und bitteren Note ein idealer Gegenpart zu Mangos. Eine ideale Sommerspezialität. Übrigens: Die leichte Mangocreme ist eine Weiterentwicklung unserer leichten Vanillecreme des Bienenstichs.

Ripe mangoes are very sweet and full of flavour. Grapefruits, with their acidic and more bitter taste, are an ideal counterpart to mangoes: an ideal summer speciality. By the way: this light mango cream is a further development from our light vanilla cream or custard we use for Bienenstich.

Ingredients

- Light mango cream
- Shortcrust case for blind baking
- Pine nut crust
- Grapefruit fillets (segments without the pith)
- Chocolate décor
- Mango wedges

4 Cakes, Ø 20 cm
2 Cakes, Ø 28 cm

Zusammensetzung

- Leichte Mangocreme
- Mürbeteigboden zum Blindbacken
- Pinienboden
- Grapefruitfilets
- Schokoladendekor
- Mangospalten

4 Torten, Ø 20 cm
2 Torten, Ø 28 cm

Leichte Mangocreme

3	*Blatt Gelatine*
300 g	*Mangopüree*
120 g	*Eigelb*
40 g	*Zucker*
50 g	*Joghurt*
15 g	*Weizenpuder*
150 g	*Eiweiß*
70 g	*Zucker*

Gelatine in kaltem Wasser einweichen. Mangopüree, Eigelb, Zucker, Joghurt und Weizenpuder zu Creme kochen. Gelatine ausdrücken und unterrühren. Eiweiß und Zucker zu Schnee schlagen und unter die noch heiße Masse ziehen. Weiterverarbeitung siehe Stepps.

Light mango cream

3	*sheets of gelatine*
300 g	*mango puree*
120 g	*egg yolk*
40 g	*sugar*
50 g	*yoghurt*
15 g	*wheat powder*
150 g	*egg white*
70 g	*sugar*

Soak the gelatine in cold water. Boil the mango puree, egg yolk, sugar, yoghurt and wheat powder into a cream. Squeeze out the gelatine and stir under. Add sugar to the egg white and beat until stiff; then fold into the mixture while it is still hot. For further processing, see stages.

Mürbeteigboden zum Blindbacken

100 g	*Butter*
200 g	*Zucker*
25 g	*Marzipanrohmasse*
	Mark von einer 1/2 Vanilleschote
20 g	*Eigelb*
1 g	*Salz*
300 g	*Mehl*

Butter mit Zucker, Marzipan, Vanillemark und Eigelb glatt arbeiten, Salz sowie Mehl dazugeben und schnell zu einem Teig zusammenwirken.

Vor der Verarbeitung kühl stellen. Bei 160 °C trocken vorbacken.

Shortcrust case for blind baking

100 g	*butter*
200 g	*sugar*
25 g	*marzipan paste*
	pith of 1/2 vanilla pod
20 g	*egg yolk*
1 g	*salt*
300 g	*flour*

Blend the butter, sugar, marzipan, vanilla pith and egg yolk until smooth, then add the salt and the flour and quickly work into a dough.

Leave in a cool place before using. Pre-bake blind at 160 °C.

1

2

3

4

5

Leichte Mangocreme in einen Ring einfüllen, glatt streichen und tiefkühlen

Fill the light mango cream into a ring, spread out until smooth and deep-freeze

Oberfläche mit Zucker bestreuen ...

Sprinkle sugar over the top ...

... und mit dem Gasbrenner karamellisieren

... and caramelise with a gas torch

Den Vorgang wiederholen

Repeat this process

Die gefrorene Mangocreme mit dem Gasbrenner ausformen

Use the gas torch to help you turn out the frozen mango cream

Pine nut crust

300 g	butter
300 g	icing sugar
300 g	pine nuts
75 g	grated pistachios
40 g	wheat powder
40 g	aniseed brandy
225 g	whole egg
600 g	yoghurt
100 g	pine nut paste

Dissolve the butter and stir in the other ingredients until smooth.

Fill the mixture into the pre-baked shortcrust case and spread the grapefruit fillets over it. Bake at 180 °C for about 20 minutes.

Pinienboden

300 g	Butter
300 g	Puderzucker
300 g	Pinien, gehackt
75 g	Pistaziengrieß
40 g	Weizenpuder
40 g	Anisschnaps
225 g	Vollei
600 g	Joghurt
100 g	Pinienpaste

Butter auflösen und mit restlichen Zutaten zu einer glatten Masse verrühren.

Masse in den vorgebackenen Mürbeteigboden einfüllen, Mit Grapefruitfilets belegen. Bei 180 °C etwa 20 Minuten backen.

Putting it all together

Spread the light mango cream on the almond crust and then place the grapefruit fillets around the edge; flame off the fillets, apply jelly icing and any further decoration.

Zusammensetzung Torte

Leichte Mangocreme auf den Mandelboden auflegen, mit Grapefruitfilets umlegen, Filets leicht abflämmen, mit Kaltgelee abglänzen und ausdekorieren.

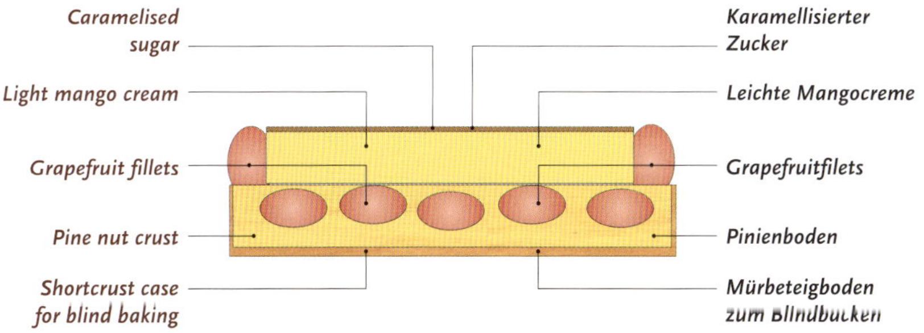

HIMBEER-NOIR-BUTTERCREME

RASPBERRY NOIR BUTTER CREAM

Fruchtbuttercreme ist eine ideale Ergänzung für die Tortentheke im Sommer. Himbeeraromen finden sich in Schokolade, insbesondere in den Criollo-Kakaobohnen.

Fruit butter cream makes an ideal addition to the gateau counter in summer. Raspberry flavour can be found in chocolate, especially in the Criollo cocoa beans.

Ingredients	Zusammensetzung
Raspberry jelly	Himbeergelee
French butter cream with raspberry puree	Französische Buttercreme mit Himbeerpüree
Feuilletine mixture	Feuilletinemasse
Chocolate sponge without flour	Schokoladenbiskuit ohne Mehl
Spray couverture	Sprühkuvertüre
Chocolate décor and icing	Schokoladendekor und -glasur
Fruit	Früchte
4 Cakes, Ø 20 cm	4 Torten, Ø 20 cm
2 Cakes, Ø 28 cm	2 Torten, Ø 28 cm

Himbeergelee

300 g	*Himbeerpüree*
60 g	*Zucker*
8	*Blatt Gelatine*

Himbeerpüree mit Zucker verrühren. Gelatine einweichen, ausdrücken und auflösen. Dann Himbeeren zugeben. In einer flachen Silikonform tiefgefrieren.

Raspberry jelly

300 g	*raspberry puree*
60 g	*sugar*
8	*sheets of gelatine*

Stir the sugar into the raspberry jelly. Soak the gelatine, squeeze it out and dissolve. Add to the raspberries. Deep-freeze in a shallow silicon mould.

Französische Buttercreme mit Himbeerpüree

750 g	*Butter*
300 g	*Vollei*
250 g	*Zucker*
200 g	*Himbeerpüree*

Butter schaumig rühren. Ei mit Zucker auf 85 °C pasteurisieren, kalt schlagen, dann unter die Buttermasse heben. Himbeerpüree unterziehen.

French butter cream with raspberry puree

750 g	*butter*
300 g	*whole egg*
250 g	*sugar*
200 g	*raspberry puree*

Beat the butter until frothy. Pasteurise the egg with sugar at 85 °C, beat cold and fold into the butter mixture. Fold in the raspberry puree.

Feuilletinemasse

100 g	*Mandelbitternugat*
20 g	*Feuilletine*
20 g	*Amaranthpopcorn*

Mandeltbitternugat erwärmen, Feuilletine und Amaranthpopcorn unterrühren.

Feuilletine mixture

100 g	*bitter almond nougat*
20 g	*feuilletine*
20 g	*amaranth popcorn*

Heat the bitter almond nougat and stir in the feuilletine and amaranth popcorn.

1

2

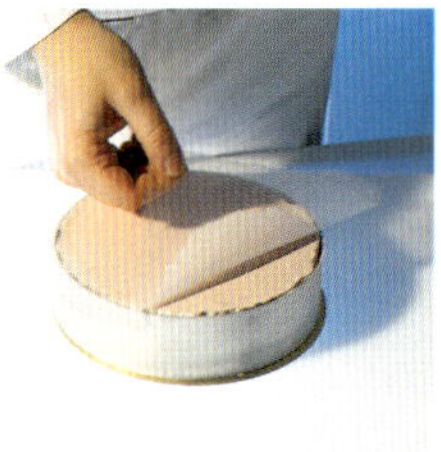

3

4

5

Tortenring auf Folie stellen und Relieffolie einlegen

Place the cake ring onto the foil and insert relief foil

Buttercreme eindressieren und in umgekehrter Reihenfolge einsetzen

Pipe in the butter cream and insert in reverse order

Torte tiefgefrieren, Folie abziehen

Deep-freeze the cake and then pull off the foil

Torte ausformen und Relieffolie abziehen

Turn out the cake and pull off the relief foil

Mit Kuvertüre absprühen

Spray with couverture

Chocolate sponge without flour

320 g	marzipan
320 g	egg yolk
520 g	egg white
520 g	sugar
170 g	cocoa powder

Beat the egg yolk and marzipan until frothy. Beat the egg white with the sugar until stiff. Fold the beaten egg and the cocoa powder, in turns, into the marzipan mixture. Bake at 180 °C for about 20 minutes.

Schokoladenbiskuit ohne Mehl

320 g	Marzipan
320 g	Eigelb
520 g	Eiweiß
520 g	Zucker
170 g	Kakaopulver

Marzipan und Eigelb schaumig schlagen. Eiweiß und Zucker zu Schnee schlagen. Eischnee und Kakaopulver im Wechsel unter die Marzipanmasse ziehen. Bei 180 °C etwa 20 Minuten backen.

Putting it all together

Dress the raspberry butter cream onto the relief foil which has been placed into the cake ring. Insert a chocolate sponge layer, spread a second layer of butter cream over the sponge and then place another chocolate sponge on top. Add the raspberry jelly and top up with butter cream. Spread feuilletine mixture over the third layer of chocolate sponge and place on top. Deep-freeze the cake. Then pull off the foil, turn out the cake, pull off the relief foil and spray the cake with spray couverture. Add the finishing touches.

Zusammensetzung Torte

In den mit Relieffolie ausgelegten Tortenring Himbeerbuttercreme eindressieren. Einen Schokoladenbiskuit einlegen, eine zweite Schicht Buttercreme eindressieren, dann wiederum einen Schokoladenbiskuit einlegen. Himbeergelee auflegen, mit Buttercreme anfüllen. Die dritte Schicht Schokoladenbiskuit mit Feuilletinemasse bestreichen und zuletzt einlegen. Torte tiefgefrieren. Dann Folie abziehen, Torte ausformen, Relieffolie abziehen und Torte mit Sprühkuvertüre absprühen. Ausgarnieren.

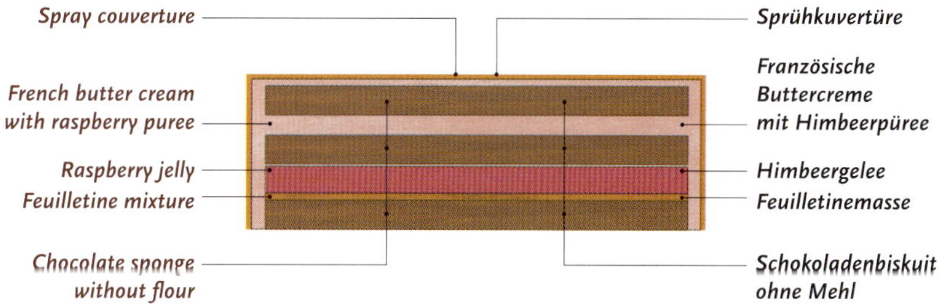

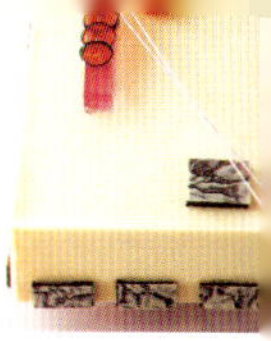

CHAMPAGNER ROSÉ

CHAMPAGNE ROSÉ

Champagner ist etwas Leckeres, und Blütenaromen mag ich sehr, sehr gerne. Eine richtige Mischung zu finden ist immer sehr schwer, aber wenn sie gefunden ist, ist es ein vollkommener Genuss.

Champagne is something quite delicious, and I am very, very fond of flower aromas. It's always very hard to find the right mixture, but once you've found it, it's a real delight.

Ingredients	Zusammensetzung
Champagne cream	Champagnersahnecreme
Rose jelly	Rosengelee
Mandarin rice cake	Mandarinenreiskuchen
Mandarin segments	Mandarinenspalten
Slices of grapes	Traubenscheiben
Chocolate décor	Schokoladendekor
Sugar threads	Zuckerfäden
White spray couverture	Weisse Sprühkuvertüre
4 Cakes, Ø 20 cm	4 Torten, Ø 20 cm
2 Cakes, Ø 28 cm	2 Torten, Ø 28 cm

Champagnersahnecreme

4	*Blatt Gelatine*
170 g	*Zucker*
25 g	*Cremepulver*
20 g	*Eigelb*
250 g	*Champagner*
50 g	*Marc de Champagne*
100 g	*Champagner*
700 g	*geschlagene Sahne*

Gelatine einweichen. Zucker und Cremepulver mischen. Eigelb und Champagner unterrühren, zu einer Creme kochen. Gelatine auspressen und in der heißen Masse auflösen. Kalt rühren, Marc de Champagne sowie Champagner zugeben und die Sahne unterheben.

Champagne cream

4	*sheets of gelatine*
170 g	*sugar*
25 g	*cream powder*
20 g	*egg yolk*
250 g	*champagne*
50 g	*Marc de Champagne*
100 g	*champagne*
700 g	*whipped cream*

Soak the gelatine. Mix the sugar and cream powder. Stir the egg yolk into the champagne and cook to a cream. Squeeze out the gelatine and dissolve in the hot mixture. Stir until cold, add the Marc de Champagne and the champagne and fold in the cream.

Rosengelee

8	*Rosen, ungespritzt und stark duftend*
750 g	*Champagner*
15	*Blatt Gelatine*
150 g	*Zucker*
60 g	*Rosenwasser*

Die Blätter der 8 Rosen über Nacht in Champagner einlegen. Gelatine einweichen, auspressen und auflösen. Dann Zucker und Rosenchampagner zugeben und durch ein Sieb dem Rosenwasser zugießen. Rosengelee in Silikonformen gießen und tiefgefrieren

Rose jelly

8	*roses, unsprayed and with a strong scent*
750 g	*champagne*
15	*sheets of gelatine*
150 g	*sugar*
60 g	*rose water*

Steep the petals of the 8 roses in champagne over night. Soak the gelatine, squeeze it out and dissolve. Add sugar and rose champagne and pour through a strainer into the rose water. Pour the rose jelly into suitable silicon moulds and deep-freeze.

1

2

3

4

5

Alufolie vorbereiten …

Prepare the aluminium foil and …

6

Dunkle Kuvertüre aufgießen

Pour on the dark couverture

… knüllen

… crumple it up

7

Mit einer Winkelpalette ausstreichen und anziehen lassen

Spread out with an angled spatula and leave to set

Alufolie wieder glatt streichen

Spread out the aluminium foil again and flatten it

8

Stücke zurechtschneiden

Cut suitable pieces

Weiße Kuvertüre auf die Folie gießen

Pour white couverture onto the foil

9

Von der Folie abziehen

Pull off from the foil

Mit einer Winkelpalette dünn ausstreichen

Spread out thinly with an angled spatula

10

Fertiger Dekor

Finished décor

Mandarinenreiskuchen

500 g	Milch
500 g	Mandarinensaft
125 g	Risottoreis
25 g	Mandarinenolivenöl
1 g	Salz
100 g	Eigelb
250 g	Marzipanrohmasse
	Abrieb von 5 Mandarinen
100 g	Eiweiß
60 g	Zucker
25 g	Mehl

Milch, Mandarinensaft und Reis zu einem cremigen Risotto kochen. Mandarinenolivenöl zugeben und pürieren. Salz, Eigelb, Marzipanrohmasse und den Mandarinenabrieb schaumig schlagen. Eiweiß mit Zucker zu Schnee schlagen. Schnee, Reiscreme, Marzipanmasse und Mehl zu einer Masse rühren, in eine Silikonform füllen und bei 180 °C etwa 30 Minuten backen.

Mandarin rice cake

500 g	milk
500 g	mandarin juice
125 g	risotto rice
25 g	mandarin olive oil
1 g	salt
100 g	egg yolk
250 g	marzipan paste
	grated rind from 5 mandarins
100 g	egg white
60 g	sugar
25 g	flour

Boil the milk, mandarin juice and rice into a creamy risotto. Add the mandarin olive oil and puree the mixture. Beat the egg yolk, salt, marzipan paste and mandarin rind until frothy. Add sugar to the egg white and beat until stiff. Stir the beaten egg, the rice cream, the marzipan mixture and the flour into a mixture, fill into a silicon mould and bake at 180 °C for about 30 minutes.

Putting it all together

Place the mandarin rice cake into a ring, spread over the rose jelly and then top up with champagne cream. Put in the deep-freeze, turn out and spray with white spray couverture; add the finishing touches. I have chosen sugar threads as décor element for the display cake. Of course, these have only a limited shelf life.

Zusammensetzung Torte

Mandarinenreiskuchen in einen Ring einlegen, Rosengelee auflegen und dann mit Champagnersahne auffüllen. Tiefgefrieren, ausformen, mit weißer Sprühkuvertüre absprühen und ausgarnieren. Für die Formtorte habe ich als Dekorelement Zuckerfäden gewählt. Diese sind natürlich nur beschränkt haltbar.

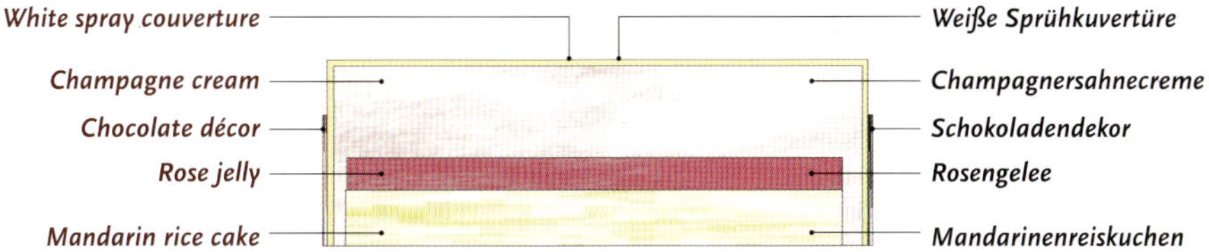

Brombeer-Birnen-Torte

Pear and Blackberry Cake

Der Herbst in meiner Region ist ein absoluter Knaller: ein Übermass an Früchten, Beeren und eine Explosion der Aromen.

In the area where I come from, the autumn is an absolute riot: there is an abundance of fruit and berries and an explosion of aromas.

Ingredients

- Poppy seed sponge
- Bavarian cream of pear
- Feuilletine mixture
- Caramel cream
- Blackberry jelly filling
- Poppy seed macaroons
- Dried slices of pear
- Chocolate icing Noir and Blanc
- Chocolate décor
- Fruits
- Sugar thread

4 Cakes, Ø 20 cm
2 Cakes, Ø 28 cm

Zusammensetzung

- Mohnbiskuit
- Bayerische Creme von der Birne
- Feuilletinemasse
- Karamellsahnecreme
- Brombeergeleekern
- Mohnmacarons
- Getrocknete Birnenscheibe
- Schokoladenglasur Noir und Blanc
- Schokoladendekor
- Früchte
- Zuckerfaden

4 Torten, Ø 20 cm
2 Torten, Ø 28 cm

Mohnbiskuit

200 g	*Eigelb*
325 g	*Zucker*
300 g	*Eiweiß*
125 g	*Mehl*
125 g	*Weizenpuder*
75 g	*Mohn, gemahlen*
50 g	*Krokant*

Eigelb mit 175 g Zucker schaumig schlagen. Eiweiß mit 150 g Zucker zu Schnee schlagen. Trockene Zutaten mischen und im Wechsel mit dem Eischnee unter die Eigelbmasse ziehen. Bei 180 °C etwa 15 Minuten backen.

Poppy seed sponge

200 g	*egg yolk*
325 g	*sugar*
300 g	*egg white*
125 g	*flour*
125 g	*wheat powder*
75 g	*poppy seeds, ground*
50 g	*almond brittle*

Beat the egg yolk with 175 g sugar until frothy. Beat egg white with 150 g of sugar until stiff. Mix the dry ingredients together and then fold the mixture and the beaten egg white, in turn, into the egg yolk mixture. Bake at 180 °C for about 15 minutes.

1

2

3

Bayerische Creme von der Birne

6	*Blatt Gelatine*
330 g	*Milch*
70 g	*Zucker*
1	*Vanilleschote*
120 g	*Eigelb*
110 g	*Zucker*
330 g	*Birnenpüree*
330 g	*geschlagene Sahne*
20 g	*Birnengeist*
40 g	*Krokant*

Gelatine in kaltem Wasser einweichen. Milch, 70 g Zucker sowie Vanillemark und -schote aufkochen. Eigelb und 110 g Zucker schaumig schlagen, Vanille-Zucker-Milch zugießen und bei 85 °C pasteurisieren. Gelatine auspressen und in die heiße Masse einrühren. Sehr kaltes Birnenpüree zugeben und abkühlen lassen. Die Sahne, Birnengeist und Krokant unterziehen.

Bavarian cream of pear

6	*sheets of gelatine*
330 g	*milk*
70 g	*sugar*
1	*vanilla pod*
120 g	*egg yolk*
110 g	*sugar*
330 g	*pear puree*
330 g	*whipped cream*
20 g	*pear brandy*
40 g	*almond brittle*

Soak the gelatine in cold water. Bring the milk, 70 g sugar, pith of vanilla and vanilla pod to boil. Beat the egg yolk and 110 g sugar until frothy, add the vanilla flavoured milk and pasteurise at 85 °C. Squeeze out the gelatine and stir into the hot mixture. Add very cold pear puree and leave to cool. Fold in the cream, pear brandy and brittle.

Birne in feine Scheiben schneiden

Cut the pear into fine slices

4

... trocken tupfen

... and dab dry

Birnenscheiben in Fruchtsäure wenden

Turn the pear slices in fruit acid

5

In Zucker wenden und auf Backmatte legen

Place in some sugar, turn over and put onto the baking mat

Auf Küchenkrepp legen ...

Place on kitchen roll ...

6

Bei maximal 70 °C trocknen

Dry at max. 70 °C

Feuilletine mixture

100 g	light almond gianduja
50 g	feuilletine

Dissolve the almond nougat and stir in the feuilletine.

Feuilletinemasse

100 g	Mandelnugat, hell
50 g	Feuilletine

Mandelnugat auflösen und Feuilletine unterrühren.

Karamellsahnecreme

8	*Blatt Gelatine*
225 g	*Zucker*
850 g	*Milch*
60 g	*Zucker*
25 g	*Cremepulver*
175 g	*Eigelb*
450 g	*geschlagene Sahne*

Gelatine in kaltem Wasser einweichen. 225 g Zucker karamellisieren und mit Milch ablöschen. 60 g Zucker, Cremepulver und Eigelb verrühren, Karamellsahne zugeben, zu einer Creme kochen, ausgedrückte Gelatine einrühren, abkühlen und die Sahne unterziehen.

Caramel cream

8	*sheets of gelatine*
225 g	*sugar*
850 g	*milk*
60 g	*sugar*
25 g	*cream powder*
175 g	*egg yolk*
450 g	*whipped cream*

Soak the gelatine in cold water. Caramelise 225 g sugar and then add the milk. Stir together the 60 g sugar, cream powder and egg yolk, add the caramel cream and boil to a creamy consistence, stir in the squeezed-out gelatine, leave to cool and fold in the cream.

Brombeergeleekern

8	*Blatt Gelatine*
500 g	*Brombeerpüree*
60 g	*Zucker*
2	*Orangen (Saft und Abrieb)*

Gelatine in kaltem Wasser einweichen. Brombeerpüree mit Zucker, Orangensaft und -abrieb verrühren. Gelatine ausdrücken, auflösen und das Fruchtpüree zugeben. Brombeergelee in einer flachen Silikonform tiefgefrieren.

Blackberry jelly filling

8	*sheets of gelatine*
500 g	*blackberry puree*
60 g	*sugar*
2	*oranges (juice and zest)*

Soak the gelatine in cold water. Stir the sugar, orange juice and zest into the blackberry puree. Squeeze out the gelatine, dissolve and add the fruit puree. Deep-freeze the blackberry jelly in a shallow silicon mould.

Macaroons

60 g	*egg whites*
125 g	*icing sugar*
20 g	*cornflour*
50 g	*finely chopped almonds*
	poppy seed for topping

Beat the egg white with 75 g icing sugar and cornflour until stiff, then mix the almonds and the remaining icing sugar and carefully fold in. Now use a piping bag with round nozzle size 8 to arrange onto a baking sheet that has been covered with baking paper, sprinkle on the poppy seed and bake in the preheated oven at 160 °C for 15 to 20 minutes.

Macaron

60 g	*Eiweiß*
125 g	*Puderzucker*
20 g	*Speisestärke*
50 g	*fein gemahlene Mandeln*
	Mohn zum Bestreuen

Eiweiß mit 75 g Puderzucker und Speisestärke zu einem festen Schnee schlagen, die Mandeln sowie den restlichen Puderzucker mischen und vorsichtig unterheben, dann auf ein mit Backpapier belegtes Backblech mit einem Dressierbeutel und 8er-Lochtülle aufdressieren, mit Mohn bestreuen und im vorgeheizten Ofen bei 160 °C 15 bis 20 Minuten backen.

Putting it all together

Fill half of a hemispheric mould with the pear cream. Spread the poppy seed sponge, fill up with caramel cream, add the blackberry jelly filling and then cover with the poppy seed sponge, onto which you have spread the feuilletine mixture. Put into the deep-freeze until frozen, then take the cake out of the mould and use the dark and white chocolate icing to achieve a marbled effect. Place the poppy seed macaroons along the lower side of the cake. Use fruit and chocolate décor to apply the finishing touches.

Zusammensetzung Torte

Birnencreme in eine Halbkugelform zur Hälfte einfüllen. Mohnbiskuit einlegen, Karamellsahnecreme auffüllen, Brombeergeleekern auflegen und den mit Feuilletinemasse bestrichenen Mohnbiskuit abdeckeln. Tiefgefrieren, ausformen, mit Schokoladenglasur Noir überziehen und mit Schokoladenglasur Blanc marmorieren. Mohnmacarons am unteren Rand anlegen. Torte mit Früchten und Schokoladendekor abschließen.

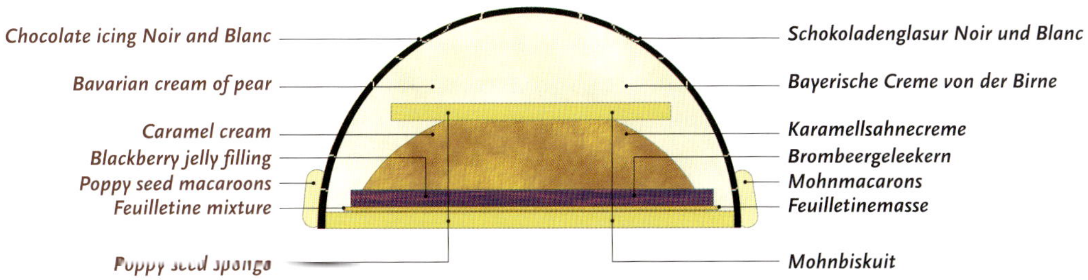

VAN GOGHS ABSINTH-KISSEN

VAN GOGH'S ABSINTHE CUSHION

Ich hoffe nicht, dass sich unsere Kunden im Absinthrausch die Ohren abschneiden, wie es Van Gogh einst getan haben soll. Aber das französische Macaron mit dem wiederauferstandenen Absinth ist einfach unwiderstehlich.

I trust that our customers won't cut off their ears under the effects of absinthe, as Van Gogh is supposed to have done. Whatever the truth of this story, French macaroons with the now legalised absinthe are simply irresistible.

Ingredients	Zusammensetzung
Macaroon	Macaron
Absinthe butter cream	Absinthbuttercreme
Chocolate décor	Schokoladendekor
Candied angelica	Kandiertes Angelika
4 Cakes, Ø 20 cm	4 Torten, Ø 20 cm
2 Cakes, Ø 28 cm	2 Torten, Ø 28 cm

Macaron

480 g	*Eiweiß*
1000 g	*Puderzucker*
160 g	*Weizenpuder*
400 g	*fein gemahlene Mandeln*

Eiweiß mit 600 g Puderzucker und Weizenpuder zu einem festen Schnee schlagen, die Mandeln und den restlichen Puderzucker mischen und vorsichtig unterheben und auf ein mit Backpapier belegtes Backblech mit einem Dressierbeutel und 8er-Lochtülle aufdressieren (siehe Stepps). Im vorgeheizten Ofen bei 160 °C 15 bis 20 Minuten backen.

Macaroon

480 g	*egg white*
1,000 g	*icing sugar*
160 g	*wheat powder*
400 g	*finely grounded almonds*

Beat the egg white with 600 g icing sugar and wheat powder stiff, mix the almonds and the remaining icing sugar and carefully fold in. Use a piping bag with a round size 8 nozzle to arrange the mixture onto a baking sheet covered with baking paper (see stages). Bake in a preheated oven at 160 °C for 15 to 20 minutes.

1
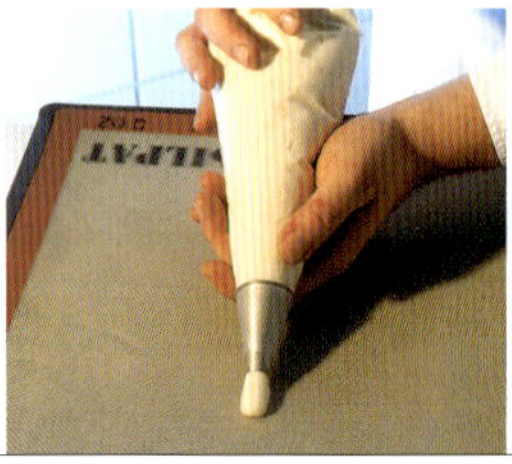

2
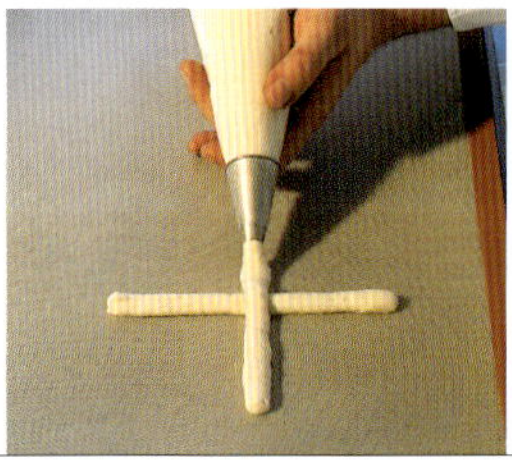

2
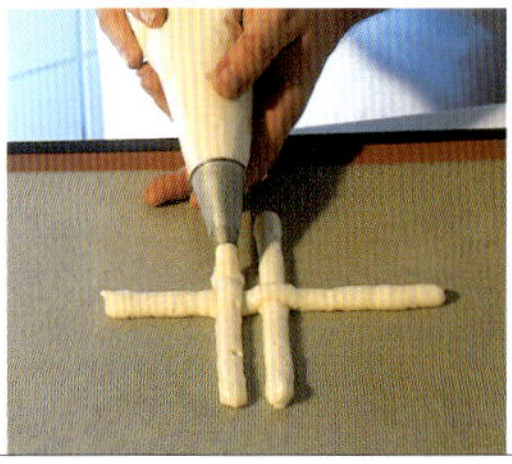

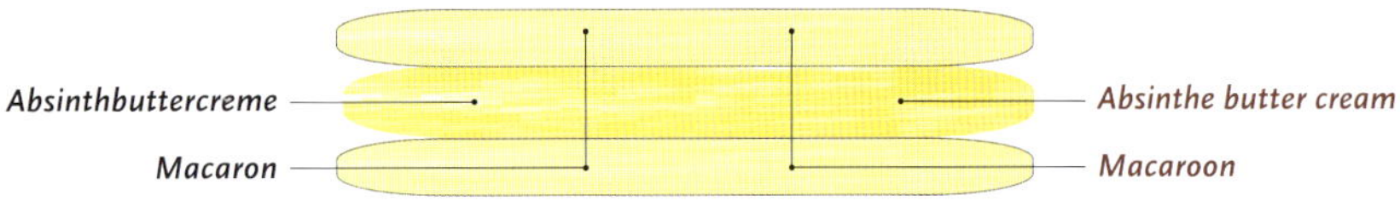

Macaronmasse in einer Linie aufdressieren

Arrange the macaroon mixture in a straight line

4

Ein 20 x 20 cm großes Quadrat herstellen

Make a square measuring 20 x 20 cm

Kreuzförmig die zweite Linie aufdressieren

Then add the second line at right angles

5

Fertiges Macaron

Finished macaroon

Dritte Linie parallel zur zweiten aufspritzen

Place the third line parallel to the second

Absinthe butter cream

200 g	*whole egg*
160 g	*sugar*
500 g	*butter*
100 g	*absinthe liqueur*

Beat the eggs with the sugar in a hot water bath until creamy. Then beat to cool. Stir the butter with the absinthe until frothy and then fold in the egg mixture.

Absinthbuttercreme

200 g	*Vollei*
160 g	*Zucker*
500 g	*Butter*
100 g	*Absinthlikör*

Eier und Zucker im heißen Wasserbad zu einer cremigen Masse aufschlagen. Danach kalt schlagen. Die Butter mit Absinth schaumig rühren und die Eiermasse unterheben.

Putting it all together

Dress the absinthe butter cream onto a cooled down macaroon, put on a second macaroon and decorate with small filled macaroons, chocolate décor and angelica.

Zusammensetzung Torte

Absinthbuttercreme auf ein abgekühltes Macaron dressieren, ein zweites Macaron auflegen und mit kleinen gefüllten Macarons und Schokoladendekor sowie Angelika garnieren.

BERND SIEFERT

UGANDA HILL

Ein Teil meiner Familie lebt in Afrika – sozusagen Siefert international. Bananen sind für mich Afrika pur. In Verbindung mit Schokolade ist dieses Tarte ein Traum.

One part of my family lives in Africa – Siefert International Inc. For me, bananas embody Africa at its purest. Together with chocolate, this tart is a dream.

Ingredients	Zusammensetzung
Chocolate shortcrust case	Schokoladen-Mürbeteig-Boden
Chocolate tart	Schokoladentarte
Dark chocolate mousse	Bitterschokoladenmousse
White chocolate mousse	Weisse Schokoladenmousse
White and black spray couverture	Sprühkuvertüre, weiss und schwarz
Chocolate décor	Schokoladendekor
Bananas	Bananen
4 Cakes, Ø 20 cm	4 Torten, Ø 20 cm
2 Cakes, Ø 28 cm	2 Torten, Ø 28 cm

1

Mit einer Garniertüte gelb gefärbte Kakaobutter auf eine Folie aufbringen

Use a piping bag to arrange the yellow-coloured cocoa butter onto a foil.

2

Grün gefärbte Kakaobutter daneben aufbringen

Add the green-coloured cocoa butter next to it

3

Mit einem Pinsel linienförmig verstreichen

Use a brush to spread it out in lines

4

5

6

7

Schokoladen-Mürbeteigboden zum Blindbacken

50 g	*Kakaomasse*
25 g	*Wasser*
100 g	*Butter*
200 g	*Zucker*
	Mark von einer ½ Vanilleschote
1 g	*Salz*
25 g	*Mandelstaub*
300 g	*Mehl*

Kakaomasse und Wasser zu einer Ganache verarbeiten. Butter, Zucker sowie Vanillemark dazugeben und glatt arbeiten. Salz, Mandelstaub und Mehl zufügen und schnell zu einem Teig zusammenwirken.

Vor der Verarbeitung kühl stellen. Bei 160 °C trocken vorbacken.

Chocolate Shortcrust Case for Blind Baking

50 g	*cocoa paste*
25 g	*water*
100 g	*butter*
200 g	*sugar*
	pith of ½ vanilla pod
1 g	*salt*
25 g	*almond dust*
300 g	*flour*

Work the cocoa paste and water into a ganache. Add the butter, sugar and vanilla pith and stir until smooth. Add the salt, almond dust and flour and work together quickly to make the pastry.

Put into a cool place before using it. Prebake blind at 160 °C.

Weiße Kakaobutter mit einem Pinsel dünn auftragen

Apply the white cocoa butter thinly with a brush

Dunkle Kuvertüre mit einer Winkelpalette auftragen

Spread on the dark couverture with an angled spatula

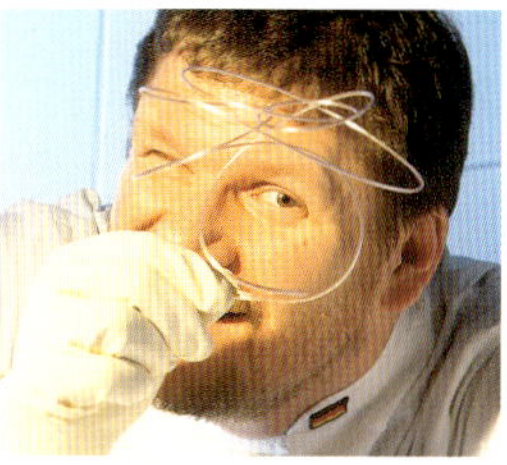

Sobald die Kuvertüre angezogen hat, Dekor schneiden

As soon as the couverture has set, cut the décor

Fertiges Schokoladendekor

Finished chocolate décor

Chocolate tart

360 g	*marzipan paste*
335 g	*whole egg*
70 g	*flour*
50 g	*cocoa powder*
4 g	*baking powder*
110 g	*butter*
2	*fresh bananas*
50 g	*banana chips*

Knead the marzipan paste with the whole egg and beat until frothy. Mix the flour, cocoa powder and baking powder and fold into the marzipan mixture. Melt the butter and stir in. Fill the chocolate tart mixture into the pre-baked chocolate shortcrust pastry and spread on the banana pieces and chips. Bake at 180 °C for about 20 minutes.

Schokoladentarte

360 g	*Marzipanrohmasse*
335 g	*Vollei*
70 g	*Mehl*
50 g	*Kakaopulver*
4 g	*Backpulver*
110 g	*Butter*
2	*Bananen, frisch*
50 g	*Bananenchips*

Marzipanrohmasse mit Vollei verkneten und schaumig schlagen. Mehl, Kakaopulver und Backpulver mischen und unter die Marzipanmasse heben. Butter aufgelöst unterrühren. Schokoladentartemasse in den vorgebackenen Schokoladenmürbeteig einfüllen, Bananenstückchen und Bananenchips ausstreuen. Bei 180 °C etwa 20 Minuten backen.

Bitterschokoladenmousse

125 g	*Milch*
125 g	*Sahne*
35 g	*Zucker*
65 g	*Eigelb*
390 g	*Bitterkuvertüre, 75 %*
530 g	*geschlagene Sahne*

Milch, Sahne, Zucker und Eigelb mischen. Bei 85 °C pasteurisieren. Klein gehackte Kuvertüre in die heiße Masse geben. Kuvertüre unterrühren, bis eine homogene Masse entsteht, dann die Sahne unterziehen. In einer Silikonform tiefgefrieren.

Dark chocolate mousse

125 g	*milk*
125 g	*cream*
35 g	*sugar*
65 g	*egg yolk*
390 g	*dark couverture, 75 %*
530 g	*whipped cream*

Mix the milk, cream, sugar and egg yolk together. Pasteurise at 85 °C. Chop up the couverture into small pieces and add to the hot mixture. Stir in the couverture until the mixture is smooth and even, then fold in the cream. Deep-freeze in a silicon mould.

White chocolate mousse

200 g	milk
20 g	sugar
20 g	cream powder
50 g	egg yolk
1	vanilla pod
130 g	white couverture
10 g	cocoa butter powder
300 g	whipped cream

Boil the milk, sugar, cream powder, egg yolk and pith of the vanilla pod into a cream. Stir the white couverture and cocoa butter into the hot mixture until they dissolve and then fold in the cream. Deep-freeze in different sizes of hemispheric silicon moulds.

Weisse Schokoladenmousse

200 g	Milch
20 g	Zucker
20 g	Cremepulver
50 g	Eigelb
1	Vanilleschote
130 g	weiße Kuvertüre
10 g	pulverisierte Kakaobutter
300 g	geschlagene Sahne

Milch, Zucker, Cremepulver, Eigelb und Mark der Vanilleschote zu Creme kochen. Die weiße Kuvertüre und die Kakaobutter in der heißen Masse unter Rühren auflösen, dann die Sahne unterziehen. In verschieden großen Silikonhalbkugelformen tiefgefrieren.

Putting it all together

Place the white half-round chocolate mousse "domes" onto the dark chocolate mousse. First spray with dark spray couverture and then follow on by spraying white spray couverture flat from one side. Now place onto the chocolate tart. Decorate with chocolate décor and jellied banana.

Zusammensetzung Torte

Bitterschokoladenmousse mit den weißen Schokoladenmousse-Halbkugeln belegen. Zuerst mit Bittersprühkuvertüre absprühen, dann flach von einer Seite mit weißer Sprühkuvertüre absprühen. Jetzt auf die Schokoladentarte auflegen. Mit Schokoladendekor und gelierter Banane dekorieren.

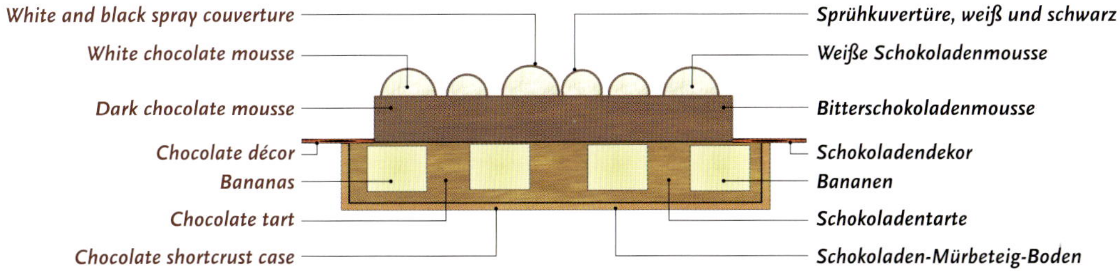

EXOTIC WALDBEER

EXOTIC WILD BERRY

Grüsse vom Kap. Exotische Früchte vereint mit heimischen Waldbeeren. Leichte Mousse, wie ich sie in Frankreich kennen gelernt habe, gepaart mit der leckeren Kokosdacquoise, kommt immer sehr gut an.

Greetings from the Cape. Exotic fruit together with native wild berries – this is a light mousse I got to know in France which, together with a tasty coconut dacquoise, is always popular with the punters.

Ingredients	Zusammensetzung
Coconut dacquoise	Kokosdacquoise
Wild berry jelly	Waldbeergelee
Exotic fruit mousse	Exotisches Fruchtmousse
Décor sponge	Dekorbiskuit
Mango sauce	Mangosauce
Jelly icing	Kaltgelee
Fresh fruit	Frische Früchte
Chocolate décor	Schokoladendekor
4 Cakes, Ø 20 cm	4 Torten, Ø 20 cm
2 Cakes, Ø 28 cm	2 Torten, Ø 28 cm

1 *Kakaozigarettenmasse auf eine Dekormatte geben*

Put the cocoa cigarette mixture onto a décor mat

2 *Mit einer Winkelpalette gleichmäßig dünn verstreichen*

Use an angled spatula to spread out evenly and thinly

3 *Überschüssige Masse abziehen*

Remove any excess mixture

4 *Dekorbiskuitmasse aufgießen*

Pour on the décor sponge mixture

5

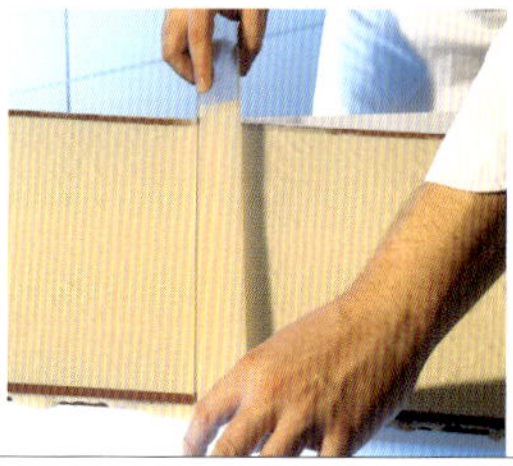

6

7

8

Kokosdacquoise

375 g	Eiweiß
125 g	Zucker
65 g	Mandelgrieß
310 g	Puderzucker
250 g	Kokosraspel
65 g	Mehl

Eiweiß mit Zucker zu Schnee schlagen. Mandelgrieß, Puderzucker, Kokosraspel sowie Mehl mischen und vorsichtig unter den Schnee ziehen. Dacquoise bei 160 °C etwa 15 Minuten backen.

Coconut dacquoise

375 g	egg white
125 g	sugar
65 g	grated almonds
310 g	icing sugar
250 g	grated coconut
65 g	flour

Add sugar to the egg white and beat until stiff. Mix the grated almonds, icing sugar, grated coconut and flour and then carefully fold into the beaten egg. Bake the dacquoise at 160 °C for about 15 minutes.

Mit einer Winkelpalette verstreichen

Use an angled spatula to spread out

Überschüssige Masse abziehen

Remove any excess mixture

Nach dem Backen mit Zucker bestreuen, dann Dekormatte abziehen

After baking, sprinkle on sugar and then pull off the décor mat.

Zurechtgeschnittener Dekorrand

Side décor strip in the finished shape

Cigarette mixture for the décor sponge

100 g	*butter*
100 g	*icing sugar*
100 g	*liquid egg white*
100 g	*flour*
	cocoa powder

Stir the butter with icing sugar until smooth, then blend in the egg white and flour alternately. Apply the cocoa powder. Use an angled spatula to spread the mixture into a silicon relief mould.

Zigarettenmasse für den Dekorbiskuit

100 g	*Butter*
100 g	*Puderzucker*
100 g	*flüssiges Eiweiß*
100 g	*Mehl*
	Kakaopulver

Butter mit Puderzucker glatt rühren, das Eiweiß und Mehl abwechselnd unterrühren. Mit Kakaopulver einfärben. Masse mit einer Winkelpalette in Silikonreliefform einstreichen.

Décor sponge

500 g	*whole egg*
375 g	*grated almonds*
375 g	*icing sugar*
100 g	*flour*
325 g	*egg white*
75 g	*sugar*
75 g	*melted butter*

Stir the egg with grated almonds, icing sugar and flour until frothy. Add sugar to the egg white and beat until stiff; then fold into the egg mixture. Finally fold in the butter. Fill the sponge mixture into the prepared silicon relief mould and bake at 220 °C for about 10 minutes. When taking the relief mould from the oven, sprinkle on the sugar immediately so that the moisture remains in the sponge.

Dekorbiskuit

500 g	*Vollei*
375 g	*Mandelgrieß*
375 g	*Puderzucker*
100 g	*Mehl*
325 g	*Eiweiß*
75 g	*Zucker*
75 g	*zerlassene Butter*

Ei mit Mandelgrieß, Puderzucker und Mehl schaumig rühren. Eiweiß mit Zucker zu Schnee schlagen und unter die Eimasse heben. Zuletzt die Butter unterziehen. Den Biskuit in die vorbereitete Silikonreliefform einfüllen und bei 220 °C etwa 10 Minuten backen. Sobald die Reliefmatte aus dem Ofen kommt, mit Zucker bestreuen, damit die Feuchtigkeit im Biskuit bleibt.

Waldbeergelee

8	*Blatt Gelatine*
500 g	*Waldbeerpüree*
60 g	*Zucker*

Gelatine einweichen. Das Waldbeerpüree mit Zucker mischen und unter die ausgedrückte, aufgelöste Gelatine rühren. Waldbeergelee in einer flachen Silikonform tiefgefrieren.

Wild berry jelly

8	*sheets of gelatine*
500 g	*puree of wild berries*
60 g	*sugar*

Soak the gelatine. Mix the wild berry puree with the sugar and then stir into the squeezed-out and dissolved gelatine. Deep-freeze the wild berry jelly in a shallow silicon mould.

Exotic fruit mousse

12	*sheets of gelatine*
400 g	*mango puree*
400 g	*passion fruit puree*
180 g	*egg white*
220 g	*sugar*
600 g	*whipped cream*

Soak the gelatine in cold water. Mix the mango puree with the passion fruit puree. Dissolve the squeezed-out gelatine and add the fruit puree. Beat the egg white with the sugar until stiff and then fold in. Finally fold in the cream.

Exotisches Fruchtmousse

12	*Blatt Gelatine*
400 g	*Mangopüree*
400 g	*Maracujapüree*
180 g	*Eiweiß*
220 g	*Zucker*
600 g	*geschlagene Sahne*

Gelatine in kaltem Wasser einweichen. Mangopüree mit Maracujapüree mischen. Ausgedrückte Gelatine auflösen, Fruchtpüree zugeben. Das Eiweiß mit Zucker zu Schnee schlagen und unterziehen. Zuletzt die Sahne unterheben.

Putting it all together

Place the décor sponge and a layer of coconut dacquoise into the mould. Spread the wild berry jelly, fill up half with the exotic fruit mousse, insert another coconut dacquoise and then fill in the remaining part of the exotic fruit mousse; put into the deep-freeze. Drip the mango sauce over it and cover with jelly icing. Turn out of the mould and finish the decoration with fruit and chocolate décors.

Zusammensetzung Torte

Form mit dem Dekorbiskuit und einer Lage Kokosdacquoise auslegen. Das Waldbeergelee einlegen, halb mit exotischem Fruchtmousse auffüllen, weitere Kokosdacquoise einlegen und mit dem restlichen exotischem Fruchtmousse auffüllen, dann tiefgefrieren. Mit Mangosauce überspinnen und mit Kaltgelee abgelieren. Torte ausformen und mit Früchten sowie Schokoladendekoren fertig stellen.

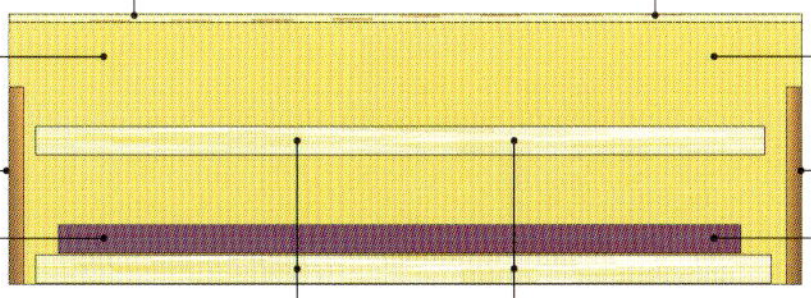

DESSERTS

DESSERTS

CALIFORNIA

Als ich bei einer meiner ersten Seminarreisen in den USA durch Kalifornien fuhr, kam ich durch die unendlichen Orangen- und Mandelhaine, und da ich am Abend nichts anderes als Himbeeren für die Deko hatte, war einer meiner Klassiker geboren.

When I was driving through California during one of my first workshop tours in the United States, I was inspired by the endless orange and almond groves I travelled through and since I had nothing but raspberries for the decoration that night, the recipe for one of my classics was born.

Ingredients	**Zusammensetzung**
Couverture cornucopia	Kuvertürefüllhorn
Citrus fruit mousse with white chocolate	Zitrusfrüchtemousse mit weisser Schokolade
Raspberry sorbet	Himbeersorbet
Bitter almond jelly	Bittermandelgelee
Raspberry sauce and raspberries cut in half	Himbeersauce und halbierte Himbeeren
Ingredients for 10 desserts	Zutaten für 10 Desserts

Himbeersauce

200 g	*Himbeerpüree*
50 g	*Zucker*
10 g	*Zitronensaft*

Leicht angefrorenes Himbeerpüree mit Zucker und Zitronensaft mischen und stabil aufmixen.

Bittermandelgelee

3	*Blatt Gelatine*
250 g	*Weißwein*
25 g	*Marzipan*
20 g	*Zucker*
1	*Tropfen Bittermandelöl*
10 g	*Amaretto*

Gelatine einweichen. Alle anderen Zutaten mixen. Gelatine auspressen, auflösen und in die Masse laufen lassen. Sofort in Silikonformen gießen. Kühl stellen oder für besseres Handling tiefgefrieren.

Raspberry sauce

200 g	*raspberry puree*
50 g	*sugar*
10 g	*lemon juice*

Mix the slightly frozen raspberry puree with sugar and lemon juice until firm.

Bitter almond jelly

3	*sheets of gelatine*
250 g	*white wine*
25 g	*marzipan*
20 g	*sugar*
1	*drop of bitter almond oil*
10 g	*Amaretto*

Soak the gelatine. Mix the other ingredients together. Squeeze out the gelatine, dissolve and let it run into the mixture. Pour it into the silicon moulds immediately. Put in a cool place or, for better handling, deep-freeze.

1

2

3

4

5

Plastikfolie kreisrund zurechtschneiden

Cut the plastic foil into a circle

6

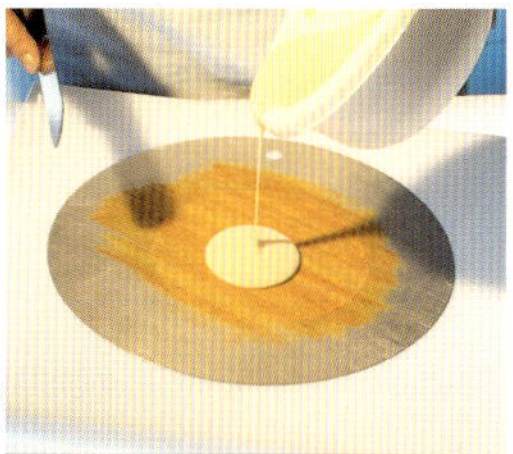

Sobald die Farbe fest ist, temperierte Kuvertüre aufgießen

As soon as the colour is firm, pour on the tempered couverture

---

Blech mit Wasser benetzen, damit die Folie besser haften bleibt

Moisten the sheet with water so that the foil sticks to it better

7

Mit einer Winkelpalette dünn verstreichen

Use an angled spatula to spread out thinly

Gelbe Kakaobutter streifenförmig auf die Folie träufeln

Sprinkle the yellow cocoa butter in strips onto the foil

8

Gefärbte Kuvertüre mit der Folie abnehmen

Take off the coloured couverture together with the foil

Rote Kakaobutter in die Zwischenräume der gelben träufeln

Sprinkle the red cocoa butter in the gaps between the yellow

9

Sobald die Kuvertüre anzieht, zu einer Tüte rollen

When the couverture begins to set, roll it into the shape of a pointed paper bag

---

Mit einem festen Pinsel streifenförmig verstreichen

Use a stiff brush to spread it out in lines

10

Folie abziehen. Je länger man wartet, desto glänzender wird das Füllhorn

Pull off the foil. The longer you wait, the shinier the cornucopia will be

Zitrusfrüchtemousse mit weisser Schokolade

2	*Blatt Gelatine*
30 g	*Puderzucker*
40 g	*Eigelb*
80 g	*Orangensaft*
60 g	*Grapefruitsaft*
60 g	*Bitterorangensaft*
	Abrieb von 2 Orangen
125 g	*weiße Kuvertüre*
250 g	*geschlagene Sahne*

Gelatine einweichen. Puderzucker, Eigelb, Fruchtsaft und Orangenabrieb bei 85 °C pasteurisieren. Ausgepresste Gelatine zugeben und auflösen, dann alles über die fein gehackte Kuvertüre gießen, glatt rühren und so bald es anfängt zu gelieren, die Sahne unterziehen. Sofort aufdressieren. Wenn die Mousse auf Vorrat hergestellt wird, nicht mehr dressieren, sondern Nocken ausstechen oder in Formen füllen.

Citrus fruit mousse with white chocolate

2	*sheets of gelatine*
30 g	*icing sugar*
40 g	*egg yolk*
80 g	*orange juice*
60 g	*grapefruit juice*
60 g	*bitter orange juice*
	grated rind from 2 oranges
125 g	*white couverture*
250 g	*cream*

Soak the gelatine. Pasteurise the icing sugar, egg yolk, fruit juice and orange rind at 85 °C. Add the squeezed-out gelatine and dissolve, then pour everything over the finely chopped couverture, stir until smooth and as soon as it starts to thicken, fold in the whipped cream. Pipe on immediately. When making extra mousse to keep, do not pipe it but rather cut out the required shapes or fill into moulds later.

Raspberry sorbet

70 g	*sugar*
10 g	*dry glucose*
135 g	*water*
180 g	*raspberry puree*
5 g	*lemon juice*

Mix the dry ingredients and then add the water, raspberry puree and lemon juice. Mix everything together with the hand blender until firm. Use the refractometer to adjust to 30 °Brix. If the sugar concentration is too high, add water, if it is too low, add sugar. This method is for making the sorbet without heating. The advantage of the cold production method is a larger volume and greater stability of the sorbet.

With the hot production method, the dry ingredients are mixed and then brought to boil with water. Then proceed as in the cold production method.

With the hot production method one can achieve a shinier sorbet that melts a bit more readily.

Put the mixture into the ice-cream maker and freeze.

Himbeersorbet

70 g	*Zucker*
10 g	*Trockenglukose*
135 g	*Wasser*
180 g	*Himbeerpüree*
5 g	*Zitronensaft*

Die trockenen Zutaten mischen, Wasser, Himbeerpüree und Zitronensaft zugeben. Alles mit dem Stabmixer stabil aufmixen. Mit dem Refraktometer auf 30 °Brix einstellen. Bei zu hoher Zuckerdichte Wasser zugeben, bei zu niedriger Dichte Zucker zugeben. Dies ist die kalte Herstellung von Sorbets. Der Vorteil bei kalter Herstellungsweise ist ein höheres Volumen und stabileres Sorbet.

Bei der warmen Herstellung werden die trockenen Zutaten gemischt und mit Wasser aufgekocht. Der restliche Vorgang ist gleich wie bei der kalten Herstellung.

Bei der warmen Herstellung erhält man ein glänzenderes, schmelzigeres Sorbet.

Masse in die Sorbetière geben und abfrieren.

Drink recommendation

1999 Arkezia Muffo di San Sisto, Fazi Marche Bianco, Bataglia, Italy

Getränkeempfehlung

1999 Arkezia Muffo di San Sisto, Fazi Marche Bianco, Bataglia, Italien

ENGLISCHER FRÜHLING

ENGLISH SPRING

Ohne Soufflés gehts einfach nicht, und sie sind ja auch so lecker. Dieses Frühlingsdessert ist leicht und erfrischend – selbst die Queen hatte Spass daran.

Soufflés are simply a must, and besides they are a real treat. This spring dessert is light and refreshing – even the Queen enjoys it.

Ingredients

- Cottage cheese soufflé with verbena
- Rhubarb and apple compote
- Riesling-Sabayon
- Raspberries
- Caramel limes
- Rhubarb chips

Ingredients for 10 desserts

Zusammensetzung

- Topfensoufflé mit Verveine
- Rhabarber-Apfel-Kompott
- Riesling-Sabayon
- Himbeeren
- Karamelllimetten
- Rhabarberchips

Zutaten für 10 Desserts

Topfensoufflé mit Verveine

200 g	*Schichtkäse*
60 g	*Eigelb*
	Mark von einer 1/2 Vanilleschote
	Abrieb von einer 1/2 Limette
90 g	*Eiweiß*
1	*Prise Salz*
60 g	*Zucker*
	Verveine oder Zitronenmelisse, fein gehackt

Schichtkäse durchpassieren, dann Eigelb, Vanillemark und Limettenabrieb zugeben und miteinander verrühren. Das Eiweiß mit der Prise Salz und Zucker zu Schnee schlagen. Fein gehackte Verveine oder Zitronenmelisse unter die Schichtkäsemasse heben, dann den Eischnee unterziehen. Topfensoufflé in gebutterte und gezuckerte Souffléförmchen füllen. Im Wasserbad bei 250 °C Oberhitze und 80 °C Unterhitze etwa 15 Minuten stocken lassen.

Cottage cheese soufflé with verbena

200 g	*cottage cheese*
60 g	*egg yolk*
	pith of 1/2 vanilla pod
	zest of 1/2 lime
90 g	*egg white*
1	*pinch of salt*
60 g	*sugar*
	verbena or lemon balm, finely chopped

Strain the cottage cheese, then add the egg yolk, vanilla pith and lime zest and stir together. Beat the egg white with the salt and sugar until stiff. Fold the chopped verbena or lemon balm into the fromage frais mixture and then carefully add the beaten egg white. Pour the soufflé into buttered and sugared ramekins. Place the ramekins into a pot with water and allow to thicken for about 15 minutes, with top heat at 250 °C and bottom heat at 80 °C.

1

2

3

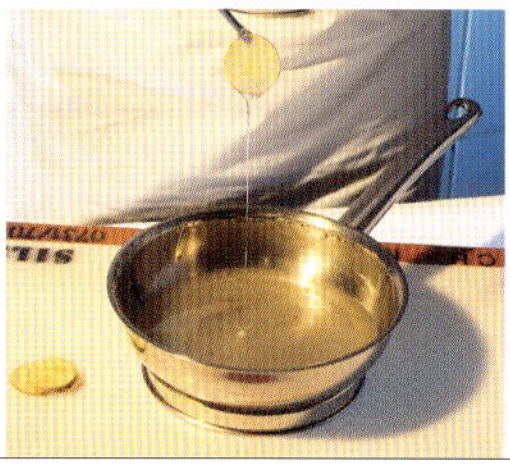
4

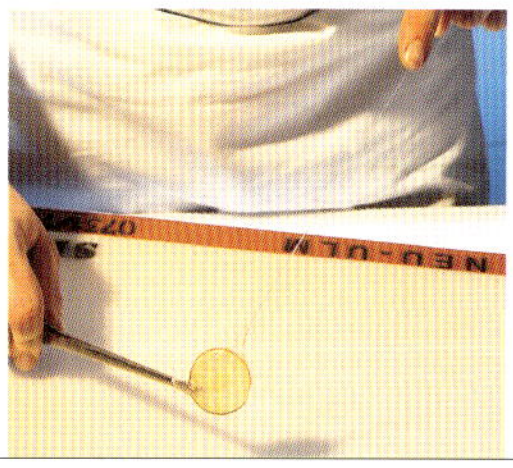
5

Limette in dünne Scheiben schneiden

Cut the lime into thin slices

Limettenscheiben in Zucker wenden und im Ofen bei 70 °C trocknen

Coat the lime slices with sugar on both sides and dry in the oven at 70 °C.

In geschmolzenen Isomalt tauchen

Dip into melted Isomalt

Limettenscheiben herausnehmen, so dass ein Zuckerfaden gezogen wird

Take out the slices of lime in such a way as to pull out a sugar thread

Fertiger Limettendekor

Completed lime decor

Rhubarb and apple compote

2	*small apples*
2	*sticks of red rhubarb*
50 g	*sugar*
20 ml	*Grand Marnier*
	pith of 1/2 vanilla pod

Peel and core the apples and cut into small cubes. Likewise, peel the red rhubarb and cut into small cubes. Caramelise the sugar and douse with Grand Marnier. Add the vanilla pith as well as the apple and rhubarb cubes, heat up briefly and then pour into cutting shapes directly onto a plate. Push down slightly and then pull off the cutting shape.

Rhabarber-Apfel-Kompott

2	*kleine Äpfel*
2	*Stangen Himbeerrhabarber*
50 g	*Zucker*
20 ml	*Grand Marnier*
	Mark von einer 1/2 Vanilleschote

Äpfel schälen, entkernen und in kleine Würfel schneiden. Den Himbeerrhabarber ebenfalls schälen und in kleine Würfel schneiden. Zucker karamellisieren und mit Grand Marnier ablöschen. Vanillemark sowie Apfel- und Rhabarberwürfel zugeben, einmal kurz heiß werden lassen, dann in einen Ausstecher direkt auf den Teller geben. Leicht anpressen und den Ausstecher abziehen.

Riesling-Sabayon

120 g	*Riesling, Auslese*
80 g	*egg yolk*
20 g	*sugar*

Beat the Riesling, egg yolk and sugar in a water bath until firmly stiff.

Riesling-Sabayon

120 g	*Riesling, Auslese*
80 g	*Eigelb*
20 g	*Zucker*

Riesling, Eigelb und Zucker im Wasserbad zu einem stabilen Schaum schlagen.

Drink recommendation

Riesling Auslese, Enkircher Steffensberg 2003, Estate Kaspari Kappel, Moselle, Germany

Getränkeempfehlung

Riesling Auslese, Enkircher Steffensberg 2003, Weingut Kaspari Kappel, Mosel, Deutschland

MEXIKANISCHER EISBERG

MEXICAN ICEBERG

Ein Grundrezept für alle möglichen Granités mit hochprozentigem Alkohol. Superlecker im Sommer, entweder als Zwischengang oder als Pre-Dessert.

A basic recipe for all kinds of granités, with concentrated alcohol. Specially delicious in the summer, either as an entremets or before a dessert.

Ingredients

Granité
Salt sugar glass
Ice-cream waffles

Ingredients for 10 desserts

Zusammensetzung

Granité
Salzzuckerglas
Eisgebäck

Zutaten für 10 Desserts

Granité

200 g	*Zucker*
700 g	*Wasser*
100 g	*Tequila*
100 g	*Zitronensaft*

Zucker mit Wasser zu Sirup kochen, abkühlen lassen, dann Tequila und Zitronensaft zugießen. In ein flaches Gefäß geben, gefrieren und von Zeit zu Zeit mit einer Gabel zerbrechen, so dass eine raue Struktur entsteht. Alternativ in einer Granitamaschine gefrieren.

Granité

200 g	*sugar*
700 g	*water*
100 g	*Tequila*
100 g	*lemon juice*

Boil the sugar with water into a syrup, allow to cool down, then add Tequila and lemon juice. Pour into a shallow dish, place in deepfreeze and break up from time to time with a fork so that it becomes rough in texture. Alternatively, freeze in a Granita machine.

Salzzuckerglas

20 g	*Wasser*
250 g	*Isomalt*
20 g	*Salz*

Die Zutaten mischen, auf 170 °C erhitzen, Topf auf eine Steinplatte stellen und die Masse langsam abkühlen. Sobald die gewünschte Konsistenz erreicht ist, Cocktailglasrand in die salzige Karamellmasse eintauchen. Beim Herausziehen ergibt sich die dekorative Eisspitze.

Salt sugar glass

20 g	*water*
250 g	*Isomalt*
20 g	*salt*

Mix the ingredients together, heat up to 170 °C, place the pan onto a stone slab and allow the mixture to cool down slowly. As soon as it has the required consistency, dip the rim of the cocktail glass into the salty caramel mixture. The decorative ice point is formed when pulling out the glass.

1

2

3

4

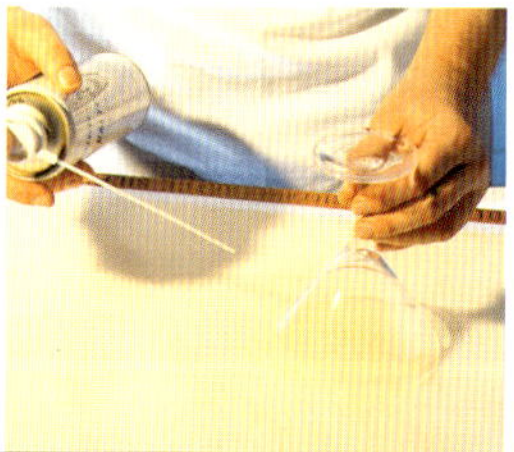
5

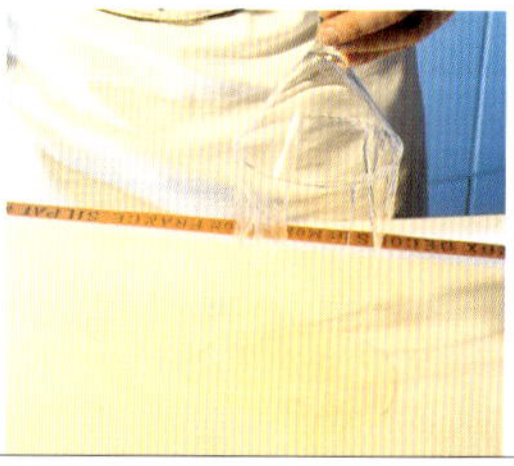
6

7

Isomalt in einen Topf geben

Place the Isomalt into a pan

Salz mit Wasser vermischen

Stir the salt into water

Auflösen

Dissolve

Wenn der gesalzene Zucker die gewünschte Konsistenz hat, auf Backmatte gießen

When the salted sugar has the required consistency, pour onto a baking mat

Glas in den Zucker tauchen

Dip the glass into the sugar

Beim Herausziehen den Zucker mit einem Kältespray stabilisieren

When pulling out the sugar, stabilise it with a cooling spray

Jedes Glas erhält individuelle Zuckerspitzen

Each glass receives individual sugar points

Ice-cream waffles

150 g	*sugar*
2.5 g	*pectin*
15 g	*grated almonds*
100 g	*butter*
50 g	*glucose syrup*
50 g	*lemon juice*
	zest from 1 lemon
4 g	*sea salt*

Mix the sugar and pectin together. Add the grated almonds, butter, glucose syrup, lemon juice and zest and salt and bring to boil. Transfer to a cool place and then use a plastic piping bag to arrange the mixture onto a silicon mat. Allow to bake at 170 °C for about 10 minutes, cut and roll over a tube while still hot.

Eisgebäck

150 g	*Zucker*
2,5 g	*Pektin*
15 g	*Mandelgrieß*
100 g	*Butter*
50 g	*Glukosesirup*
50 g	*Zitronensaft*
	Abrieb von 1 Zitrone
4 g	*Meersalz*

Zucker und Pektin mischen. Mandelgrieß, Butter, Glukosesirup, Zitronensaft und -abrieb sowie Salz zugeben und aufkochen. Kühl stellen, dann mit einem Plastikspritzsack auf eine Silikonbackmatte aufdressieren. Bei 170 °C etwa 10 Minuten backen, schneiden und noch heiß über ein Rohr rollen.

Drink recommendation

Nectar Imperial Moët & Chandon, Champagne Sec, Epernay, France

or

Limoncello liqueur, Italy

Getränkeempfehlung

Nectar Imperial Moët & Chandon, Champagne Sec, Epernay, Frankreich

oder

Limoncello Likör, Italien

Alpenrauschen

Alpine Delight

Wildkräuter sind in! Sei es bei uns im Odenwald oder bei einem 3-Sterne-Koch, wie Herrn Veyrat. Heu mit Kräutern, von der Bergwiese gepflückt und zum Dessert verarbeitet, ist zwar absolut verrückt, aber überraschend lecker. Einfach mal probieren. Besonders mit dem empfohlenen Dessertwein.

Wild herbs are in fashion! Both here in the Odenwald region and with 3-star chefs, such as Mr Veyrat. Picking hay with herbs from a mountain meadow and working it into a dessert may sound totally crazy, but it's surprisingly tasty. Just give it a try! Especially together with the recommended dessert wine.

Ingredients	Zusammensetzung
Hay mousse with white chocolate on almond sponge	Heumousse mit weisser Schokolade auf Mandelbiskuit
Seasoned chocolate espuma	Gewürztes Schokoladenespuma
Gingerbread cookies	Aachener Printen
Chocolate and caramel sauce	Schokoladen- und Karamellsauce
Chocolate décor	Schokoladendekor
Berries	Beeren
Candied cumquat wedges	Konfierte Kumquatspalten
Ingredients for 10 desserts	Zutaten für 10 Desserts

Heumousse mit weisser Schokolade auf Mandelbiskuit

1,5	*Blatt Gelatine*
60 g	*Milch*
60 g	*Prosecco*
1	*große Hand voll Heu mit Bergkräutern*
25 g	*Eigelb*
75 g	*weiße Kuvertüre, fein gehackt*
150 g	*geschlagene Sahne*
120 g	*weiße Sprühkuvertüre*

Gelatine in kaltem Wasser einweichen. Milch mit Prosecco sowie dem Heu etwa 1 Minute aufkochen. 5 Minuten ziehen lassen, abpassieren und gut abpressen. Eigelb einrühren und bei 85 °C pasteurisieren. Gelatine auspressen und in der heißen Masse auflösen. Weiße Kuvertüre einrühren und sobald die Masse etwas abgekühlt ist, in die Sahne unterziehen. In Silikon-Halbkugelformen füllen, tiefkühlen, ausformen und mit aufgelöster Sprühkuvertüre samtig absprühen.

Hay mousse with white chocolate on almond sponge

1,5	*sheets of gelatine*
60 g	*milk*
60 g	*Prosecco*
1	*large handful of hay with mountain herbs*
25 g	*egg yolk*
75 g	*white couverture, finely chopped*
150 g	*whipped cream*
120 g	*white spray couverture*

Soak the gelatine in cold water. Boil the milk with the Prosecco and the hay for about 1 minute. Leave to steep for 5 minutes, strain and squeeze the liquid out of the hay. Stir in the egg yolk and pasteurise at 85 °C. Squeeze out the gelatine and dissolve in the hot mixture. Stir in the white couverture and as soon as the mixture has cooled down a little, fold into the cream. Fill into semi-spherical silicon shapes, deep-freeze, remove from the shapes and cover with a velvety coat of spray couverture.

1

2

3

4

Heu in Milch und Prosecco aufkochen

Boil the hay in milk and Prosecco

5

Weiße Kuvertüre darin auflösen

Dissolve the white couverture into this

Heu abpassieren

Strain the hay

6

Sahne unterziehen

Fold in the cream

Eigelb zugießen

Add the egg yolk

7

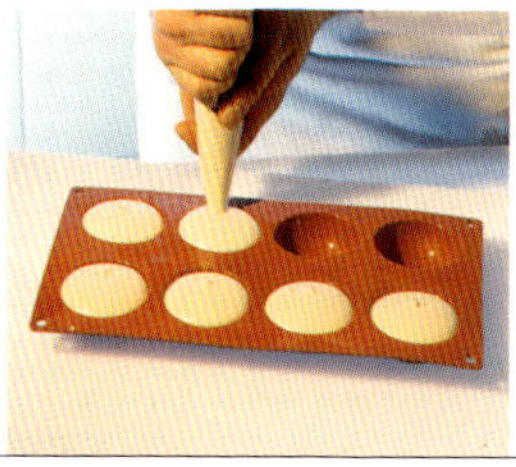

Mit einem Dressierbeutel in Silikonförmchen eindressieren

Use a piping bag to arrange into small silicon cups

Ausgepresste Gelatine im Fond auflösen

Dissolve the squeezed-out gelatine in the stock

8

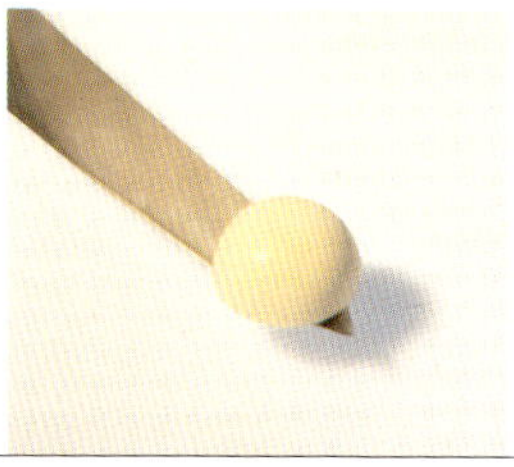

Fertig abgesprühte Heumousse

The completed hay mousse

Almond sponge

45 g	sugar
20 g	grated almonds
50 g	egg yolk
75 g	egg white
35 g	sugar
30 g	wheat powder
30 g	flour

Beat the egg yolk with grated almonds and sugar until frothy. Add sugar to the egg white and beat until stiff. Add the wheat powder and the flour and the beaten egg white, in turn, into the egg mixture. Use a piping bag and arrange in the required shape onto a baking mat. Bake the sponge cake at 180 °C for about 15 minutes.

Mandelbiskuit

45 g	Zucker
20 g	Mandelgrieß
50 g	Eigelb
75 g	Eiweiß
35 g	Zucker
30 g	Weizenpuder
30 g	Mehl

Den Zucker mit Mandelgrieß und Eigelb schaumig schlagen. Eiweiß mit Zucker zu Schnee schlagen. Weizenpuder und Mehl mischen und im Wechsel mit dem Eischnee unter die Eimasse melieren. Mit 8er-Lochtülle in der gewünschten Form auf eine Backmatte aufdressieren. Biskuit bei 180 °C etwa 15 Minuten backen.

Schokoladenmousse mit kandierten Früchten

10 g	*Zucker*
25 g	*Eigelb*
60 g	*Sahne*
60 g	*Milch*
10 g	*kandiertes, fein gehacktes Orangeat und Zitronat*
10 g	*kandierter Ingwer, fein gehackt*
180 g	*Bitterkuvertüre, 70 %*
225 g	*geschlagene Sahne*

Zucker mit Eigelb schaumig schlagen. Parallel Sahne und Milch mit den kandierten Früchten und kandiertem Ingwer aufkochen, zu der Eigelbmasse laufen lassen und bei 85 °C pasteurisieren.

Masse über die fein gehackte Kuvertüre gießen und zu einer glatten Masse verarbeiten. Sahne vorsichtig in 3 Schritten unterziehen, dann in Gläser abfüllen.

Chocolate mousse with candied fruits

10 g	*sugar*
25 g	*egg yolk*
60 g	*cream*
60 g	*milk*
10 g	*candied orange and lemon, finely chopped*
10 g	*candied ginger, finely chopped*
180 g	*dark couverture, 70 %*
225 g	*whipped cream*

Beat the egg yolk with sugar until frothy. Boil up the cream and milk with the candied fruits and candied ginger at the same time, pour into the egg yolk mixture and pasteurise at 85 °C.

Pour the mixture over the finely chopped couverture and work into a smooth mixture. Carefully fold in the cream in 3 stages, and fill into the glasses.

Aachener-Printen-Schokoladen-Sauce

50 g	*Zucker*
50 g	*Glukose*
10 g	*Aachener Printengewürz*
100 g	*Sahne*
75 g	*Bitterkuvertüre, 65 %*
20 g	*Butter*

Zucker mit der Glukose, dem Printengewürz und der Sahne aufkochen, durch ein Sieb über die fein gehackte Kuvertüre gießen und mit der Butter zu einer glatten Sauce mixen.

Gingerbread cookies/ chocolate sauce

50 g	*sugar*
50 g	*glucose*
10 g	*gingerbread spice*
100 g	*cream*
75 g	*dark couverture, 65 %*
20 g	*butter*

Bring the cream to boil with the sugar, the glucose and the gingerbread spices, pour over the finely chopped couverture through a sieve and blend with the butter until smooth.

Caramel sauce

100 g	*sugar*
20 g	*glucose*
50 g	*cream*
2 g	*sea salt*
20 g	*butter*

Caramelise the sugar with the glucose, add the cream and season with the salt to taste. Stir in the butter.

Karamellsauce

100 g	*Zucker*
20 g	*Glukose*
50 g	*Sahne*
2 g	*Meersalz*
20 g	*Butter*

Zucker mit der Glukose karamellisieren, mit der Sahne ablöschen und mit dem Salz abschmecken. Butter unterrühren.

Candied cumquat wedges

100 g	*sugar*
100 g	*water*
100 g	*cumquats*

Bring the sugar to boil with the water, and pierce the cumquats several times with a needle. Briefly boil in the sugar water, leave to soak overnight and then boil up again in the morning. Drain off the liquid and cut the cumquats into quarters if required.

Konfierte Kumquatspalten

100 g	*Zucker*
100 g	*Wasser*
100 g	*Kumquat*

Zucker mit Wasser aufkochen, Kumquats mit einer Nadel mehrmals einstechen. Dann im Zuckersud kurz aufkochen, über Nacht stehen lassen und am Morgen nochmals kurz aufkochen. Zuckersud abgießen und die Kumquats bei Bedarf vierteln.

Drink recommendation

Barolo Chinato, Cocchi Vino Aromatizzato, Asti, Italy

Getränkeempfehlung

Barolo Chinato, Cocchi Vino Aromatizzato, Asti, Italien

Schwarzwälder Kirsch

Black Forest Gateau

Auf der ganzen Welt werden wir für unsere Klassiker beneidet. Schwarzwälder Kirsch ist wie Donnerhall in der deutschen Konditorei. Man muss immer darüber Bescheid wissen, woher man kommt, dann kann man auch andere Wege gehen und Neues schaffen. Viel Spass beim Ausprobieren.

People all over the world envy us for our classics. Black Forest Gateau is the big drum roll in the German patisserie opera. You should always know your roots intimately – then you have the basis for venturing forth and creating something new. Have fun trying it out.

Ingredients	Zusammensetzung
Kirsch Panna Cotta	Kirschwasser-Panna-Cotta
Chocolate sponge without flour	Schokoladenbiskuit ohne Mehl
Chocolate ice-cream	Schokoladeneis
Chocolate caramel	Schokoladenkaramell
Morello cherries in Rimage	Sauerkirschen in Rimage
Custard	Vanillesauce
Chocolate décor	Schokoladendekor
Gold leaf	Blattgold
Ingredients for 10 desserts	Zutaten für 10 Desserts

1

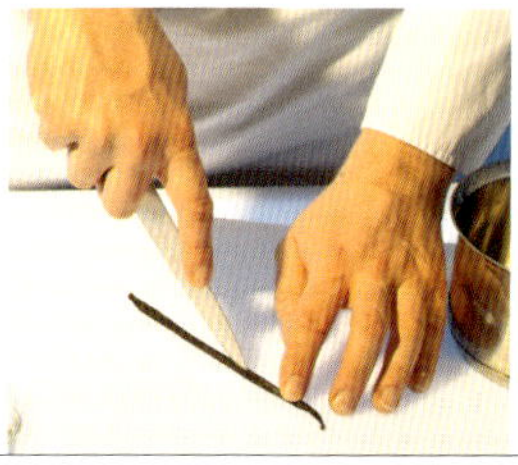

2

3

4

5

Kirschwasser-Panna-Cotta

3	*Blatt Gelatine*
340 g	*Sahne*
70 g	*Zucker*
	Mark von 1 Vanilleschote
5 g	*Zimtblüten*
20 g	*Kirschwasser, 40 %*

Gelatine in kaltem Wasser einweichen. Sahne, Zucker, Vanillemark und zerriebene Zimtblüten aufkochen. Ausgedrückte Gelatine in der heißen Masse auflösen und durch ein Sieb gießen. Kirschwasser unterrühren, dann Masse in Silikonformen gießen und tiefgefrieren.

Kirsch Panna Cotta

3	*sheets of gelatine*
340 g	*cream*
70 g	*sugar*
	pith of 1 vanilla pod
5 g	*cinnamon flowers*
20 g	*kirsch, 40 %*

Soak the gelatine in cold water. Bring the cream, sugar, vanilla pith and ground cinnamon flowers to boil. Dissolve the squeezed-out gelatine in the hot mixture and pour through a strainer. Stir in the kirsch and then pour the mixture into silicon moulds and deep-freeze.

Schokoladensorbet

35 g	*Zucker*
15 g	*Trockenglukose*
270 g	*Wasser*
80 g	*Bitterkuvertüre, 67 %*

Zucker mit der Trockenglukose mischen und mit dem Wasser aufkochen. Noch heiß über die fein gehackte Kuvertüre gießen, mit einem Mixstab gut aufmixen und in der Eismaschine abfrieren.

Chocolate Sorbet

35 g	*sugar*
15 g	*dry glucose*
270 g	*water*
80 g	*dark couverture, 67 %*

Mix the sugar with the dry glucose and boil together with the water. Pour over the finely chopped couverture while still hot, blend well with a hand-held blender and freeze in the ice-cream machine.

Gelatine in kaltem Wasser einweichen

Soak the gelatine in cold water

Vanilleschote längs aufschneiden

Cut the vanilla pod open lengthways

Vanillemark herausstreichen

Scrape out the vanilla pith

Zimtblüten in einen Topf geben

Put the cinnamon flowers into a pan

Sahne, Zucker und Vanillemark zugeben und aufkochen

Add the cream, sugar and the vanilla pith and boil it

6

Gelatine aus dem Wasser nehmen, auspressen und in der heißen Masse auflösen

Take the gelatine out of the water, squeeze out and dissolve in the hot mixture

7

Masse durch ein Sieb gießen

Pour the mixture through a strainer

8

Kirschwasser unterrühren

Stir in the kirsch

9

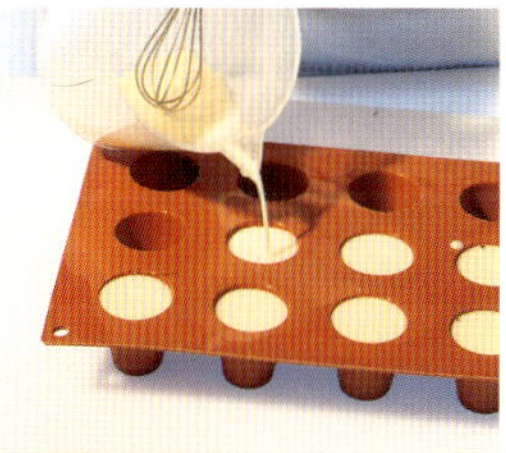

In Silikonformen gießen und tiefgefrieren

Pour into silicon moulds and deep-freeze

10

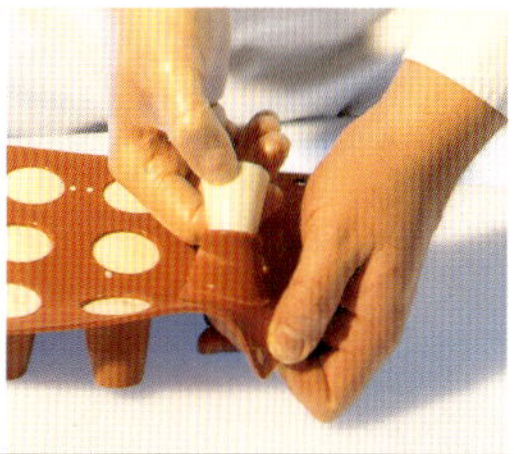

Kirschwasser-Panna-Cotta ausformen

Take the kirsch Panna Cotta out of the forms

Schokoladenkaramelldeko

25 g	*Wasser*
250 g	*Isomalt*
30 g	*Kakaopulver*

Wasser mit dem Isomalt auf 165 °C kochen, dann das Kakaopulver unterrühren. Auf eine Backmatte gießen und mit einer zweiten Backmatte bedecken. Dünn ausrollen, in Rechtecke schneiden, diese unter eine Wärmelampe legen, bis sie in der Mitte erwärmt sind. Dann auseinander ziehen, so dass sich wilde Schokoladenkaramelldekore ergeben. Trocken lagern.

Chocolate caramel décor

25 g	*water*
250 g	*Isomalt*
30 g	*cocoa powder*

Heat the water with the Isomalt to 165 °C and then stir in the cocoa powder. Pour onto a baking mat and cover with a second baking mat. Roll out thinly, cut into squares, place under a heater lamp until they have warmed up in the middle. Then pull them apart so that they form "wild" shapes of chocolate caramel décors. Store in a dry place.

Schokoladenbiskuit ohne Mehl

70 g	*Marzipan*
70 g	*Eigelb*
115 g	*Eiweiß*
115 g	*Zucker*
40 g	*Kakaopulver*

Marzipan mit Eigelb schaumig schlagen, Eiweiß mit Zucker zu Schnee schlagen. Beide Massen abwechselnd mit dem Kakaopulver melieren und mit einem Dressierbeutel in der gewünschten Form auf Backpapier aufdressieren. Bei 200 °C etwa 10 Minuten backen.

Chocolate sponge without flour

70 g	*marzipan*
70 g	*egg yolk*
115 g	*egg white*
115 g	*sugar*
40 g	*cocoa powder*

Beat the marzipan with the egg yolk until frothy; add sugar to the egg white and beat until stiff. Mix the cocoa powder with both mixtures in turn, then use a piping bag to arrange it onto baking paper in the required shape. Bake at 200 °C for about 10 minutes.

Morello cherries in Rimage

400 g	*deep-frozen morello cherries*
60 g	*sugar*
20 g	*wheat powder*
100 g	*Rimage, dessert wine*

Allow the morello cherries to thaw and then drain the juice off. Mix the sugar and wheat powder, add the juice from the cherries and bring to boil while stirring continuously, then allow to cool down. Stir the morello cherries and the Rimage into the cold mixture.

Sauerkirschen in Rimage

400 g	*Sauerkirschen, tiefgekühlt*
60 g	*Zucker*
20 g	*Weizenpuder*
100 g	*Rimage, Dessertwein*

Sauerkirschen auftauen lassen, dann Saft der Sauerkirschen abgießen. Zucker mit Weizenpuder mischen, Kirschsaft zugießen und unter Rühren aufkochen, dann abkühlen lassen. Sauerkirschen und Rimage unter die kalte Masse rühren.

Custard

2	*vanilla pods*
200 g	*cream*
150 g	*milk*
80 g	*egg yolk*
85 g	*sugar*

Add the vanilla pods and pith together with the cream and milk and bring to boil. Beat the egg yolk and sugar until frothy. Add the hot liquid and pasteurise at 85 °C. Strain the mixture and place into an ice water bath to cool down to 4 °C.

Vanillesauce

2	*Vanilleschoten*
200 g	*Sahne*
150 g	*Milch*
80 g	*Eigelb*
85 g	*Zucker*

Vanilleschoten und herausgestrichenes Mark sowie Sahne und Milch aufkochen lassen. Eigelb und Zucker schaumig schlagen. Heiße Flüssigkeit zugießen und auf 85 °C pasteurisieren. Masse absieben und im Eiswasserbad auf 4 °C abkühlen.

Drink recommendation

Mas Amiel Vintage 2002, Vin Doux Naturel, Maury, France

Getränkeempfehlung

Mas Amiel Vintage 2002, Vin Doux Naturel, Maury, Frankreich

LAS VEGAS PINEAPPLE

LAS VEGAS PINEAPPLE

Ich hatte öfter das Vergnügen und die Ehre, zur WM in Las Vegas ein Seminar abhalten zu dürfen. Diese Variation kam ganz besonders gut an. Michael Schneider, einer der Organisatoren, meinte nur: "You are the gelato man."

I had the pleasure and honour several times to hold a seminar at the World Championships in Las Vegas. This variation was particularly popular. Michael Schneider, one of the organisers, said: "You are the gelato man."

Ingredients	Zusammensetzung
Pineapple sorbet	Ananassorbet
Salad with pineapple and fennel	Ananas-Fenchel-Salat
Banana/walnut sponge	Bananen-Walnuss-Biskuit
Dried pineapple slices	Getrocknete Ananasscheiben
Chocolate décor	Schokoladendekor
Green part of fennel	Fenchelgrün
Ingredients for 10 desserts	Zutaten für 10 Desserts

Ananassorbet

500 g	*Ananassaft*
80 g	*Zucker*
40 g	*Trockenglukose*
1	*Ananas, geschält, ohne Strunk*

Ananassaft mit Zucker und Trockenglukose mischen und aufkochen. Ananas würfeln und in einen Pacojetbehälter füllen. Mit Saft auffüllen, 24 Stunden bei –20 °C tiefgefrieren. Das Sorbet portionsweise mit Gewürzen nach Geschmack, z. B. Wacholder, Tahitivanille oder Sternanis, pacossieren.

Pineapple sorbet

500 g	*pineapple juice*
80 g	*sugar*
40 g	*dry glucose*
1	*pineapple, peeled and cored*

Mix the pineapple juice with the sugar and dry glucose and bring to boil, cut the pineapple into cubes and put into a Pacojet processor. Fill up with juice and deep-freeze at –20 °C for 24 hours. Pacotise individual portions of the sorbet with seasoning to taste, e.g. juniper, Tahiti vanilla or star anise.

Ananas-Fenchel-Salat

100 g	*Zucker*
250 g	*Riesling*
½	*Fenchelknolle*
½	*Ananas*

Zucker karamellisieren und mit Riesling ablöschen. Den Fenchel schälen, in Würfel schneiden, zufügen und weich dünsten. Die Ananas schälen, Strunk entfernen, in Würfel schneiden und beigeben. Alles ziehen lassen.

Salad with pineapple and fennel

100 g	*sugar*
250 g	*Riesling*
½	*fennel bulb*
½	*pineapple*

Caramelise the sugar and douse with Riesling. Peel the fennel, cut into cubes, add to the mixture and boil until soft. Peel and core the pineapple, cut into cubes and add to the mixture. Leave to steep.

1

2

3

4

5

6

7

Trockenglukose und Zucker mischen

Mix the dry glucose together with the sugar

Trockenmasse in Ananassaft einrühren und aufkochen

Stir the dry mixture into the pineapple juice and bring to boil

Ananas schälen. Strunk herausschneiden und würfeln

Peel the pineapple. Cut out the core and cut the rest into cubes

Ananaswürfel in einen Pacojetbehälter füllen

Put the pineapple cubes into a Pacojet processor

Ananassaft zugießen und tiefgefrieren

Add the pineapple juice and deep-freeze

Gewürze je nach Geschmack pro Portion zugeben

Season each portion to taste

Fertiges Sorbet

Finished sorbet

Banana/walnut sponge

50 g	*egg yolk*
30 g	*sugar*
90 g	*egg white*
25 g	*sugar*
35 g	*flour*
30 g	*butter, liquid*
25 g	*banana chips, chopped*
25 g	*walnuts, chopped*

Beat 30 g sugar with the egg yolk until frothy, and 25 g sugar with the egg white until stiff. Mix both mixtures, blend in the flour and fold in the butter. Arrange the mixture onto a baking sheet, sprinkle with the banana chips and walnuts, and bake at 200 °C for about 15 minutes.

Bananen-Walnuss-Biskuit

50 g	*Eigelb*
30 g	*Zucker*
90 g	*Eiweiß*
25 g	*Zucker*
35 g	*Mehl*
30 g	*Butter, flüssig*
25 g	*Bananenchips, gehackt*
25 g	*Walnüsse, gehackt*

Eigelb mit 30 g Zucker schaumig, Eiweiß mit 25 g Zucker zu Schnee schlagen, beide Massen mischen, Mehl untermelieren, Butter unterziehen. Masse auf ein Blech aufdressieren, Bananenchips und Walnüsse aufstreuen, bei 200 °C etwa 15 Minuten backen.

Drink recommendation

Ruster Ausbruch Essenz 2002, Feiler Artinger, Burgenland, Austria

Getränkeempfehlung

Ruster Ausbruch Essenz 2002, Feiler Artinger, Burgenland, Österreich

Venedig

Venice

Italien ist so etwas wie meine zweite Heimat geworden. Das liegt zum Teil an den Seminaren, die ich dort halte, und den Firmen, die ich berate, aber insbesondere an den Menschen, mit den denen ich dort befreundet bin. Tiramisu ist für mich das italienische Dessert schlechthin – ich hoffe, man verzeiht mir meine Version.

Italy has almost become my second home. This is partly due to the seminars I run there and the companies I do consultancy work for, but most of all the people I have made friends with over there. For me, Tiramisu is the Italian dessert par excellence – I hope you will forgive me for trying my own version.

Ingredients	Zusammensetzung
Green tea sugar tube with Isomalt	Grüntee-Zuckertubus mit Isomalt
Green tea Mascarpone mousse	Grüntee-Mascarpone-schaum
Almond sponge, soaked in mango juice	Mandelbiskuit, mit Mangosaft getränkt
Strawberry Szechuan sorbet	Erdbeer-Setchuansorbet
Mango strawberry salad	Mango-Erdbeer-Salat
Cashew brittle	Cashew-Krokant
Strawberry caramel spiral	Erdbeerkaramellspirale
Ingredients for 10 desserts	Zutaten für 10 Desserts

Grüntee-Zuckertubus mit Isomalt

100 g	*Wasser*
20 g	*grüner Tee*
400 g	*Isomalt*

Wasser aufkochen und den grünen Tee damit überbrühen. Nach 1 Minute absieben und das Teewasser mit dem Isomalt auf 170 °C kochen. Auf eine Backmatte gießen, mit einer zweiten belegen und so dünn als möglich ausrollen. In die passende Größe schneiden und noch heiß über ein Rohr biegen. Fest anpressen und nachdem das Rohr erkaltet ist, mit einem heißen Messer in Form schneiden. Trocken lagern.

Green tea sugar tube with Isomalt

100 g	*water*
20 g	*green tea*
400 g	*Isomalt*

Bring the water to boil and pour it over the green tea. Strain off after 1 minute and then heat the water with the Isomalt to 170 °C. Pour onto a baking mat, cover with a second baking mat and roll out as thinly as possible. Cut to the size needed and bend over a tube while still hot. Press home firmly and, once the tube has cooled down, use a hot knife to cut the required shape. Store in a dry place.

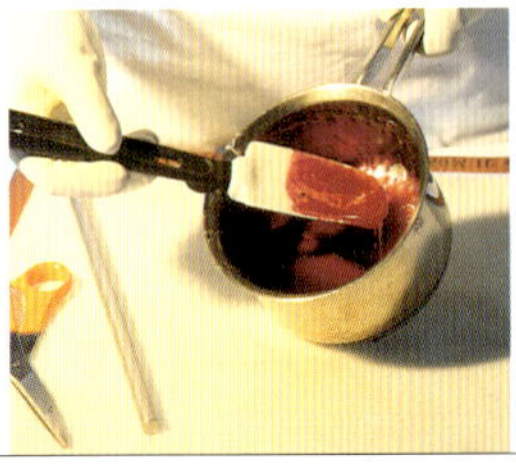
1

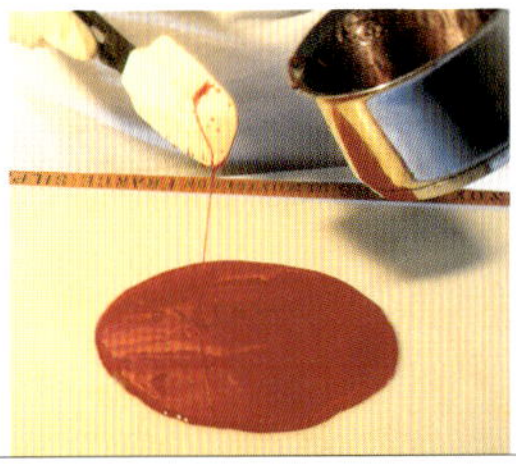
2

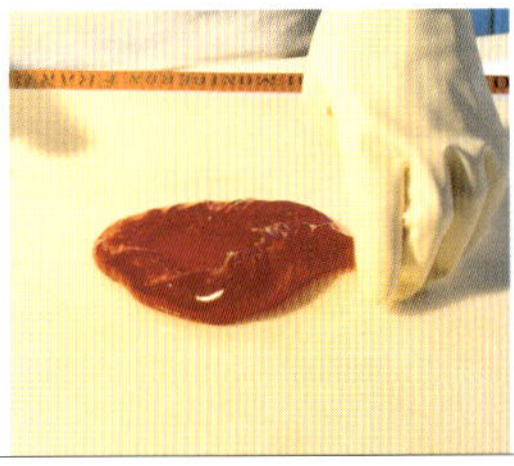
3

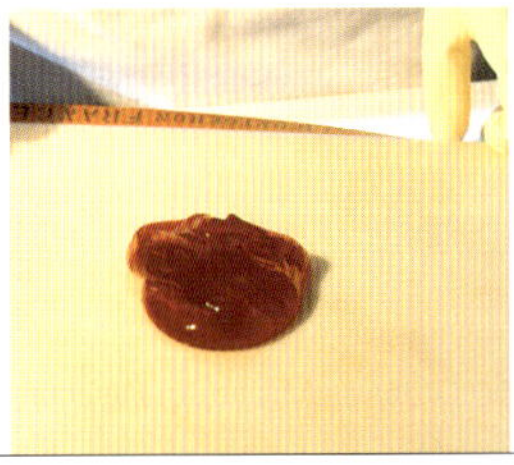
4

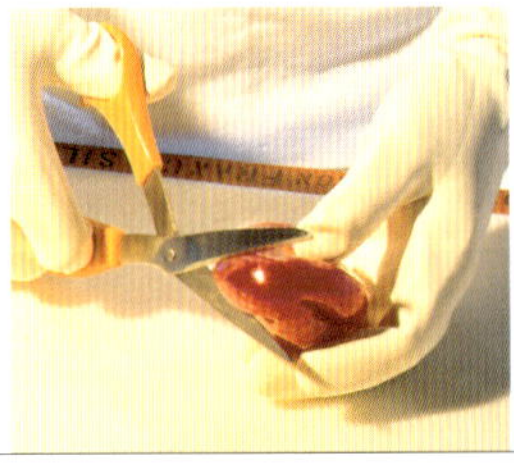
5

Grüntee-Mascarponeschaum

60 g	*Puderzucker*
10 g	*Grünteepulver (Matcha)*
200 g	*Mascarpone*
100 g	*Milch*
100 g	*Sahne*

Puderzucker mit dem Grünteepulver versieben. Mascarpone mit Milch und Sahne sowie der Teezuckermischung zu einer glatten Masse verrühren. In Espumaschäumer füllen und 2 Gaspatronen aufschrauben. Kühl stellen.

Green tea Mascarpone mousse

60 g	*icing sugar*
10 g	*green tea powder (Matcha)*
200 g	*Mascarpone*
100 g	*milk*
100 g	*cream*

Strain both the icing sugar and the green tea powder through a sieve. Stir the Mascarpone together with the milk and cream and the tea sugar mixture until it is smooth. Fill into an Espuma foaming beaker and insert 2 gas cartridges. Put in a cool place.

Erdbeerpaste unter den aufgelösten Isomalt rühren

Stir the strawberry paste into the dissolved Isomalt

6

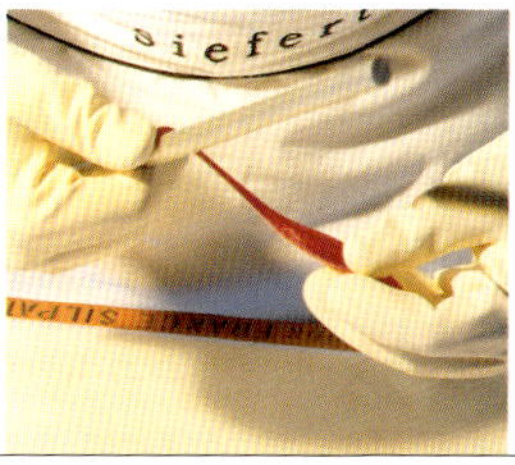

Ein Ende des Stückchens dünn herausmodellieren

Shape one end of the piece to make it thin and round

Auf Backmatte gießen

Pour onto a baking mat

7

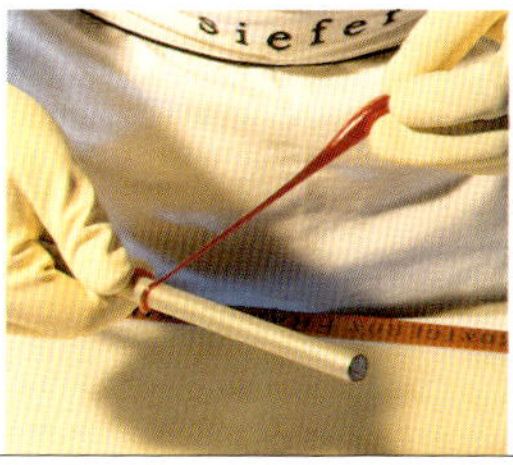

Dünnes Ende mit dem Daumen festhalten und über einen Metallstab ziehen …

Hold the thin end with your thumb and pull over a metal rod …

Immer wieder von außen nach innen einschlagen

Keep folding in from the outside inwards

8

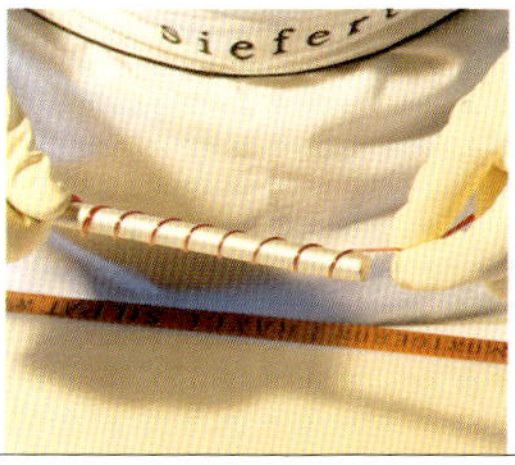

… und diesen umwickeln

… and wind it round the rod

Wenn der Zucker sich kaum mehr bewegt …

When the sugar hardly moves anymore …

9

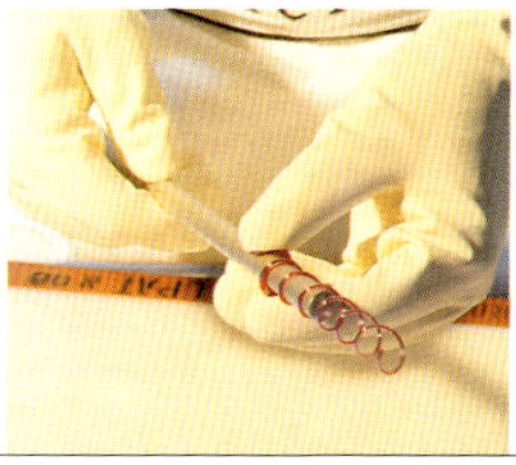

Vorsichtig herunterschieben

Carefully slide off

… mit einer Schere ein kleines Stück abschneiden

… cut off a small piece with a pair of scissors

10

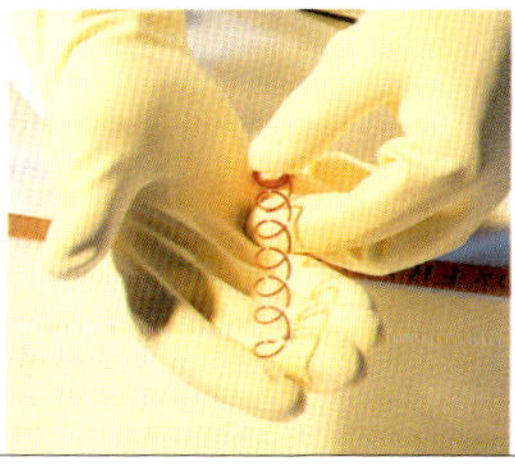

Fertige Karamellspirale

Finished caramel spiral

Mandelbiskuit, mit Mangosaft getränkt

25 g	*Mehl*
95 g	*Mandeln, fein gemahlen*
95 g	*Puderzucker*
125 g	*Vollei*
80 g	*Eiweiß*
20 g	*Zucker*
20 g	*Butter, flüssig*
100 g	*Mangopüree*

Mehl, Mandeln und Puderzucker mischen. Vollei dazugeben und bei voller Geschwindigkeit schaumig schlagen. Eiweiß und Zucker zu Schnee schlagen, dann beide Massen vermischen und zum Schluss die Butter unterheben. Die Masse auf eine Backmatte streichen. Im vorgeheizten Ofen bei 200 °C etwa 15 Minuten backen. Biskuit in Würfel schneiden und mit Mangopüree, das mit etwas Läuterzucker verdünnt ist, tränken.

Almond sponge, soaked in mango juice

25 g	*flour*
95 g	*almonds, finely ground*
95 g	*icing sugar*
125 g	*whole egg*
80 g	*egg white*
20 g	*sugar*
20 g	*butter, liquid*
100 g	*mango puree*

Mix the flour, almonds and icing sugar. Add the complete egg and beat at full speed until frothy. Add sugar to the egg white and beat until stiff; then blend both mixtures and finally fold in the butter. Spread the mixture onto a baking mat. Bake in a preheated oven at 200 °C for about 15 minutes. Cut the sponge into cubes and then soak with mango puree which has been diluted with some sugar syrup.

Erdbeer-Setchuansorbet

5 g	*Setchuanpfeffer*
200 g	*Erdbeerpüree*
80 g	*Zucker*
5 g	*Zitronensaft*
110 g	*Wasser*

Setchuanpfeffer in einer Pfanne anrösten, in das Erdbeerpüree geben und über Nacht stehen lassen. Absieben, Erdbeerpüree mit dem Zucker, Zitronensaft und dem Wasser aufmixen. Auf 30 °Brix einstellen. In der Eismaschine abfrieren.

Strawberry Szechuan sorbet

5 g	*Szechuan pepper*
200 g	*strawberry puree*
80 g	*sugar*
5 g	*lemon juice*
110 g	*water*

Slightly roast the Szechuan pepper in a pan, add to the strawberry puree and leave overnight. Strain and then blend the strawberry puree with the sugar, lemon juice and the water. Adjust to 30 °Brix. Place into the ice-cream maker to freeze.

Mango strawberry salad

200 g	*mango*
200 g	*strawberries*
50 g	*sugar*
	juice of ½ lemon

Peel and core the mango and cut into small cubes. Clean the strawberries and also cut into small cubes. Pour the lemon juice and sugar over the diced fruit and mix well.

Mango-Erdbeer-Salat

200 g	*Mango*
200 g	*Erdbeeren*
50	*Zucker*
	Saft von einer ½ Zitrone

Die Mango schälen, Kern entfernen und Fruchtfleisch in kleine Würfel schneiden. Erdbeeren putzen und ebenfalls in kleine Würfel scheiden. Zucker und Zitronensaft über die Fruchtwürfelchen geben und vermischen.

Cashew brittle

200 g	*sugar*
20 g	*glucose*
100 g	*cashew nuts, chopped*

Use the sugar and glucose to make caramel. Stir in the cashew nuts, then pour everything together onto a baking mat and leave to cool down. Chop coarsely and store in a dry place.

Cashew-Krokant

200 g	*Zucker*
20 g	*Glukose*
100 g	*Cashewkerne, gehackt*

Aus Zucker und Glukose einen Karamell herstellen. Die Cashewkerne unterrühren, dann alles auf eine Backmatte gießen und erkalten lassen. Grob hacken und trocken lagern.

Drink recommendation

Rietvallei Estate Wine, Red Muscadel 2003, Wine of Origin Robertson, South Africa

Getränkeempfehlung

Rietvallei Estate Wine, Red Muscadel 2003, Wine of Origin Robertson, Südafrika

Ägyptische Nächte

Egyptian Nights

Dieses Dessert hat seine Wurzeln in Afrika. Genauer gesagt in Ägypten. Einer meiner ersten Events, zusammen mit meiner Frau, war in Ägypten. Leider ging unser Koffer mit der gesamten Kleidung verloren und wir mussten die ganze Zeit in kurzen Hosen und Turnschuhen arbeiten. Auf ewig unvergesslich. Spice up your Life!

This dessert originates from Africa: Egypt – to be more precise. One of my first events, together with my wife, was in Egypt. Unfortunately, our suitcase with all of our clothes went missing and we had to work in shorts and trainers the whole time, something I won't forget in a hurry. Spice up your Life!

Ingredients

- White coffee crème brûlée
- Spicy coffee jelly
- Orange foam
- Black caraway seed cookies
- Citrus fruit/ grapefruit segments
- Orange thyme sorbet
- Corn flowers

Zusammensetzung

- Weisse-Kaffee-Crème-brûlée
- Gewürztes Kaffeegelee
- Orangenschaum
- Schwarzkümmelgebäck
- Zitrusfrüchte-Grapefruitfilets
- Orangen-Thymian-Sorbet
- Kornblumen

1

Eigelb und Orangensaft zum Zucker geben

Add the egg yolk and orange juice to the sugar

2

Orangenschale zugeben

Add the orange peel

3

4

Weisse-Kaffee-Crème-brûlée

75 g	*Kaffee Arabica in Bohnen*
145 g	*Milch*
145 g	*Sahne*
50 g	*Zucker*
50 g	*Eigelb*
50 g	*brauner Rohrzucker*

Kaffee in einer Pfanne kurz anrösten. Mit Milch und Sahne übergießen und über Nacht gekühlt ziehen lassen. Absieben und mit Zucker und Eigelb zu einer glatten Masse verrühren. Masse in Espressotasse einfüllen und im Wasserbad im Ofen bei 100 °C etwa 45 Minuten stocken lassen. Dann etwa 3 Stunden kühl stellen. Crème brûlée 2-mal mit Rohrzucker übersieben und jeweils mit einem Gasbrenner karamellisieren.

White coffee crème brûlée

75 g	*Arabica coffee beans*
145 g	*milk*
145 g	*cream*
50 g	*sugar*
50 g	*egg yolk*
50 g	*brown cane sugar*

Slightly roast the coffee in a frying pan. Pour the milk and cream over it and leave to soak overnight. Strain and stir in the sugar and egg yolk until smooth. Fill the mixture into an espresso cup and allow to thicken in a water bath in the oven at 100 °C for about 45 minutes. Then transfer to a cool place for about 3 hours. Go over the crème brûlée twice with a sprinkling of cane sugar and caramelise each time with a gas torch.

Koriander aus der Mühle zugeben und zu einem stabilen Schaum schlagen

Add coriander from the mill and beat into a stiff foam

Orangenlikör zum Schaum zugeben

Add the orange liqueur to the foam

Spicy coffee jelly

6	*sheets of gelatine*
250 g	*coffee*
60 g	*sugar*
1	*vanilla pod*
1	*star anise*

Soak the gelatine in cold water and bring the coffee to boil with the sugar and spices. Squeeze out the gelatine and dissolve in the coffee brew. Pour through a fine sieve into a silicon mould and leave to set; cut into cubes if required.

Gewürztes Kaffeegelee

6	*Blatt Gelatine*
250 g	*Kaffee*
60 g	*Zucker*
1	*Vanilleschote*
1	*Sternanis*

Gelatine in kaltem Wasser einweichen, Kaffee mit Zucker und den Gewürzen aufkochen. Die Gelatine auspressen und im Kaffeesud auflösen. Durch ein feines Sieb in eine Silikonform gießen und erstarren lassen, bei Bedarf in Würfel schneiden.

Orangenschaum

60 g	*Orangensaft*
	Abrieb von 1 unbehandelten Orange
30 g	*Eigelb*
30 g	*Zucker*
2 g	*Zitronensaft*
	Koriander aus der Mühle
10 g	*Orangenlikör*

Alle Zutaten bis auf den Likör im Wasserbad zu einem stabilen Schaum aufschlagen. Zum Schluss den Likör unterrühren.

Orange foam

60 g	*orange juice*
	zest from 1 untreated orange
30 g	*egg yolk*
30 g	*sugar*
2 g	*lemon juice*
	milled coriander
10 g	*orange liqueur*

Beat all the ingredients, except for the liqueur, in a water bath until they turn into a stiff foam. Stir in the liqueur at the end.

Schwarzkümmelgebäck

50 g	*Butter*
50 g	*Puderzucker*
	Abrieb von 1 Orange
50 g	*Eiweiß*
50 g	*Mehl*
30 g	*Schwarzkümmel*

Alle Zutaten auf Zimmertemperatur bringen, Butter mit Puderzucker und Orangenabrieb zu einer glatten Masse verrühren, Eiweiß und Mehl abwechselnd unterrühren. Die Masse mit einer Palette auf eine Backmatte aufstreichen und mit Schwarzkümmel bestreuen. Bei 180 °C etwa 15 Minuten backen und dann noch heiß in die gewünschte Form bringen.

Black caraway seed cookies

50 g	*butter*
50 g	*icing sugar*
	zest from 1 orange
50 g	*egg white*
50 g	*flour*
30 g	*black caraway seeds*

Bring all the ingredients up to room temperature, blend the butter with the icing sugar and orange zest to a smooth mixture, and stir in the egg white and flour in turn. Spread the mixture with a spatula onto a baking mat and sprinkle black caraway seeds over it. Bake at 180 °C for about 15 minutes and make the required shapes while still hot.

Citrus fruit/ grapefruit segments

Cut the grapefruit segments in half and flame off.

Zitrusfrüchte-Grapefruitfilets

Die Grapefruitfilets quer halbieren und abflämmen.

Orange thyme sorbet

75 g	*sugar*
10 g	*dry glucose*
270 g	*orange juice*
	zest from 2 oranges
1	*twig of thyme*
40 g	*water*

Mix the sugar and dry glucose, add the orange juice and zest, thyme and water and bring to boil. Pass through a sieve and adjust to 31 °Brix. Place into the ice-cream maker to freeze.

Orangen-Thymian-Sorbet

75 g	*Zucker*
10 g	*Trockenglukose*
270 g	*Orangensaft*
	Abrieb von 2 Orangen
1	*Thymianzweig*
40 g	*Wasser*

Den Zucker und Trockenglukose mischen, Orangensaft und -abrieb, Thymian sowie Wasser zugeben, alles aufkochen. Durch ein Sieb passieren und auf 31 °Brix einstellen. In der Eismaschine gefrieren.

Drink recommendation

Black Noble by de Bortoli, Bilbur, Australia

Getränkeempfehlung

Black Noble by de Bortoli, Bilbur, Australien

HAWAII SURFER

Eigentlich mag ich gar kein Snickers. Aber in diesem Pacojeteisrezept ist es unwiderstehlich.

For the most part I don't really like Snickers candy bars. But in this Pacojet ice-cream recipe it is irresistible.

Ingredients	Zusammensetzung
Deep fried ganache in a coconut coating	Frittierte Ganache im Kokosmantel
Cocoa Isomalt ship	Kakao-Isomalt-Schiff
Raspberry cocoa bean tuille	Himbeer-Kakaobohnen-Tuille
Banana chip	Bananenchip
Snickers ice-cream from the Pacojet	Snickerseis aus dem Pacojet
Papaya, finely diced	Papaya, fein gewürfelt
Lime zest	Limonenzesten
Raspberries	Himbeeren
Ingredients for 10 desserts	Zutaten für 10 Desserts

1 

Erhitzte Bananensahne über die klein geschnittene Kuvertüre gießen

Pour the heated banana cream over the finely chopped couverture

2 

Nach der Zugabe der Butter rühren, bis eine homogene Masse entsteht

Add the butter and then stir until the mixture is even and smooth

3 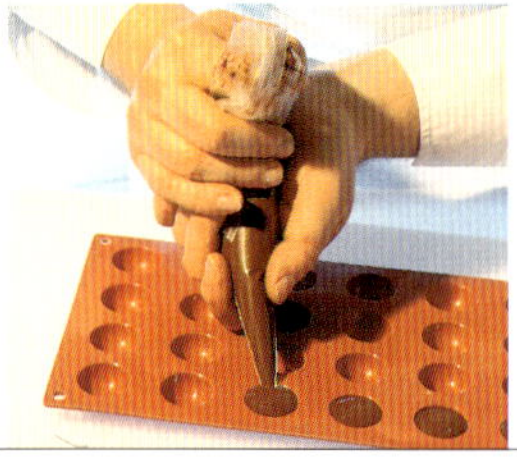

Masse in Silikonformen spritzen und tiefgefrieren

Place mixture into silicon moulds and deep-freeze

4 

Ganache zuerst in Ei …

First dip the ganache in the egg …

5 

6 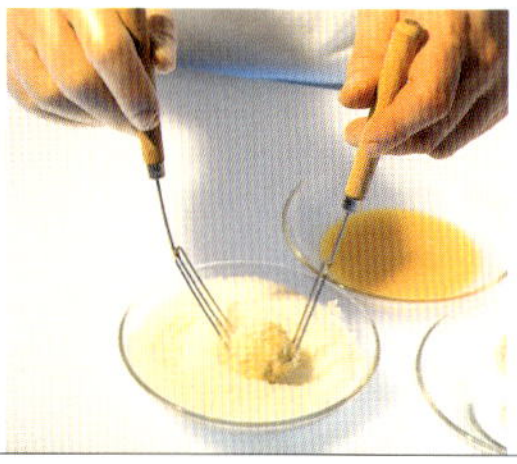

7 

8 

... dann in Kokosraspel wenden

... and then in the grated coconut

Vorgang wiederholen

Repeat this process

Panierte Ganache in heißem Frittierfett ausbacken

Deep-fry the coated ganache in hot oil

Fertig frittierte Ganache

Finished deep-fried ganache

Deep fried ganache in a coconut coating

100 g	*banana puree*
100 g	*cream*
200 g	*couverture, 66 %*
50 g	*butter*
100 g	*whole egg*
150 g	*grated coconut*

Heat up the banana puree and cream. Chop the couverture and butter into small pieces and put into a bowl. Pour the heated banana cream over it and keep stirring until the mixture is well blended and smooth. Deep-freeze the ganache in silicon moulds, take out of the moulds and then dip first in egg and then in the grated coconut. Then turn over once again in the egg and grated coconut. Deep-fry the ganache in hot oil and apply a dusting of icing sugar.

Frittierte Ganache im Kokosmantel

100 g	*Bananenpüree*
100 g	*Sahne*
200 g	*Kuvertüre, 66 %*
50 g	*Butter*
100 g	*Vollei*
150 g	*Kokosraspel*

Bananenpüree und Sahne erhitzen. Kuvertüre und Butter in kleine Stückchen schneiden und in eine Schüssel geben. Erhitzte Bananensahne darüber gießen und rühren, bis eine homogene Masse entsteht. Ganache in Silikonformen tiefgefrieren, ausformen, dann zuerst in Ei und danach in Kokosraspel wenden. Nochmals in Ei und Kokosraspel wenden. Ganache in heißem Frittierfett ausbacken und mit Puderzucker bestreuen.

Cocoa Isomalt ship

250 g	*Isomalt*
5 g	*water*
20 g	*cocoa powder, slightly fat-reduced*

Dissolve the Isomalt and douse with water, stir in the cocoa powder, roll out between two Silpat mats, cut and shape.

Kakao-Isomalt-Schiff

250 g	*Isomalt*
5 g	*Wasser*
20 g	*Kakaopulver, schwach entölt*

Isomalt auflösen mit Wasser abschrecken, Kakaopulver unterrühren, zwischen zwei Silpatmatten ausrollen, zuschneiden und formen.

Himbeer-Kakaobohnen-Tuille

150 g	*Zucker*
5 g	*Himbeerpulver (gefriergetrocknete Himbeeren)*
15 g	*Kakaobohnenbruch*
2,5 g	*Pektin*
100 g	*Butter*
50 g	*Glukosesirup*
50 g	*Himbeersaft*

Zucker, Himbeerpulver, Kakaobohnenbruch und Pektin mischen. Butter und Glukosesirup aufkochen und zusammen mit dem Himbeersaft den trockenen Zutaten zugeben. Kühl stellen, dann mit einem Plastikspritzsack auf eine Silikonbackmatte aufdressieren. Bei 170 °C etwa 10 Minuten backen, schneiden und noch heiß über ein eckiges Rohr biegen.

Raspberry cocoa bean tuille

150 g	*sugar*
5 g	*raspberry powder (freeze-dried raspberries)*
15 g	*cocoa bean bits*
2.5 g	*pectin*
100 g	*butter*
50 g	*glucose syrup*
50 g	*raspberry juice*

Mix the sugar, raspberry, cocoa bean pieces and pectin together. Bring the butter and glucose syrup to boil and add to the dry ingredients together with the raspberry juice. Transfer to a cool place and then use a plastic piping bag to arrange the mixture onto a silicon mat. Bake at 170 °C for about 10 minutes, cut and bend over a square tube while still hot.

Bananenchip

Bananen längs schneiden und in Zitronensäure wenden. Trocken tupfen und in Kristallzucker wenden. Auf Backmatte legen und bei 70 °C im Ofen trocknen. Trocken lagern.

Banana chip

Cut the bananas lengthways and roll briefly in citric acid. Dab to dry and quickly roll in granulated sugar. Place on a baking mat and dry in the oven at 70 °C. Store in a dry place.

Snickers ice-cream from the Pacojet

120 g	*Snickers (chocolate bars)*
300 g	*milk*
100 g	*egg yolk*
70 g	*sugar*
2 g	*sea salt*
200 g	*cream*

Add a little milk into the Pacojet container to freeze the Snickers into place. Bring the milk to boil, stir the egg yolk with sugar and salt until frothy, add the hot milk and pasteurise at 85 °C. Allow to cool down to 65 °C, then add the cream and cool down to 4 °C. Fill into the prepared container with the Snickers. Deep-freeze at –20 °C and pacotise after 20 hours.

Snickerseis aus dem Pacojet

120 g	*Snickers (Schokoladenriegel)*
300 g	*Milch*
100 g	*Eigelb*
70 g	*Zucker*
2 g	*Meersalz*
200 g	*Sahne*

Snickers mit etwas Milch in der Pacojetdose festfrieren. Milch aufkochen, Eigelb mit Zucker und Salz schaumig rühren, heiße Milch einlaufen lassen und bei 85 °C pasteurisieren. Auf 65 °C abkühlen, dann Sahne zugeben und auf 4 °C herunterkühlen. In die vorbereitete Snickersdose einfüllen. Bei –20 °C tiefgefrieren und nach 20 Stunden pacossieren.

Drink recommendation

Pedro Ximinez Murillo, 100 Años, Emilio Lustau, Jerez, Spain

Getränkeempfehlung

Pedro Ximinez Murillo, 100 Anos, Emilio Lustau, Jerez, Spanien

Bayerische Papstwelle

The New Pope from Bavaria

Eine grosse Ehre ist uns widerfahren. Ein Deutscher ist Papst geworden. Eine grosse Chance für das ganze Land und natürlich auch für den Papst, der ja eigentlich gehofft hatte, dass der Herr diesen Krug an ihm vorübergehen lasse, und dann feststellte, dass der Herr ihm in diesem Moment wohl nicht zugehört hatte. Sympathisch, nicht? Meine kleine Hommage an Papst Benedikt XVI.

We have been granted a great honour. A German citizen has become Pope. A big opportunity for the whole country and of course for the Pope as well, who had really hoped that the Lord would spare him, but who then realised that the Lord was probably not listening at that particular moment. Delightful. My small homage to Pope Benedict XVI.

Ingredients	Zusammensetzung
Raspberry cream	Himbeersahne
Bock beer peach sorbet	Bockbier-Pfirsich-Sorbet
Gingerbread décor	Lebkuchendekor
Caramelised peaches	Karamellisierte Pfirsiche
Spicy chocolate cake	Schokoladengewürzkuchen
Bock beer Sabayon	Bockbiersabayon
Raspberry sauce	Himbeersauce
Chocolate décor	Schokoladendekor
Ingredients for 10 desserts	Zutaten für 10 Desserts

Himbeersahne (Menge für 1 Becher)

400 g	*Sahne*
100 g	*Himbeermark*
80 g	*Puderzucker*
20 g	*Himbeergeist*
10 g	*Zitronensaft*

Alle Zutaten mischen und mit einem Schlagmesser 2-mal pacossieren, ohne die Druckluft abzulassen. In Spritzbeutel mit 10-mm-Lochtülle füllen.

Raspberry cream (quantity for 1 beaker)

400 g	*cream*
100 g	*raspberry pulp*
80 g	*icing sugar*
20 g	*Himbeergeist*
10 g	*lemon juice*

Mix all the ingredients and pacotise twice with a beating knife, without releasing the compressed air. Fill into a piping bag with a 10 mm round nozzle.

1

2

3

Bockbier-Pfirsich-Sorbet

125 g	*Honig*
400 g	*Starkbier*
400 g	*Pfirsichpüree*

Honig und Bier aufkochen, auf die Hälfte reduzieren, Pfirsichpüree zugeben und bei −20 °C 24 Stunden gefrieren. Bei Bedarf pacossieren.

Bock beer peach sorbet

125 g	*honey*
400 g	*brown ale*
400 g	*peach puree*

Bring the honey and beer to boil, reduce to half the quantity, add the puree and deep-freeze at −20 °C for 24 hours. Pacotise if required.

Lebkuchendekor

Selbst gemachten oder gekauften Lebkuchen mit einer Aufschnittmaschine schneiden und im Ofen trocknen. Im heißen Zustand formen und trocken lagern.

Gingerbread décor

Cut the selfmade or bought gingerbread with a mechanical slicer and dry in the oven. Form into shape while hot and store in a dry place.

Sahne in einen Paccojetbehälter gießen

Pour the cream into a Pacojet processor

4

Himbeergeist zugießen

Add Himbeergeist (made from raspberries and similar to raspberry brandy)

Himbeermark zugeben

Add the raspberry pulp

5

Messer in den Pacojetdeckel einsetzen

Insert the knives into the lid of the Pacojet

Puderzucker einrieseln lassen

Let the icing sugar run into it

6

Fertige Himbeersahne

Finished raspberry cream

Karamellisierte Pfirsiche

200 g	*frische Pfirsiche*
50 g	*Zucker*
100 g	*Bockbier*

Die Pfirsiche in feine Scheiben schneiden, den Zucker leicht karamellisieren und mit Bockbier ablöschen. Pfrisichspalten kurz darin schwenken.

Caramelised peaches

200 g	*fresh peaches*
50 g	*sugar*
100 g	*Bock beer*

Cut the peaches into thin slices, slightly caramelise the sugar and douse with Bock beer. Briefly roll the peach slices in the sugar.

Schokoladengewürzkuchen

60 g	*Butter*
10 g	*Zucker*
	Abrieb von einer 1/2 Zitrone
60 g	*Eigelb*
105 g	*Lebkuchenbrösel*
40 g	*Kuvertüre, 70 %, gehackt*
45 g	*Walnüsse, gehackt*
40 g	*Milch*
90 g	*Eiweiß*
45 g	*Zucker*

Butter mit 10 g Zucker, Zitronenabrieb und Eigelb schaumig schlagen. Lebkuchenbrösel, Kuvertüre, Walnüsse sowie Milch glatt rühren und zugeben. Das Eiweiß mit 45 g Zucker zu Schnee schlagen und unterziehen. Schokoladengewürzkuchen in Silikonformen geben und bei 200 °C etwa 15 Minuten backen. Leicht abkühlen lassen und aus der Form nehmen. Sie sollten als warme Komponente im Dessert auftauchen.

Spicy chocolate cake

60 g	*butter*
10 g	*sugar*
	zest from 1/2 lemon
60 g	*egg yolk*
105 g	*gingerbread crumbs*
40 g	*couverture, 70 %, chopped*
45 g	*walnuts, chopped*
40 g	*milk*
90 g	*egg white*
45 g	*sugar*

Beat the butter with 10 g sugar, lemon zest and egg yolk until frothy. Add together the gingerbread crumbs, couverture, walnuts and milk and stir until smooth. Beat the egg white with 45 g sugar until stiff and then fold in. Fill the spicy chocolate cake into silicon moulds and bake at 200 °C for about 15 minutes. Allow to cool down slightly and remove from the moulds. These should be warm when served as part of the dessert.

Bock beer Sabayon

100 g	*Bock beer*
30 g	*honey*
40 g	*egg yolk*

Beat all the ingredients in a water bath until firmly stiff.

Bockbiersabayon

100 g	*Bockbier*
30 g	*Honig*
40 g	*Eigelb*

Alle Zutaten im Wasserbad zu einem stabilen Schaum schlagen.

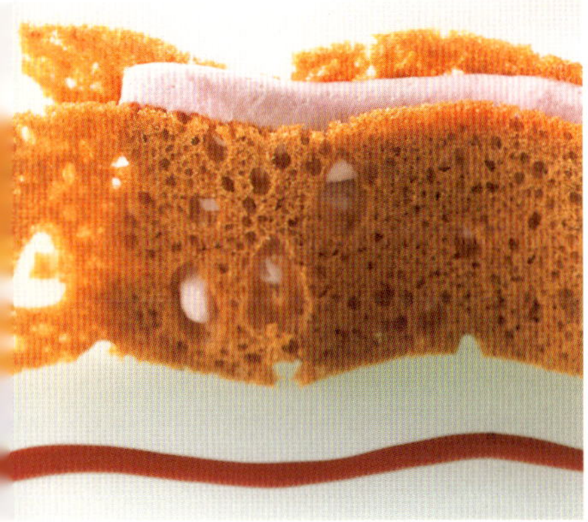

Drink recommendation

EKU 28, Doppel-Bockbier, Kulmbach, Germany

Getränkeempfehlung

EKU 28, Doppel-Bockbier, Kulmbach, Deutschland

Christoph Columbus

Christopher Columbus

Ich liebe einfache und erfolgreiche Desserts. Mit dem entsprechenden Pfiff kann auch aus heissen Kirschen mit Vanilleeis etwas Besonderes werden.

I like simple and successful desserts. With that little bit extra, even hot cherries with vanilla ice-cream can be turned into something quite special.

Ingredients

Thyme cherries
with oranges
Balsamic caramel
Spiced honey ice-cream
Filo pastry sheet
Sugar décor

Ingredients for 10 desserts

Zusammensetzung

Thymiankirschen
mit Orangen
Balsamico-Karamell
Gewürz-Honig-Eis
Filoblatt
Zuckerdekor

Zutaten für 10 Desserts

Thymiankirschen mit Orangen

100 g	*Zucker*
400 g	*Sauerkirschen*
2	*Thymianzweige*
2	*Orangen*
	(Schale und Filets, etwa 100 g)

Zucker in einer Pfanne karamellisieren lassen, dann mit dem Kirschsaft nach und nach ablöschen, restliche Zutaten zugeben und kurz aufkochen lassen.

Thyme cherries with oranges

100 g	*sugar*
400 g	*morello cherries*
2	*twigs of thyme*
2	*oranges*
	(peel and segments, about 100 g)

Let the sugar caramelise in a frying pan, then add the cherry juice bit by bit, add the other ingredients and bring to boil briefly.

Balsamico-Karamell

100 g	*Zucker*
100 g	*Balsamico-Essig*

Zucker in der Pfanne karamellisieren lassen. Nach und nach mit Balsamico-Essig ablöschen. Je nach gewünschter Saucenkonsistenz etwas mehr oder etwas weniger Balsamico-Essig zugeben.

Balsamic caramel

100 g	*sugar*
100 g	*balsamic vinegar*

Let the sugar caramelise in the frying pan. Add the balsamic vinegar bit by bit. Add a bit more or a bit less balsamic vinegar, depending on the consistency of the sauce required.

1

2

3

4

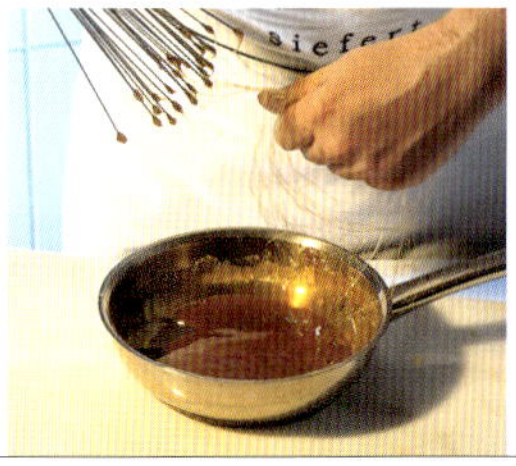

5

6

7

Zucker in eine flache Pfanne geben ...

Put the sugar into a shallow frying pan

... karamellisieren

... and then caramelise

Einen abgeschnittenen Schneebesen in die Zuckermasse tauchen

Use a cut-off whisk and dip it into the sugar mixture

Fäden ziehen

Pull threads

Zuckerfäden leicht aufwickeln

Slightly wind up the sugar threads

Eine Zuckergespinstkugel formen

Form a ball with the spun sugar threads

Fertiger Zuckerdekor

Finished sugar décor

Spiced honey ice-cream

200 g	*whole milk*
2 g	*allspice*
	pith of 1/2 vanilla pod
2 g	*macis*
60 g	*egg yolks*
25 g	*sugar*
50 g	*honey*
300 g	*cream*

Add the finely grounded spices to the milk and bring to boil. Stir the egg yolk with the sugar and honey until frothy, add the milk and then pasteurise everything in a water bath at 85 °C. Allow the mixture to cool down to 65 °C, then add the cream and cool down to 4 °C. Allow to settle for at least 4 hours. Place into the ice-cream maker to freeze.

Gewürz-Honig-Eis

200 g	*Vollmilch*
2 g	*Piment*
	Mark von einer 1/2 Vanilleschote
2 g	*Macis*
60	*Eigelb*
25 g	*Zucker*
50 g	*Honig*
300 g	*Sahne*

Milch mit der Gewürzmischung aufkochen. Eigelb mit Zucker und Honig schaumig rühren, Milch zugießen, dann alles im Wasserbad auf 85 °C pasteurisieren. Eismasse auf 65 °C abkühlen lassen, dann die Sahne zugeben und auf 4 °C abkühlen. Mindestens 4 Stunden reifen lassen. In der Eismaschine abfrieren.

Filo pastry sheet

Cut the filo pastry into 12 × 12 cm squares, deep-fry in a frying pan, place on kitchen paper and dust lightly with icing sugar.

Filoblatt

Filoteig im Format 12 × 12 cm zurechtschneiden, in Frittierfett ausbacken, danach auf Küchenpapier ablegen und mit Puderzucker leicht absieben.

Drink recommendation

Ruby Porto Burmester Vila Nova de Gaja, Portugal

Getränkeempfehlung

Ruby Porto Burmester Vila Nova de Gaja, Portugal

Bernd
Siefert
Konditor
Welt
Meister

ROUSSILLON

Quitten sind ein Saisonobst mit einem unbeschreiblichen Duft, dem ich nicht widerstehen kann. Deshalb stelle ich neben 120 Sorten Konfitüre auch Quittenkonfit her. So kann ich diese Frucht noch länger geniessen.

Quinces are a seasonal fruit with an incredible fragrance which I cannot resist. That's why I make quince jam in addition to the 120 types of jam I produce. Like this I can enjoy quinces even out of season.

Ingredients	Zusammensetzung
Liquid chocolate cake	Flüssiger Schokoladenkuchen
Quince jam in Banyuls	Quittenkonfit in Banyuls
Vanilla ginger ice-cream	Vanille-Ingwer-Eis
Rose cocoa caramel sauce	Rosen-Kakao-Karamellsauce
Chocolate décor	Schokoladendeko
Ingredients for 10 desserts	Zutaten für 10 Desserts

Flüssiger Schokoladenkuchen

120 g	*Zucker*
150 g	*Vollei*
95 g	*Bitterkuvertüre, 70 %*
90 g	*Butter weich*
40 g	*Mehl*

Zucker und Vollei etwa 10 Minuten schaumig schlagen, Kuvertüre und Butter bei 40 °C auflösen, mit dem gesiebten Mehl zugeben, alles wiederum 10 Minuten aufschlagen.

Masse für mindestens 2 Stunden im Kühlschrank lagern.

Bei 200 °C etwa 10 Minuten backen. Je nach Formgröße auch etwas länger.

Liquid chocolate cake

120 g	*sugar*
150 g	*whole egg*
95 g	*dark couverture, 70 %*
90 g	*butter, soft*
40 g	*flour*

Beat the whole egg with the sugar for about 10 minutes until frothy, dissolve the couverture and butter at 40 °C, add the flour by passing it through a sieve and then whisk everything again for 10 minutes.

Leave the mixture in a refrigerator for at least 2 hours.

Bake at 200 °C for about 10 minutes. A bit longer if it is larger.

Quittenkonfit in Banyuls

50 g	*Zucker*
150 g	*frische Quitten, fein gewürfelt*
75 g	*Banyuls*
5 g	*Pektin*

25 g Zucker leicht in der Pfanne karamellisieren, dann die Quitten darin leicht anschwenken und mit Banyuls ablöschen. Den restlichen Zucker mit dem Pektin mischen und zugeben, alles so lange leicht köcheln, bis die Quitten durch sind.

Quince jam in Banyuls

50 g	*sugar*
150 g	*fresh quinces, finely diced*
75 g	*Banyuls*
5 g	*pectin*

Caramelise 25 g sugar lightly in a frying pan, turn the quince dice in the sugar and douse with Banyuls. Blend the remaining sugar with the pectin and add to the frying pan, then simmer until the quinces are cooked through.

1

2

3

4

5

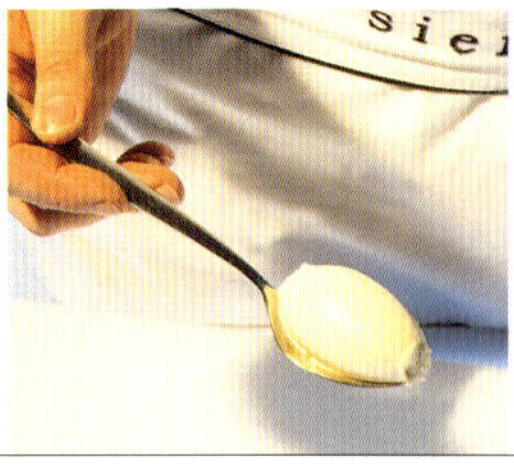

6

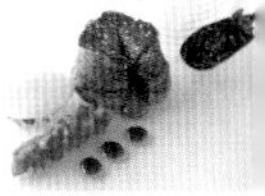

Milch und Zucker in einen Topf geben

Put the milk and sugar into a pan

Mark der Vanille zugeben

Add the vanilla pith

Eigelb und Zucker verrühren

Stir the sugar into the egg yolk

Kochende Vanillemilch zugeben

Add the boiling vanilla milk

Sahne bei 65 °C zugeben, Ingwer zum Schluss des Gefriervorgangs zugeben

Add the cream at 65 °C and the ginger at the end of the freezing process

Fertiges Eis

Finished ice cream

Vanilla ice cream with candied ginger

200 g	*whole milk*
1/2	*Tahiti vanilla pod*
70 g	*egg yolk*
75 g	*sugar*
300 g	*cream*
25 g	*candied ginger*

Bring the milk with the vanilla pith and pod to boil, stir the egg yolk with the sugar until frothy, add the milk and then pasteurise everything in a water bath at 85 °C. Allow to cool down to 65 °C, add the cream and place into the ice cream maker to freeze. Towards the end of the freezing process, add the candied and finely chopped ginger.

Rose cocoa caramel sauce

100 g	*sugar*
10 g	*cocoa beans*
50 g	*Banyuls*
25 g	*rose water*

Caramelise the sugar to a light colour, add the cocoa beans and douse with Banyuls. Add the rose water and bring to boil briefly. Then pass through a fine sieve.

Drink recommendation

Etoile Banyuls, 1989 Tuile' Vin Doux Naturel, Banyuls, France

Vanilleeis mit kandiertem Ingwer

200 g	*Vollmilch*
1/2	*Tahiti-Vanilleschote*
70 g	*Eigelb*
75 g	*Zucker*
300 g	*Sahne*
25 g	*kandierter Ingwer*

Milch mit Vanillemark und -schote aufkochen, Eigelb mit Zucker schaumig rühren, Milch zugießen, dann alles im Wasserbad bei 85 °C pasteurisieren. Auf 65 °C abkühlen und die Sahne zugeben, dann in der Eismaschine frieren. Gegen Ende des Gefriervorgangs kandierten, fein gehackten Ingwer zugeben.

Rosen-Kakao-Karamell-Sauce

100 g	*Zucker*
10 g	*Kakaobohnen*
50 g	*Banyuls*
25 g	*Rosenwasser*

Zucker hell karamellisieren, Kakaobohnen zugeben und mit Banyuls ablöschen. Rosenwasser zugeben und kurz aufkochen. Dann durch ein feines Sieb passieren.

Getränkeempfehlung

Etoile Banyuls, 1989 Tuile' Vin Doux Naturel, Banyuls, Frankreich

THAI FUSION

Pandanblätter habe ich zum ersten Mal in unserem Asia-Shop im Odenwald gesehen und dachte gleich, damit kann man doch vieles anstellen. Während einer Asienreise habe ich dann gesehen, was dort damit gemacht wird. Ein Mix aus Pandanblättern und europäischen Zutaten macht für mich den Reiz aus.

I saw pandanus leaves for the first time in our Asiatic store in the Odenwald and thought at once that they could be used for many things. While travelling through Asia I had a chance to see what they do with them there. For me, the attraction lies in the combination of pandanus leaves with European ingredients.

Ingredients

Rice soufflé with pandanus leaves
Cassis mousse
Figs in Rivesaltes
Yoghurt ice-cream
Yoghurt honey sauce
Tube of cigarette pastry

Ingredients for 10 desserts

Zusammensetzung

Reissoufflé mit Pandanblättern
Cassismousse
Feigen in Rivesaltes
Joghurteisschnee
Joghurt-Honig-Sauce
Zigarettenteigröhre

Zutaten für 10 Desserts

Reissoufflé mit Pandanblättern

50 g	*Risottoreis (Aborio)*
285 g	*Milch*
	Mark von 1 Vanilleschote
1 g	*Salz*
35 g	*Zucker*
120 g	*Eigelb*
15 g	*Pistazien*
15 g	*Pistazienpaste*
4 g	*Pandanessenz (Asia-Shop)*
180 g	*Eiweiß*

Reis in warmem Wasser gut auswaschen, Milch und Vanillemark aufkochen, Reis und Salz zufügen und etwa 20 Minuten garen. Zucker zugeben, Eigelb nach und nach unterrühren und erkalten lassen. Restliche Zutaten unterrühren, Reismasse abfüllen und 24 Stunden bei –20 °C gefrieren. Pacossieren, gebutterte Formen zu $^3/_4$ mit der Masse füllen und im Wasserbad bei 180 °C etwa 25 Minuten backen.

Rice soufflé with pandanus leaves

50 g	*risotto rice (Aborio)*
285 g	*milk*
	pith of 1 vanilla pod
1 g	*salt*
35 g	*sugar*
120 g	*egg yolk*
15 g	*pistachios*
15 g	*pistachio paste*
4 g	*pandanus essence (Asiatic shop)*
180 g	*egg white*

Thoroughly wash the rice in warm water, bring the milk and vanilla pith to boil, add the rice and salt and leave to cook slowly for about 20 minutes. Add the sugar, stir in the egg yolk bit by bit and leave to cool down. Blend in the remaining ingredients, put the rice pudding into moulds and deep-freeze at –20 °C for 24 hours. Pacotise, fill the buttered moulds up to $^3/_4$ high with the pudding and bake in a water bath at 180 °C for about 25 minutes.

1

2

3

Cassismousse

50 g	*Cassispüree*
70 g	*Puderzucker*
400 g	*Sahne*
10 g	*Crème de Cassis*

Alle Zutaten mischen und mit einem Schlagmesser im Pacojet 2-mal pacossieren, ohne die Druckluft abzulassen.

Cassis mousse

50 g	*cassis puree*
70 g	*icing sugar*
400 g	*cream*
10 g	*Crème de Cassis*

Blend all ingredients together and pacotise twice with the Pacojetknive in the Pacojet, without releasing the compressed air.

Milchreis herstellen

Make the rice pudding

4

Gefrorene Reismasse pacossieren

Pacotise the frozen rice pudding

Pandanessenz zugeben

Add pandanus essence

5

Reismasse in gebutterte und gezuckerte Formen dressieren

Arrange the rice pudding into buttered and sugared moulds

Fertige Masse in einen Pacojetbehälter geben und 24 Stunden tiefgefrieren

Fill the finished mixture into a Pacojet container and deep-freeze for 24 hours

6

Im Wasserbad gebackene Pandan-Reis-Soufflés ausformen

Bake the pandanus rice soufflés in a water bath and then take out of the moulds

Figs in Rivesaltes

200 g	*small dried figs*
200 g	*Rivesaltes*

Leave the figs to soak for at least a day in the Rivesaltes.

Feigen in Rivesaltes

200 g	*kleine getrocknete Feigen*
200 g	*Rivesaltes*

Feigen mindestens 1 Tag in Rivesaltes einlegen.

Joghurteisschnee (Pacojet)

20 g	*Zucker*
10 g	*Thymianhonig*
60 g	*Wasser*
365 g	*Joghurt*

Zucker, Honig und Wasser aufkochen. Joghurt zugeben, mixen und 24 Stunden bei −20 °C gefrieren. Mehrmals hintereinander 10 Sekunden pacossieren, so dass ein Joghurtgranulat entsteht.

Yoghurt ice cream (Pacojet)

20 g	*sugar*
10 g	*thyme honey*
60 g	*water*
365 g	*yoghurt*

Bring the water, sugar and honey to boil. Add the yoghurt, mix and freeze at −20 °C for 24 hours. Pacotise several times for 10 seconds so that you create a yoghurt granulate.

Joghurt-Honig-Sauce

100 g	*Joghurt*
25 g	*Honig*
25 g	*Sahne*

Alle Zutaten glatt und stabil aufrühren.

Yoghurt honey sauce

100 g	*yoghurt*
25 g	*honey*
25 g	*cream*

Stir all ingredients together until firm and smooth.

Tube of cigarette pastry

50 g	*butter*
50 g	*icing sugar*
50 g	*egg white*
50 g	*flour*

Bring all the ingredients up to room temperature, then beat the butter with the icing sugar until smooth and stir in the egg white and sieved flour in turn.

Use a template to spread the cigarette mixture onto a baking mat so that it ends up very thin at one end. Bake at 180 °C and immediately roll over a rolling pin. Store in a dry place.

Zigarettenteigröhre

50 g	*Butter*
50 g	*Puderzucker*
50 g	*Eiweiß*
50 g	*Mehl*

Alle Zutaten auf Zimmertemperatur bringen, dann zuerst Butter mit Puderzucker glatt rühren und abwechselnd Eiweiß und gesiebtes Mehl unterrühren.

Zigarettenmasse mit einer Schablone auf eine Backmatte streichen, so dass sie am einen Ende ganz dünn aufgebracht ist. Bei 180 °C backen und sofort über ein Rundholz aufrollen. Trocken lagern.

Drink recommendation

Rivesaltes Ambré 1986, Vin Doux Naturel, Cellier Trouillas, Roussillon, France

Getränkeempfehlung

Rivesaltes Ambré 1986, Vin Doux Naturel, Cellier Trouillas, Roussillon, Frankreich

DER KERN DER WAHRHEIT

THE SECRET OF THE HEART

Dieses Dessert war ein Vordessert zu einer Veranstaltung „Legenden in Weiss“ mit meinem „Papa“, was meine Küchenkarriere angeht, „Otto Koch“ und „Eckehard Witzigmann“. Witzigmanns Kommentar zu meiner Kreation fing an mit: „In Bewunderung ...“ Es war wie ein kleines Weihnachtsgeschenk.

This dessert was an entremets at an event entitled “Legends in White” with my “Daddy”, as far as my kitchen career is concerned, “Otto Koch”, and “Eckehard Witzigmann”. Witzigmann started his comments with these words: “In admiration ...” It was a small Christmas present.

Ingredients

- Pistachio green tea cookies with cranberries
- Mango espuma
- Raspberry sorbet
- Pineapple jam
- Almond tuille
- Raspberries

Ingredients for 10 desserts

Zusammensetzung

- Pistazien-Grüntee-Financiers mit Cranberries
- Mangoespuma
- Himbeersorbet
- Ananaskonfit
- Mandeltuille
- Himbeeren

Zutaten für 10 Desserts

Pistazien-Grüntee-Financiers mit Cranberries

15 g	*Mandelstaub*
10 g	*Puderzucker*
15 g	*Pistazien, fein gehackt*
10 g	*Mehl*
25 g	*Butter, geschmolzen*
40 g	*Eiweiß*
20 g	*Zucker*
1 g	*Matchateepulver*
40 g	*Cranberries*

Alle Zutaten miteinander verrühren und in Silikonbackform einfüllen. Bei 190 °C 15 Minuten backen. Nach dem Backen mit etwas Puderzucker besieben.

Pistachio green tea cookies with cranberries

15 g	*almond dust*
10 g	*icing sugar*
15 g	*pistachios, finely chopped*
10 g	*flour*
25 g	*butter, melted*
40 g	*egg white*
20 g	*sugar*
1 g	*Matcha tea powder*
40 g	*cranberries*

Stir all ingredients together and fill into silicon baking cups. Bake at 190 °C about 15 minutes. After baking, apply a slight dusting with icing sugar.

Mangoespuma

2	*Blatt Gelatine*
125 g	*Orangensaft*
55 g	*Zucker*
375 g	*Mangopüree*

Gelatine in kaltem Wasser einweichen, Orangensaft mit Zucker erhitzen, Gelatine ausgepresst hinzufügen, dann nach und nach das Mangopüree zugeben. Alles durch ein Haarsieb gießen, dann in einen Espumasiphon geben und 2 Gaspatronen einschrauben. Mindestens 4 Stunden sehr kalt stellen.

Mango espuma

2	*sheets of gelatine*
125 g	*orange juice*
55 g	*sugar*
375 g	*mango puree*

Soak the gelatine in cold water, heat up the orange juice with the sugar, squeeze out the gelatine and add to the juice and then add the mango puree bit by bit. Pass everything through a fine sieve, then put into an espuma siphon and insert 2 gas cartridges. Leave in a very cold place for at least 4 hours.

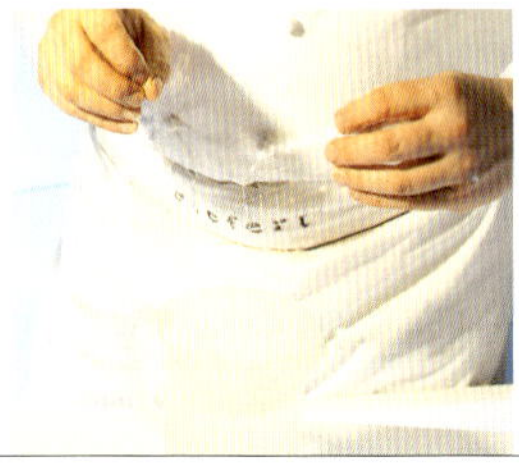

1

2

3

4

Gelatine einweichen

Soak the gelatine

5

Mangopüree nach und nach zugeben und unterrühren

Add the mango puree bit by bit and stir in

Zucker in einen Topf geben

Put the sugar into a pan

6

Masse durch ein Haarsieb gießen, dann in den Espumasiphon geben

Pass the mixture through a fine sieve and then put it into the espuma siphon

Orangensaft zugießen, verrühren und erhitzen

Pour in the orange juice, stir and heat up

7

2 Gaspatronen aufschrauben

Insert the 2 gas cartridges

Ausgedrückte Gelatine im Orangensaft auflösen

Dissolve the squeezed out gelatine in the orange juice

8

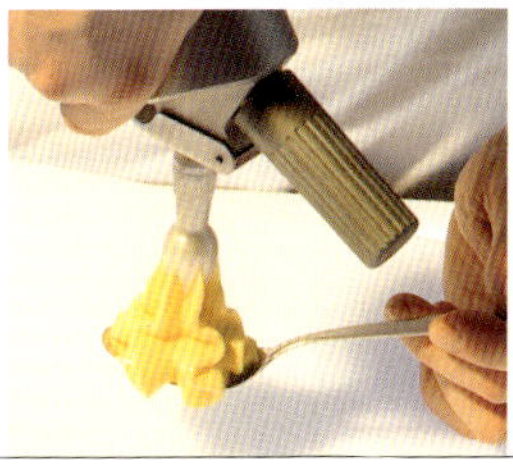

Fertiges Mangoespuma

Finished mango espuma

Himbeersorbet

60 g	*Zucker*
15 g	*Trockenglukose*
250 g	*Himbeerpüree*
125 g	*Wasser*
2 g	*Zitronensaft*

Alle trockenen Zutaten mischen, dann flüssige Zutaten zugeben und alles gut durchmixen. Mit dem Refraktometer auf 30 °Brix einstellen und abfrieren.

Raspberry sorbet

60 g	*sugar*
15 g	*dry glucose*
250 g	*raspberry puree*
125 g	*water*
2 g	*lemon juice*

Mix all dry ingredients, then add the liquid ingredients and blend everything well. Use a refractometer to adjust to 30 °Brix and then freeze.

Ananaskonfit

100 g	*Gelierzucker, 2 zu 1*
150 g	*Weißwein (Silvaner)*
1	*Vanilleschote*
2	*Rosmarinzweige*
500 g	*Ananas, geschält und fein gewürfelt*

Gelierzucker karamellisieren, mit Weißwein ablöschen, Vanille und Rosmarin zugeben und kurz aufkochen lassen. Ananaswürfel zufügen und ziehen lassen. Gewürze vor dem Anrichten entfernen.

Pineapple jam

100 g	*gelling sugar, 2 to 1*
150 g	*white wine (Silvaner)*
1	*vanilla pod*
2	*twigs of rosemary*
500 g	*pineapple, peeled and finely diced*

Caramelise the gelling sugar, douse with the white wine, add the vanilla and rosemary and bring to boil briefly. Add the diced pineapple and allow to steep. Remove the rosemary twigs and vanilla pod before serving.

Almond tuille

150 g	*sugar*
2.5 g	*pectin*
100 g	*butter*
50 g	*glucose syrup*
50 g	*liquid (water or juice)*
20 g	*almond semolina*

Mix the sugar and pectin, bring to boil with butter and glucose syrup together with the liquid, add to the almond semolina. Cool the mixture and then use a plastic piping bag to arrange the mixture onto a silicon mat. Bake at 180 °C for about 15 minutes.

Mandeltuille

150 g	*Zucker*
2,5 g	*Pektin*
100 g	*Butter*
50 g	*Glukosesirup*
50 g	*Flüssigkeit (Wasser/Saft)*
20 g	*Mandelgrieß*

Zucker und Pektin mischen, mit Butter und Glukosesirup aufkochen und mit Flüssigkeit dem Mandelgrieß zugeben. Kühlen, dann mit einem Plastikspritzsack auf eine Silikonbackmatte aufdressieren. Bei 180 °C etwa 15 Minuten backen.

Drink recommendation

Muscat de Rivesaltes, Domaine Cazes, 2001, Vin Doux Naturel Rivesaltes, Roussillon, France

Getränkeempfehlung

Muscat de Rivesaltes, Domaine Cazes, 2001, Vin Doux Naturel Rivesaltes, Roussillon, Frankreich

Wilder Sommer

Wild Summer

Dass ich der Süsse bei den „Jungen Wilden“ bin, ist ja bekannt. Die Idee zum „Wilden Sommer“ kam von Stefan Marquard, dem Punksternekoch, auf einem Event in Tunesien. Anfangs dachte ich, Stefans Idee wäre gar nicht umzusetzen. Aber einer meiner Leitsätze ist, dass es nichts gibt, was nicht geht. So habe ich aus Stefans Idee den „Wilden Sommer“ gemacht. Ein super leckeres Sommerdessert. Selbst Stefan war überrascht …

It's a well known fact that I'm the sweetie at "Young And Wild Club" Chef Association. The idea for "Wild Summer" came from Stefan Marquard, the punk star chef, at an event in Tunisia. At first I thought that it was impossible to make Stefan's idea a reality. But one of my mottos is that nothing is impossible. So I produced "Wild Summer" from Stefan's idea. A super-duper summer dessert. Even Stefan was surprised.

Ingredients

- Saffron vinaigrette
- Sweet basil pesto
- Balsamic caramel
- Rosemary honey parfait
- Salad with cucumbers and apricots
- Cigarette spaghetti
- Cigarette spaghetti crumbs (to be placed under the parfait)
- Candied violets

Ingredients for 10 desserts

Zusammensetzung

- Safranvinaigrette
- Süsses Basilikumpesto
- Balsamico-Karamell
- Rosmarinhonigparfait
- Salatgurken-Aprikosen-Salat
- Zigarettenspaghetti
- Zigarettenspaghettibrösel (kommen unter das Parfait)
- Kandierte Veilchen

Zutaten für 10 Desserts

Safranvinaigrette

10	*Safranfäden*
100 g	*Orangensaft*
100 g	*Zitronensaft*
100 g	*Apfelsaft*

Alle Zutaten aufkochen und auf Saucenkonsistenz reduzieren.

Saffron vinaigrette

10	*saffron threads*
100 g	*orange juice*
100 g	*lemon juice*
100 g	*apple juice*

Bring all the ingredients to boil, then maintain on low heat to reduce to sauce consistency.

1

2

Süsses Basilikumpesto

75 g	*Basilikum*
10 g	*Minze*
10 g	*Pinienkerne*
10 g	*Kokosraspel*
25 g	*Olivenöl*
10 g	*Zucker*
50 g	*Honig*

Alle Zutaten mit einem Mörser zu einem Pesto mörsern.

Oder alles gefrieren und pacossieren – wird supergrün, aber sehr fein.

Sweet basil pesto

75 g	*basil*
10 g	*mint*
10 g	*pine kernels*
10 g	*grated coconut*
25 g	*olive oil*
10 g	*sugar*
50 g	*honey*

Use pestle and mortar to pulp all the ingredients into a pesto.

Alternatively, freeze everything and pacotise it – it will become very green, but very fine.

3

4

Basilikum in das Mörserschälchen geben

Place the basil into the mortar

Minze zugeben

Add the mint

Pinienkerne, Kokosraspel, Olivenöl, Zucker und Honig zugeben

Add the pine kernels, grated coconut, olive oil, sugar and honey

Zu einer gleichmäßigen Masse mörsern

Use the pestle to grind an even mixture

Balsamic caramel

100 g	*sugar*
100 g	*balsamic vinegar*

Caramelise the sugar and douse with balsamic vinegar.

Tip: the caramel should not be boiling, otherwise it will become bitter.

Balsamico-Karamell

100 g	*Zucker*
100 g	*Balsamico-Essig*

Zucker karamellisieren und mit Balsamico-Essig ablöschen.

Tipp: Karamell darf nicht mehr kochen, sonst wird es bitter.

Rosemary honey parfait (Pacojet)

160 g	*milk*
	rosemary to taste
80 g	*egg yolk*
100 g	*honey*
10 g	*crème fraîche*
160 g	*cream*

Boil up the milk and rosemary, leave to steep, remove the rosemary, beat the egg yolk and honey and add the milk. Pasteurise the mixture in a bowl in hot water at 85 °C, then cool down quickly in ice water. Heat up the crème fraîche and cream to 60 °C and mix in.

Deep-freeze at –20 °C for about 24 hours. Then pacotise, fill into moulds and continue freezing.

Variation without Pacojet: fold the whipped cream into the mixture, which has been stirred in an ice water bath to cool down, fill into moulds and freeze.

Rosmarinhonigparfait (Pacojet)

160 g	*Milch*
	Rosmarin je nach Geschmack
80 g	*Eigelb*
100 g	*Honig*
10 g	*Crème fraîche*
160 g	*Sahne*

Milch und Rosmarin aufkochen, ziehen lassen, Rosmarin entfernen, Eigelb und Honig aufschlagen, Milch dazugießen. Masse im Wasserbad bei 85 °C pasteurisieren, dann im Eiswasserbad schnell abkühlen lassen. Crème fraîche und Sahne auf 60 °C erwärmen und untermixen.

Bei –20 °C etwa 24 Stunden gefrieren. Pacossieren, in Förmchen abfüllen und weiter gefrieren.

Variante ohne Pacojet: Geschlagene Sahne unter die im Eiswasserbad kalt gerührte Masse heben, in Formen füllen und gefrieren.

Salatgurken-Aprikosen-Salat

200 g	*Salatgurke*
100 g	*Aprikosen in Spalten*
50 g	*Rivesaltes, Dessertwein*
1	*Orange, Abrieb und Saft*
1	*Zitrone, Abrieb und Saft*

Salatgurke schälen, halbieren, entkernen und in feine Scheiben schneiden. Aprikosen in Rivesaltes einlegen. Saft und Abrieb der Zitrusfrüchte mit den Gurkenscheiben und den Aprikosenspalten mischen und im Kühlschrank ziehen lassen.

Salad with cucumbers and apricots

200 g	*cucumber*
100 g	*apricots in wedges*
50 g	*Rivesaltes, dessert wine*
1	*orange, zest and juice*
1	*lemon, zest and juice*

Peel, halve and core the cucumber and then cut into fine slices. Place the apricots into Rivesaltes to soak. Mix the juice and zest of the citrus fruits with the cucumber slices and apricots and allow to steep in the refrigerator.

Cigarette spaghetti

50 g	*butter*
50 g	*icing sugar*
50 g	*egg white*
50 g	*flour*

Stir all ingredients together at room temperature until smooth, then use a comb to spread onto the Silpat. Bake at 190 °C and shape while still warm.

Zigarettenspaghetti

50 g	*Butter*
50 g	*Puderzucker*
50 g	*Eiweiß*
50 g	*Mehl*

Alle Zutaten bei Zimmertemperatur glatt verrühren, mit einem Kamm auf Silpat aufstreichen. Bei 190 °C backen und im warmen Zustand formen.

Cigarette spaghetti crumbs (to be placed under the parfait)

Crush some of the cigarette spaghetti into crumbs, put on the plate and then place the parfait on top of the crumbs.

Zigarettenspaghettibrösel (kommen unter das Parfait)

Einige Zigarettenspaghetti zerbröseln, auf den Teller legen und Parfait darauf platzieren.

Drink recommendation

Terassous, Rivesaltes Ambré 1995, Vin Doux Naturel, Terrats, Roussillon, France

Getränkeempfehlung

Terassous, 95er Rivesaltes Ambré, Vin Doux Naturel, Terrats, Roussillon, Frankreich

PROVENCE

Schokolade ist ein ganz grosses Thema, gerade für mich, und ich habe versucht, eine kleine Hommage an die Region zu kreieren, die den Schokoladenboom auf der Welt ausgelöst hat.

Chocolate is a huge subject, especially for me, and so I have tried to create a small homage to the region that triggered the worldwide chocolate boom.

Ingredients

- Chocolate sponge without flour
- Apricot sorbet
- Faux crème brûlée with lavender honey
- Chocolate mousse
- Fruits
- Sugar and chocolate décor

Ingredients for 10 desserts

Zusammensetzung

- Schokoladenbiskuit ohne Mehl
- Aprikosensorbet
- Falsche Lavendelhonig-Crème-brûlée
- Schokoladenmousse
- Früchte
- Zucker- und Schokoladendekor

Zutaten für 10 Desserts

Schokoladenbiskuit ohne Mehl

70 g	*Marzipan*
70 g	*Eigelb*
115 g	*Eiweiß*
115 g	*Zucker*
35 g	*Kakaopulver*

Marzipan mit Eigelb schaumig rühren. Eiweiß mit Zucker zu Schnee schlagen. Eischnee unter die Marzipanmasse heben. Kakaopulver vorsichtig unterrühren. Mit einer Lochtülle auf Backpapier aufdressieren. Schokoladenbiskuit bei 180 °C etwa 15 Minuten backen.

Chocolate sponge without flour

70 g	*marzipan*
70 g	*egg yolk*
115 g	*egg white*
115 g	*sugar*
35 g	*cocoa powder*

Stir the egg yolk and marzipan until frothy. Add sugar to the egg white and beat until stiff. Fold the beaten egg white into the marzipan mixture. Carefully blend in the cocoa powder. Use a round piping nozzle to arrange onto baking paper. Bake the chocolate sponge at 180 °C for about 15 minutes.

Aprikosensorbet

340 g	*Aprikosen aus der Dose*
60 g	*Puderzucker*
	Mark von einer 1/4 Tahiti-Vanilleschote
5 g	*Zitronensaft*

Aprikosen pürieren, Puderzucker, Vanillemark und Zitronensaft unterrühren und auf 30 °Brix einstellen. In die Sorbetière geben und tiefgefrieren.

Apricot sorbet

340 g	*canned apricots*
60 g	*icing sugar*
	pith of 1/4 Tahiti vanilla pod
5 g	*lemon juice*

Puree the apricots, stir in the icing sugar, vanilla pith and lemon juice and adjust to 30 °Brix. Place the mixture into a sorbetière and deep-freeze.

1

2

3

4

5

Milch in einen Topf gießen und erhitzen

Put the milk into a pan and heat up

Eigelb mit Zucker glatt rühren

Stir the egg yolk with sugar until smooth

Heiße Milchsahne unterrühren

Stir in the hot milk/cream

Masse über klein geschnittene Kuvertüre gießen

Pour the mixture over the finely chopped couverture

Glatt arbeiten

Work until smooth

6

Geschlagene Sahne unterheben

Fold in the whipped cream

7

Zu einer homogenen Masse verrühren

Stir until the mixture is no longer streaky

8

Mit einem Spritzbeutel in Silikon-Halbkugelformen spritzen

Use a piping bag to pipe into semi-spherical silicon moulds

9

Lavendelhonig-Crème-brûlée einlegen und tiefgefrieren

Fill in the crème brûlée with lavender honey and deep-freeze

10

Fertiges Schokoladenmoussetörtchen

Finished little chocolate mousse cake

Falsche Lavendelhonig-Crème-brûlée

2½	*Blatt Gelatine*
50 g	*Eigelb, pasteurisiert*
200 g	*Sahne*
80 g	*Lavendelhonig*
1	*Tropfen Lavendelöl (je nach Intensität variieren)*

Gelatine in kaltem Wasser einweichen. Eigelb mit Sahne und Honig verrühren, dann Lavendelöl zugeben. Gelatine ausdrücken, auflösen und die Masse in die Gelatine einrühren. In halbrunde Silikonformen füllen und tiefgefrieren.

Faux crème brûlée with lavender honey

2½	*sheets of gelatine*
50 g	*egg yolk, pasteurised*
200 g	*cream*
80 g	*lavender honey*
1	*drop of lavender oil (more or less, depending on required taste)*

Soak the gelatine in cold water. Stir the egg yolk with cream and honey, then add the lavender oil. Squeeze out and dissolve the gelatine and then stir the mixture into the gelatine. Fill into semi-spherical silicon moulds and deep-freeze.

Chocolate mousse

30 g	*egg yolk*
20 g	*sugar*
60 g	*milk*
65 g	*cream*
195 g	*dark couverture, 66 %*
265 g	*whipped cream*

Stir the egg yolk with the sugar until smooth, bring the milk with 65 g of cream to boil and pasteurise at 85 °C. Then pour immediately over the finely chopped couverture. Work until smooth, then fold in the 265 g cream. Use a piping bag to pipe the chocolate mousse into hemispheric silicon moulds and then place the deep-frozen lavender honey crème brûlée on top. Top off with chocolate sponge and deep-freeze.

Take out of the moulds and spray with dark spray couverture to a velvety finish. Using freezing technology, place a thin couverture ribbon around it.

Schokoladenmousse

30 g	*Eigelb*
20 g	*Zucker*
60 g	*Milch*
65 g	*Sahne*
195 g	*Bitterkuvertüre, 66 %*
265 g	*geschlagene Sahne*

Eigelb und Zucker glatt rühren, Milch mit 65 g Sahne aufkochen und bei 85°C pasteurisieren. Sofort über die klein geschnittene Bitterkuvertüre gießen. Glatt arbeiten, dann die 265 g Sahne unterziehen. Schokoladenmousse mit einem Spritzbeutel in Silikon-Halbkugelformen spritzen, tiefgekühlte Lavendelhonig-Crème-brûlée einlegen. Schokoladenbiskuit auflegen und tiefgefrieren.

Ausformen und mit Bittersprühkuvertüre samtig absprühen. Mit Frostertechnik ein dünnes Kuvertüreband umlegen.

Drink recommendation

Maury Cuvée Prestige, 15 Ans d'Age, Mas Amiel, Vin Doux Naturel, Maury, Roussillon, France

Getränkeempfehlung

Maury Cuvée Prestige, 15 Ans d'Age, Mas Amiel, Vin Doux Naturel, Maury, Roussillon, Frankreich

SINGAPORE SOUP

SINGAPORE SOUP

Die asiatische Küche wäre ohne Sago und Zitronengras viel ärmer, und da so ein Sommersüppchen, mit Champagner angegossen, eine erfrischende Sache ist, hier mein Sagosüppchen à la Singapour.

Asian cuisine would be far poorer without sago and lemon grass, and since a little summer soup with a touch of champagne is so refreshing, I would like to present my little sago soup "à la Singapore".

Ingredients	**Zusammensetzung**
Sago lemon grass mixture	Sagozitronengrasmasse
Fruit pearls	Fruchtperlen
Deep fried sweet potato mixture	Frittierte Süsskartoffelmasse
Coconut sorbet	Kokossorbet
Coconut twirl	Kokoslocke
Lemon grass lolly	Zitronengraslolly
Ingredients for 10 desserts	Zutaten für 10 Desserts

Sagomasse

3	*Zitronengrasstangen*
100 g	*Sago*
100 g	*Maracujasaft*
500 g	*Apfelsaft*
400 g	*Wasser*
100 g	*Zucker*

3 Zitronengrasstangen, 1-mal über Kreuz geschnitten. Sago mit den anderen Zutaten aufkochen und langsam zu einem Brei kochen, Zitronengras entfernen, schnell herunterkühlen und bei Bedarf in Tellern anrichten.

Sago mixture

3	*sticks of lemon grass*
100 g	*sago*
100 g	*passion fruit juice*
500 g	*apple juice*
400 g	*water*
100 g	*sugar*

Prepare 3 sticks of lemon grass, cut once crosswise. Bring the sago and the other ingredients to boil and keep simmering until it is mushy, remove the lemon grass, cool down quickly and then serve onto plates if required.

Kokosmilchsorbet

75 g	*Zucker*
10 g	*Trockenglukose*
90 g	*Wasser*
10 g	*Ingwer, frisch*
250 g	*Kokospüree*

Trockene Zutaten mischen. Wasser mit frisch gemahlenem Ingwer zugeben und aufkochen lassen. Masse zu dem Kokospüree geben und mixen. Mit dem Refraktometer auf 32 °Brix einstellen und in der Eismaschine gefrieren.

Coconut milk sorbet

75 g	*sugar*
10 g	*dry glucose*
90 g	*water*
10 g	*fresh ginger*
250 g	*coconut puree*

Mix the dry ingredience, add the water and the fine grated ginger. Bring it to boil and add it to the coconut puree. Mix it and bring the mix to 32 °Brix. Freeze the mix in a ice-cream machine.

1

2

3

4

5

6

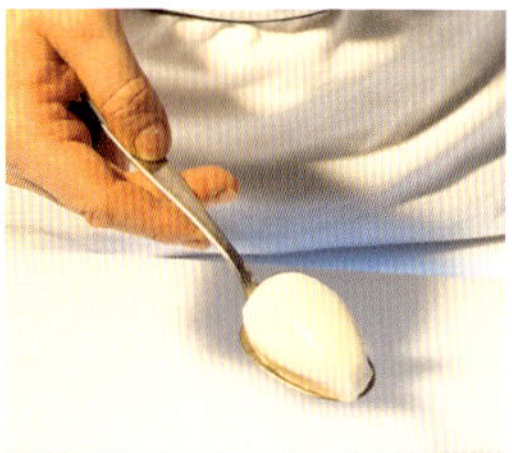

7

Trockene Zutaten mischen

Mix the dry ingredients

Wasser zugeben

Add water

Frischen Ingwer dazuraspeln und aufkochen

Add grated fresh ginger and bring to boil

Kokospüree in einen Topf geben

Pour the coconut puree into a pan

Zuckersud dazumixen

Add in the sugar water and mix

Sorbet mit dem Refraktometer einstellen

Use the refractometer to adjust the sorbet

Fertiges Sorbet

Finished sorbet

Lemon grass lolly

	Lemon grass, cut into individual leaves
200 g	*sugar*
100 g	*water*
40 g	*glucose*

Bring the sugar and water to boil, add the glucose and boil everything to 155 °C. Allow to cool down slightly, then pull the leaves through the liquid, one by one, and stabilise with ice spray.

Sweet potato egg white pastry

200 g	*sweet potato, boiled and pureed*
200 g	*egg white*
50 g	*tempura flour*
50 g	*sugar*

Stir all ingredients until smooth and then deep-fry by the spoonful, leave to drain off and apply a slight dusting with icing sugar.

Drink recommendation

Iniskillin Sparkling Ice Wine 2001, Niagara on the Lake, Canada

or

Kerner Sekt Halbtrocken, Deutscher Sekt b. A., Umstädter Winzergenossenschaft, Hessische Bergstraße, Bereich Umstadt, Germany

Zitronengraslolly

	Zitronengras, in einzelne Blätter geschnitten
200 g	*Zucker*
100 g	*Wasser*
40 g	*Glukose*

Zucker und Wasser aufkochen, dann Glukose zugeben und alles auf 155 °C kochen. Leicht abkühlen lassen, dann nacheinander je ein Blatt durchziehen und mit Eisspray stabilisieren.

Süsskartoffeleiweissteig

200 g	*Süßkartoffeln, gekocht und püriert*
200 g	*Eiweiß*
50 g	*Tempuramehl*
50 g	*Zucker*

Alle Zutaten glatt rühren und löffelweise in Frittieröl ausbacken, abtropfen lassen, leicht mit Puderzucker bestäuben.

Getränkeempfehlung

Iniskillin Sparkling Ice Wine 2001, Niagara on the Lake, Kanada

oder

Kerner Sekt Halbtrocken, Deutscher Sekt b. A., Umstädter Winzergenossenschaft Hessische Bergstraße, Bereich Umstadt, Deutschland

CHINESE AMARO

Meine Freundin Judy in Singapur hatte mir mal ein chinesisches Dessert gezeigt, das mich beim Probieren unweigerlich an bitteren deutschen Kräuterlikör erinnerte. Ich musste einfach ein Fusion-Kitchen-Dessert machen: West meets far east. Eat and Digest.

My friend Judy in Singapore once showed me a Chinese dessert that reminded me strongly of a bitter-tasting German herbal liqueur. I just had to make a dessert that combines the two cuisines: West meets Far East. Eat and digest.

Ingredients

- Herbal liqueur jelly
- Honey mousse
- Dandelion flower sorbet
- Pumpkin seed caramel ring
- Honey
- Pumpkin seed oil
- Caramelised yellow plums

Ingredients for 10 desserts

Zusammensetzung

- Kräuterlikörgelee
- Honigcreme
- Löwenzahnblütensorbet
- Kürbiskernkaramellring
- Honig
- Kürbiskernöl
- Karamellisierte gelbe Pflaumen

Zutaten für 10 Desserts

Kräuterlikörgelee

8	*Blatt Gelatine*
375 g	*Kräuterlikör*
375 g	*Riesling, Weißwein*

Gelatine in kaltem Wasser einweichen, ausdrücken, auflösen. Kräuterlikör und Riesling zugeben und verrühren. Die Masse in eine Silikonform, etwa 3 mm hoch, eingießen. Erkalten lassen und in Form schneiden.

Herbal liqueur jelly

8	*sheets of gelatine*
375 g	*herbal liqueur*
375 g	*Riesling, white wine*

Soak the gelatine in cold water, squeeze out and dissolve. Add the herbal liqueur and Riesling and stir well. Pour the mixture into a silicon mould, about 3 mm high. Allow to cool down and cut into shape.

Honigcreme (Pacojet)

500 g	*Sahne*
50 g	*Blütenhonig*

Sahne mit dem Honig verrühren und mit dem Schlagmesser im Pacojet zu einer stabilen Sahne aufschlagen. Tipp: Bei der Auswahl des Honigs kann man sehr kreativ sein, von Akazienhonig bis indischer Zimtblütenhonig kann alles, je nach Kräuterlikör, passen. Soll das Dessert vorbereitet werden, kann man 2 Blatt Gelatine zum Stabilisieren zugeben.

Honey mousse (Pacojet)

500 g	*cream*
50 g	*flower honey*

Stir the honey in with the cream and pacotise with the beater until stiff. Tip: When selecting the honey you can be very creative; depending on the herbal liqueur, you can choose anything from acacia to Indian cinnamon flower. If you want to prepare the dessert, you can add 2 sheets of gelatine to stabilise it.

1

2

3

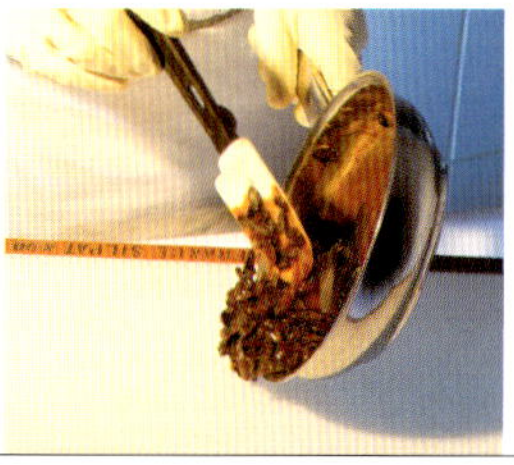

4

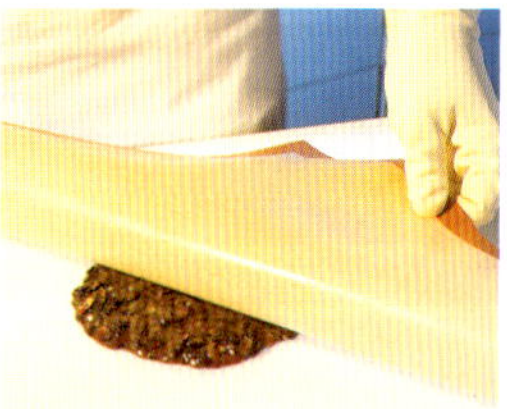

5

Zucker und Glukose in eine Pfanne geben

Put the sugar and the glucose into a pan ...

Karamellisieren

... then caramelise

Kürbiskerne unterrühren

Stir in the pumpkin seeds

Auf eine Backmatte ausgießen

Pour onto a baking mat

Zweite Backmatte auflegen

Place a second baking mat on top

6

Mit einem Rollholz dünn ausrollen

Use a rolling pin to roll out thinly

7

Backmatten entfernen
und schmale Streifen schneiden

Remove the baking mats
and cut into narrow strips

8

Streifen noch warm in einen Ring einlegen

Put the strips into a ring while they are
still warm

9

Fertiger Kürbiskernkaramellring

Finished pumpkin seed caramel ring

Löwenzahnblütensorbet

500 g	*Löwenzahnblüten*
1500 g	*Wasser*
2	*Zitronen*
2	*Orangen*
750 g	*Zucker*

Blüten mit Wasser, abgeriebenen Schalen und Saft der Zitrusfrüchte für 1 Stunde bei schwacher Hitze köcheln lassen. Durch ein Sieb passieren und den Zucker zugeben, mit dem Refraktometer auf 30 °Brix einstellen und dann in der Eismaschine gefrieren.

Dandelion flower sorbet

500 g	*dandelion flowers*
1,500 g	*water*
2	*lemons*
2	*oranges*
750 g	*sugar*

Let the flowers, water, zest and juice of the citrus fruits simmer on low heat for an hour. Pass through a sieve and add the sugar, use the refractometer to adjust to 30 °Brix and then freeze in the ice cream machine.

Kürbiskernkaramellring

50 g	*Glukosesirup*
500 g	*Zucker*
250 g	*Kürbiskerne*

Glukosesirup in einer Pfanne auflösen, dann nach und nach den Zucker zugeben und zu einem hellen Karamell schmelzen. Weitere Verarbeitung siehe Stepps.

Pumpkin seed caramel ring

50 g	*glucose syrup*
500 g	*sugar*
250 g	*pumpkin seeds*

Dissolve the glucose syrup in a frying pan, then add the sugar in small portions and melt to a light coloured caramel. Further processing see under Stages.

Caramelised yellow plums

100 g *sugar*
50 g *plum wine*
300 g *yellow plums, cut into segments*

Caramelise the sugar in a frying pan, pour the plum wine over it and briefly heat up the plums in the liquid.

Karamellisierte gelbe Pflaumen

100 g *Zucker*
50 g *Pflaumenwein*
300 g *gelbe Pflaumen, in Spalten geschnitten*

Zucker in einer Pfanne karamellisieren, mit dem Pflaumenwein ablöschen und die Pflaumen kurz darin erhitzen.

Drink recommendation

2002 Kiedricher Gräfenberg, Riesling Eiswein, Weingut Robert Weil, Kiedrich, Germany

Getränkeempfehlung

2002er Kiedricher Gräfenberg, Riesling Eiswein, Weingut Robert Weil, Kiedrich, Deutschland

MEXIKO

MEXICO

Eigentlich hatte ich mir vorgenommen, in Mexiko ein ganz tolles Ananasdessert mit viel Vanille herzustellen. Aber auf ganz Yucatan war zu diesem Zeitpunkt keine anständige Ananas und schon gar keine Vanille zu finden. Also was machen? Das, was ich immer mache, wenn ich in einem fremden Land bin. Ich gehe zuerst auf den Markt und schaue, was es gibt. In diesem Fall waren Bananen da, Kokos, Mangos und Chili. Siehe da, einer meiner Klassiker war geboren.

In Mexico I had really planned to make a fantastic pineapple dessert with a lot of vanilla. But at that point in time, no decent pineapple could be found in the whole of Yucatan and even less so vanilla. So what could I do? What I always do when I am in a foreign country. I first go to the market to see what's available. In this case there were bananas, coconuts, mangos and chillis. And lo and behold, one of my classics was born.

Ingredients

- Coconut dacquoise
- Cigarette pastry for ball
- Curd cheese chilli sorbet
- Mango sorbet
- Caramelised spicy bananas
- Mango scoops and fresh fruits
- Chocolate rolls
- Mango sauce

Ingredients for 10 desserts

Zusammensetzung

- Kokosdacquoise
- Zigarettenteig für Knäuel
- Quark-Chili-Sorbet
- Mangosorbet
- Karamellisierte Gewürzbananen
- Mangobällchen und frische Früchte
- Schokoladenröllchen
- Mangosauce

Zutaten für 10 Desserts

Kokosdacquoise

150 g	*Eiweiß*
50 g	*Zucker*
25 g	*Mandelgrieß*
125 g	*Puderzucker*
100 g	*Kokosraspel*

Das Eiweiß mit Zucker zu Schnee schlagen. Mandelgrieß, Puderzucker und Kokosraspel mischen und vorsichtig unter den Eischnee ziehen. Mit einem Spritzbeutel und 8er-Lochtülle, etwa 8 cm im Durchmesser, auf Backpapier dressieren. Bei 160 °C etwa 15 Minuten backen.

Coconut dacquoise

150 g	*egg white*
50 g	*sugar*
25 g	*grated almonds*
125 g	*icing sugar*
100 g	*grated coconut*

Beat the egg white with sugar until stiff. Mix the grated almonds, icing sugar and grated coconut and then carefully fold into the beaten egg. Use a piping bag with a round size 8 nozzle to arrange the mixture in a diameter of about 8 cm on baking paper. Bake at 160 °C for about 15 minutes.

Zigarettenteig für Knäuel

100 g	*Butter*
100 g	*Puderzucker*
100 g	*Eiweiß*
100 g	*Mehl*

Butter mit Puderzucker verrühren. Abwechselnd Eiweiß und Mehl einarbeiten, zu einer glatten Masse verrühren. Masse auf eine Backmatte streichen und mit einem breiten Kamm abziehen. Bei 180 °C etwa 10 Minuten backen. Im noch heißen Zustand zu einem Knäuel formen.

Cigarette pastry for ball

100 g	*butter*
100 g	*icing sugar*
100 g	*egg white*
100 g	*flour*

Blend the butter with the icing sugar. Add egg white and flour in turns and work into a smooth mixture. Spread the mixture onto a baking mat and drag a wide comb across it. Bake at 180 °C for about 10 minutes. Make the shape of the ball while the pastry is still hot.

1

2

3

4

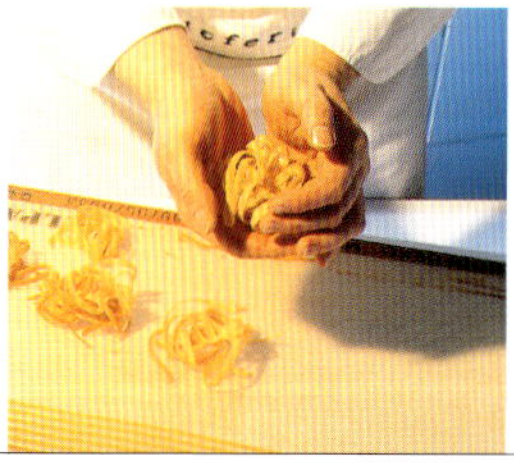
5

Butter mit Puderzucker verrühren

Blend the butter with the icing sugar

Eiweiß abwechselnd ...

Work in the egg white ...

... mit Mehl einarbeiten

... and the flour, in turns

Masse auf einer Backmatte verstreichen und mit einem breiten Kamm abziehen

Spread the mixture on a baking mat and drag a wide comb across it

Nach dem Backen mehrere noch heiße Streifen zu einem Knäuel formen

After baking, take several strips, while still hot, to form a ball

Curd cheese chilli sorbet

125 g	*curd cheese (quark)*
185 g	*water*
75 g	*sugar*
	chilli pod or Tabasco

Mix all ingredients and deep-freeze in the sorbetière. Or process using a Pacojet.

Mango sorbet

250 g	*mango puree*
100 g	*sugar*
100 g	*water*
10 g	*lemon juice*

Mix all the ingredients together, adjust to 30 °Brix with a refractometer and then deep-freeze in the sorbetière.

Caramelised spicy bananas

5	*bananas*
1	*nutmeg seed*
200 g	*cane sugar*

Cut the bananas into slices, place them in a circle in a cutting shape, sprinkle on some freshly grated nutmeg and then some cane sugar and caramelise.

Drink recommendation

Scharzhofberger Riesling 2003, Beerenauslese, Reichsgraf von Kesselstatt, Saar, Germany

Quark-Chili-Sorbet

125 g	*Quark*
185 g	*Wasser*
75 g	*Zucker*
	Chilischote oder Tabasco

Zutaten mischen und in der Sorbetière frieren. Oder mit einem Pacojet verarbeiten.

Mangosorbet

250 g	*Mangopüree*
100 g	*Zucker*
100 g	*Wasser*
10 g	*Zitronensaft*

Alle Zutaten mischen, mit dem Refraktometer auf 30 °Brix einstellen und in der Sorbetière tiefgefrieren.

Karamellisierte Gewürzbananen

5	*Bananen*
1	*Muskatnuss*
200 g	*Rohrzucker*

Bananen in Scheiben schneiden, in einem Ausstecher rund auslegen, mit frisch geriebener Muskatnuss und danach mit Rohrzucker bestreuen, dann karamellisieren.

Getränkeempfehlung

Scharzhofberger Riesling 2003, Beerenauslese, Reichsgraf von Kesselstatt, Saar, Deutschland

SHANGHAI

Shanghai, eine Stadt, die so schnell wächst, dass man Desserts nur noch im Glas anbieten kann. Glasdesserts sind in und haben viele Vorteile, wie z. B. dass sie gut vorzuproduzieren und leicht zu lagern sind.

In Shanghai people are in such a hurry that they only offer desserts in glasses there these days. Glass desserts have become fashionable and they are easy to make in advance and easy to store.

Ingredients	**Zusammensetzung**
Lychee aloe vera jelly	Litschi-Aloevera-Gelee
Blackberry tayberry mousse	Brombeeren-Tayberry-Mousse
Deep-fried glass noodles	Frittierte Glasnudeln
Tarry lapsang souchong rice cream	Tarry-lapsang-souchong-Reiscreme
Meringue	Baiser
Bubble sugar from Isomalt	Blasenzucker aus Isomalt
Ingredients for 10 desserts	Zutaten für 10 Desserts

Litschi-Aloevera-Gelee

5	*Blatt Gelatine*
100 g	*Zucker*
	Mark von 1 Vanilleschote
250 g	*Wasser*
100 g	*gewürfelte Litschis*
100 g	*geschälte und gewürfelte Aloevera*

Gelatine in kaltem Wasser einweichen. Zucker, Vanillemark sowie 250 g Wasser aufkochen und die Früchte damit überbrühen. Über Nacht ziehen lassen, dann nochmals kurz aufkochen und Gelatine in kaltem Wasser einweichen. Die Gelatine ausgepresst in der noch heißen Fruchtsuppe auflösen. In Gläser füllen und gelieren lassen.

Lychee aloe vera jelly

5	*sheets of gelatine*
100 g	*sugar*
	pith of 1 vanilla pod
250 g	*water*
100 g	*diced lychees*
100 g	*peeled and diced aloe vera*

Add the sugar and vanilla pith to the 250 g water, bring to boil and use it to scald the fruit. Leave to steep overnight, then boil again briefly; soak the gelatine in cold water and dissolve the squeezed-out gelatine in the fruit soup while this is still hot. Fill into glasses and leave to set.

Brombeeren-Tayberry-Mousse

3	*Blatt Gelatine*
400 g	*Brombeerpüree*
1,5	*Zitronengrasstangen*
100 g	*halbierte Tayberries (Kreuzung aus Himbeeren und Brombeeren*
35 g	*Eiweiß*
45 g	*Zucker*
125 g	*geschlagene Sahne*

Gelatine in kaltem Wasser einweichen, Brombeerpüree mit über Kreuz eingeschnittenem Zitronengras aufkochen und ziehen lassen. Zitronengras entfernen, Gelatine auspressen und darin auflösen. Tayberries zugeben. Eiweiß mit Zucker zu Schnee schlagen, erkaltetes Püree unterlaufen lassen und die Sahne unterziehen. Auf das Litschi-Aloevera-Gelee füllen.

Blackberry tayberry mousse

3	*sheets of gelatine*
400 g	*blackberry puree*
1,5	*sticks of lemon grass*
100 g	*tayberries cut in half (cross between raspberries and blackberries)*
35 g	*egg white*
45 g	*sugar*
125 g	*whipped cream*

Soak the gelatine in cold water, bring the blackberry puree and the cross-cut lemon grass to boil and allow to steep. Remove the lemon grass, squeeze out the gelatine and dissolve into the blackberry puree. Add the tayberries. Add sugar to the egg white and beat until stiff; allow the cooled puree to run into it and then fold in the cream. Fill up the glasses on top of the lychee aloe vera jelly.

1

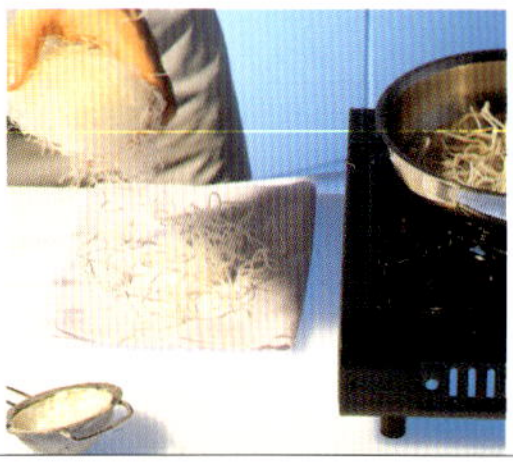

2

3

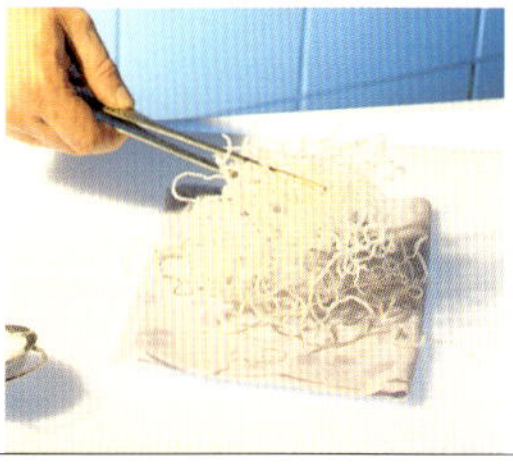

4

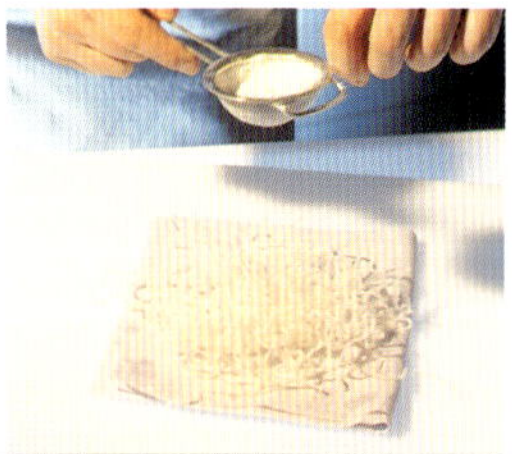

5

Öl in einer Pfanne erhitzen
Heat the oil in a frying pan

Reisnudeln in das heiße Öl geben
Place the rice noodles into the hot oil

Nach dem Frittieren herausnehmen
Once they are fried, remove them ...

Auf Küchenpapier abtropfen lassen
... and drain off on a paper towel

Mit Puderzucker bestreuen
Apply a dusting of icing sugar

Tarry lapsang souchong rice cream

2	*sheets of gelatine*
375 g	*milk*
5 g	*Tarry lapsang souchong tea (smoked tea)*
40 g	*sugar*
40 g	*rice for rice pudding*
50 g	*whipped cream*

Soak the gelatine in cold water, bring the milk to boil and use it to brew the tea. Allow to brew for about 5 minutes, then drain off, add the sugar and rice and cook into a thick rice pudding. Squeeze out the gelatine, dissolve in the mixture and leave to cool down. When it starts to gel, fold in the cream. Fill on top of the blackberry mousse.

Meringue

100 g	*egg white*
100 g	*sugar*

Add sugar to the egg white, heat to 40 °C and beat until stiff. Coat the glasses thinly with the egg and flame off with torch.

Bubble sugar from Isomalt

See the stages in "Austrian Evolution".

Drink recommendation

Zibibbo, Fiori d'uva buffa vino liquoroso, Sicily, Italy

Tarry-lapsang-souchong-Reiscreme

2	*Blatt Gelatine*
375 g	*Milch*
5 g	*Tarry-lapsang-souchong-Tee (geräucherter Tee)*
40 g	*Zucker*
40 g	*Milchreis*
50 g	*geschlagene Sahne*

Gelatine in kaltem Wasser einweichen, Milch aufkochen und den Tee damit überbrühen. Etwa 5 Minuten ziehen lassen, abseihen und mit dem Zucker und dem Milchreis zu einer dicken Reiscreme kochen. Die Gelatine auspressen und in der Masse auflösen, erkalten lassen. Wenn es anfängt zu gelieren, die Sahne unterziehen. Auf die Brombeermousse füllen.

Baiser

100 g	*Eiweiß*
100 g	*Zucker*

Eiweiß mit dem Zucker auf 40 °C erwärmen und dann zu Schnee schlagen. Gläser dünn damit abstreichen und abflämmen.

Blasenzucker aus Isomalt

Siehe Stepps „Austrian Evolution".

Getränkeempfehlung

Zibibbo, Fiori d'uva buffa vino liquoroso, Sizilien, Italien

AUSTRIAN EVOLUTION

Kaiserschmarren ist etwas total Leckeres. Wenn ich bei meinem Freund Tobias im Zillertal bin, ist dieser Dessertklassiker Pflicht. Dass sich in Österreich die Zeiten geändert haben, merkt man daran, dass neben „Red Bull“ jetzt auch „Kombucha“ produziert wird. Hier mein Wellness-dessert zum Thema k.-u.-k.-Monarchie.

“Emperor’s pancakes” taste truly delicious. When I stay with my friend Tobias in Zillertal, this classic dessert is a must. You can see that times have changed in Austria from the fact that they now produce not only “Red Bull” but also “Kombucha”. Here’s my wellness dessert as a tribute to the Austro-Hungarian Empire.

Ingredients

- Blueberry blini
- Kombucha jelly with fresh wild berries
- Strawberry Kombucha sorbet
- Raspberry paprika jam
- Fresh berries
- Bubble sugar from Isomalt
- Raspberry sauce

Ingredients for 10 desserts

Zusammensetzung

- Heidelbeer-Blini
- Kombuchagelee mit frischen Waldbeeren
- Erdbeer-Kombucha-Sorbet
- Himbeer-Paprika-Konfit
- Frische Beeren
- Blasenzucker aus Isomalt
- Himbeersauce

Zutaten für 10 Desserts

Heidelbeer-Blini

120 g	*Mehl*
60 g	*Heidelbeersaft, gefriergetrocknet*
250 g	*Milch*
80 g	*Eigelb*
120 g	*Eiweiß*
50 g	*Zucker*
1	*Prise Salz*

Mehl mit Heidelbeersaftpulver mischen, mit Milch und Eigelb zu einem Teig rühren. Eiweiß mit Zucker und Salz zu einem steifen Schnee schlagen, beide Massen mischen. In einer Pfanne kleine Pfannkuchen anbraten und im Ofen bei 200 °C fertig backen.

Blueberry blini

120 g	*flour*
60 g	*blueberry juice, freeze-dried*
250 g	*milk*
80 g	*egg yolk*
120 g	*egg white*
50 g	*sugar*
1	*pinch of salt*

Mix the flour with the blueberry juice powder, add milk and egg yolk and stir into a batter. Add sugar and salt to the egg white and beat until stiff, then blend both mixtures together. Start frying the small pancakes in a frying pan and finish off in the oven at 200 °C.

Kombuchagelee mit frischen Waldbeeren

3	*Blatt Gelatine*
100 g	*Kombucha*
100 g	*Waldbeeren*

Die Gelatine in kaltem Wasser einweichen, auspressen und auflösen. Kombucha zugeben und wieder erkalten lassen. Kombuchagelee durch ein mittelgrobes Sieb drücken. So bekommt man Kombuchakaviar. Auf Tellern anrichten und mit Waldbeeren dekorieren.

Kombucha jelly with fresh wild berries

3	*sheets of gelatine*
100 g	*Kombucha*
100 g	*wild berries*

Soak the gelatine in cold water, squeeze out and dissolve. Add the Kombucha and allow to cool down again. Pass the Kombucha jelly through a coarse sieve. That's how you make Kombucha caviar. Arrange on plates and decorate with wild berries.

1

2

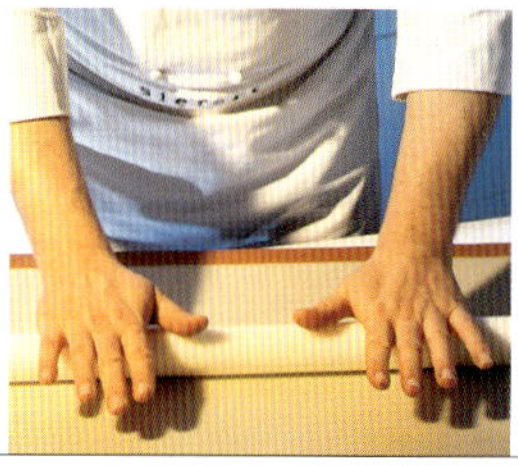

3

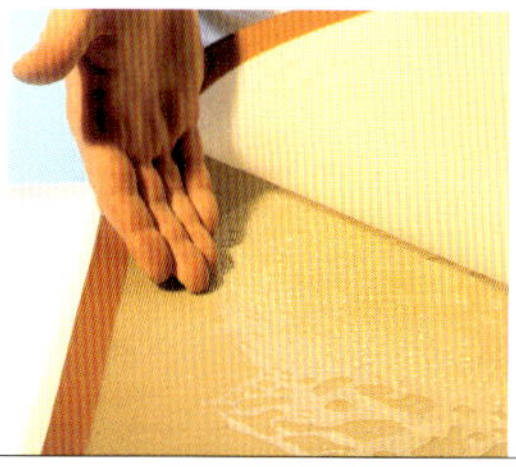

4

5

Isomalt auf Backmatte aufstreuen

Sprinkle the Isomalt onto a baking mat

Zweite Backmatte auflegen und bei 200 °C backen, bis das Isomalt Blasen wirft

Place a second baking mat on top and bake at 200 °C until the Isomalt starts bubbling up

Mit dem Rollholz gleichmäßig ausrollen

Roll out evenly with a rolling pin

Nochmals backen, auskühlen lassen und Backmatten abziehen

Bake again, leave to cool down and pull off the baking mats

Fertiger Blasenzucker

Finished bubble sugar

Strawberry Kombucha sorbet

215 g	*strawberry puree*
85 g	*sugar*
95 g	*Kombucha*
	lemon juice

Mix all ingredients cold for at least 3 minutes and adjust to 30 °Brix with the refractometer. It is advantageous to leave this mixture in a cool place for about 4 hours as this gives the pectins a better chance to swell up and the whole thing develops a finer texture. Place into the ice-cream maker to freeze.

Erdbeer-Kombucha-Sorbet

215 g	*Erdbeerpüree*
85 g	*Zucker*
95 g	*Kombucha*
	Zitronensaft

Alle Zutaten im kalten Zustand mindestens 3 Minuten mixen und mit dem Refraktometer auf 30 °Brix einstellen. Es ist von Vorteil, wenn man diesen Mix für etwa 4 Stunden kühl stellt, da dann die Pektine besser quellen können und das Ganze eine feinere Struktur bekommt. In der Eismaschine abfrieren.

Raspberry paprika jam

100 g	*sugar*
2 g	*pectin*
125 g	*red peppers, peeled, cored and diced*
125 g	*raspberries*
	pith of 1/2 Tahiti vanilla pod

Mix the sugar with the pectin. Bring to boil together with the remaining ingredients, then allow to cool down.

Himbeer-Paprika-Konfit

100 g	*Zucker*
2 g	*Pektin*
125 g	*rote Paprika, geschält, entkernt und in Würfel geschnitten*
125 g	*Himbeeren*
	Mark von einer 1/2 Tahiti-Vanilleschote

Zucker mit Pektin mischen. Mit den restlichen Zutaten kurz aufkochen, dann erkalten lassen.

Drink recommendation

Recioto della Valpolicella 2001, Domini Veneti Vigneti di Moron Classico, Italy

Getränkeempfehlung

Recioto della Valpolicella 2001, Domini Veneti Vigneti di Moron Classico, Italien

Süsses Rosensushi

Sweet Rose Sushi

Blumen und Blüten sind in Deutschland nicht gerade häufig auf der Speisekarte zu finden. Ich denke, das hat einfach damit zu tun, dass in unseren Breitengraden die Blumen nur noch aus dem Treibhaus kommen und die Esskultur, wie wir sie früher hatten, nicht erhalten blieb. Schade, denn das Dessert ist so lecker.

In Germany, you don't often find flowers and blossoms on the menu. The reason for this, I think, is that at our latitudes flowers are only cultivated in greenhouses these days and our traditional cuisine has not survived. Too bad, because this dessert is so tasty.

Ingredients	Zusammensetzung
Raspberry jelly	Himbeergelee
Rose parfait	Rosenhalbgefrorenes
Raspberry vinegar caramel sauce	Himbeeressig-Karamell-Sauce
Raspberries and pistachios	Himbeeren und Pistazien
Chocolate décor	Schokoladendekor
Ingredients for 10 desserts	Zutaten für 10 Desserts

Himbeergelee

15	*Blatt Gelatine*
450 g	*Himbeerpüree*
150 g	*Zucker*
300 g	*Rosenmuskateller*

Gelatine in kaltem Wasser einweichen, Himbeerpüree mit Zucker mischen, erwärmen und ausgepresste Gelatine darin auflösen. Zuletzt den Rosenmuskateller zugeben.

Himbeergelee etwa 2 mm hoch in eine flache Silikonform gießen. Erstarren lassen und rechteckig, in gewünschter Größe, zurechtschneiden.

Raspberry jelly

15	*sheets of gelatine*
450 g	*raspberry puree*
150 g	*sugar*
300 g	*rose muscat wine*

Soak the gelatine in cold water, mix the raspberry puree with sugar, heat up and dissolve the squeezed-out gelatine into the puree. Finally add the rose muscat wine.

Pour about 2 mm of raspberry jelly into a shallow silicon mould. Allow to set and cut into rectangles of the required size.

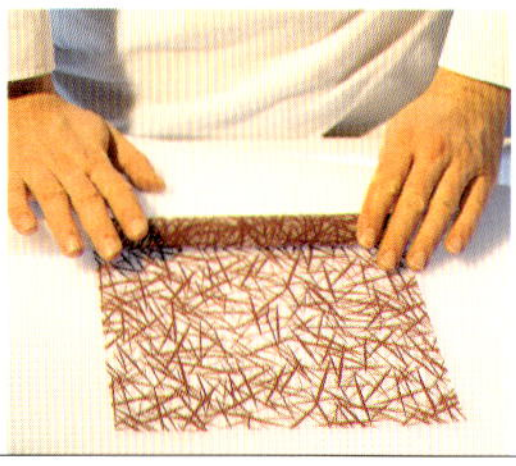

1

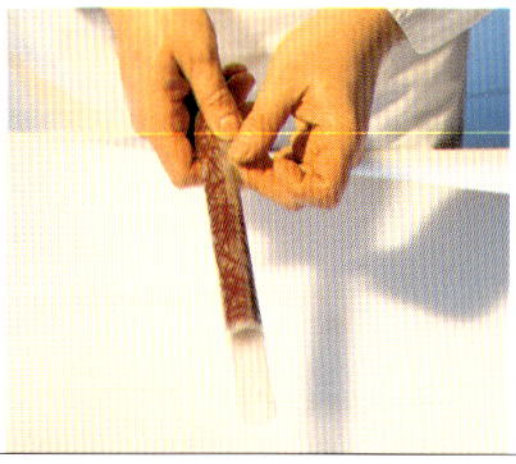

2

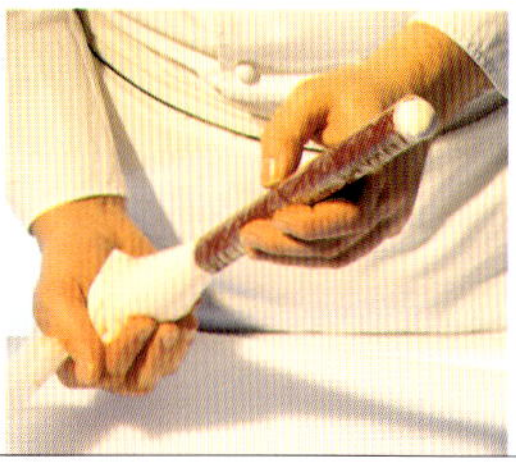

3

Rosenhalbgefrorenes

175 g	*Milch*
2	*Duftrosen, unbehandelt*
70 g	*Eigelb*
55 g	*Zucker*
265 g	*geschlagene Sahne*
35 g	*Rosenwasser (die Intensität beachten)*

Milch aufkochen, über die Rosenblätter gießen, etwa 15 Minuten ziehen lassen und dann abseihen. Eigelb mit Zucker schaumig rühren, Rosenmilch zugeben und in einem Wasserbad bei 85 °C pasteurisieren. Schnell auf 4 °C herunterkühlen und dann die Sahne sowie das Rosenwasser unterziehen. Weiterverarbeitung siehe Stepps.

Rose parfait

175 g	*milk*
2	*scented roses, untreated*
70 g	*egg yolk*
55 g	*sugar*
265 g	*whipped cream*
35 g	*rose water (of the right intensity)*

Boil the milk, pour over the rose petals, allow to steep for about 15 minutes and then drain off. Beat the egg yolk with sugar until frothy, add the rose milk and pasteurise in a water bath at 85 °C. Quickly cool down to 4 °C and then fold in the cream and the rose water. For further processing see Stages.

Bedruckte Folie auf eine Rolle aufrollen

Roll the printed foil onto a roll

4

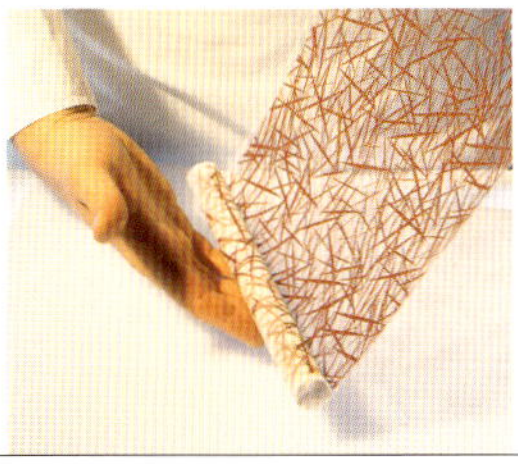

Tiefgefrorenen Stab ausformen

Shape the deep-frozen baton

Mit Klebeband fixieren

Attach with adhesive tape

5

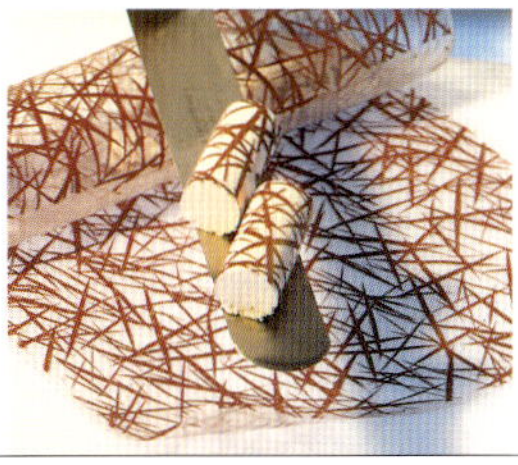

Fertiges bedrucktes Rosenhalbgefrorenes

Finished printed rose parfait baton

Rosenhalbgefrorenes mit einem Spritzbeutel eindressieren und tiefgefrieren

Pipe in the rose parfait, using a piping bag, and deep-freeze

Raspberry vinegar caramel sauce

100 g	*sugar*
50 g	*raspberry vinegar*
25 g	*raspberry brandy*

Process the sugar to caramel and douse with the raspberry vinegar. Add the raspberry brandy and adjust to the required consistency.

Himbeeressig-Karamell-Sauce

100 g	*Zucker*
50 g	*Himbeeressig*
25 g	*Himbeergeist*

Zucker zu Karamell verarbeiten und mit dem Himbeeressig ablöschen. Himbeergeist zugießen und auf die gewünschte Konsistenz bringen.

Drink recommendation

Abtei Muri, Rosenmuskateller, 2002, South Tyrol, Italy

Getränkeempfehlung

Abtei Muri, Rosenmuskateller, 2002, Südtirol, Italien

Budapester Herbst

Autumn in Budapest

Ungarn mit seiner k.-u.-k.-Vergangenheit ist einer der grossen Eckpfeiler im deutschsprachigen Raum für Desserts. In ungarischen Konditoreien hatte ich das Vergnügen, diese Desserts probieren zu dürfen. Hier meine Variante eines ungarischen Klassikers.

As a former part of the Austro-Hungarian Empire, Hungary established itself as a stronghold for desserts. I had the privilege and pleasure of trying out some of these desserts in Hungarian patisseries. Here is my version of a Hungarian classic.

Ingredients	**Zusammensetzung**
Viennese crêpes	Palatschinken-Crêpes
Chocolate sauce	Schokoladensauce
Hazelnut meringue	Haselnussbaiser
Vanilla cream	Vanillesahne
Rum Marsala raisins	Rum-Marsala-Rosinen
Hazelnut brittle	Haselnusskrokant
Sugar threads	Zuckerfäden
Ingredients for 10 desserts	Zutaten für 10 Desserts

Palatschinken-Crêpes

390 g	*Milch*
300 g	*Mehl*
150 g	*Vollei*
60 g	*Eigelb*
195 g	*Sahne*
45 g	*Öl*
45 g	*Zucker*
2 g	*Salz*

Alle Zutaten mit einem Mixstab aufmixen, dann durch ein Sieb passieren. Mindestens 1 Stunde stehen lassen. Auf einem Crêpeseisen oder in der Pfanne dünne Crêpes backen.

Viennese crêpes

390 g	*milk*
300 g	*flour*
150 g	*whole egg*
60 g	*egg yolk*
195 g	*cream*
45 g	*oil*
45 g	*sugar*
2 g	*salt*

Use a hand-held blender to blend all ingredients and then pass through a sieve. Leave to rest for at least 1 hour. Bake thin crêpes on a crêpe maker or in a frying pan.

1

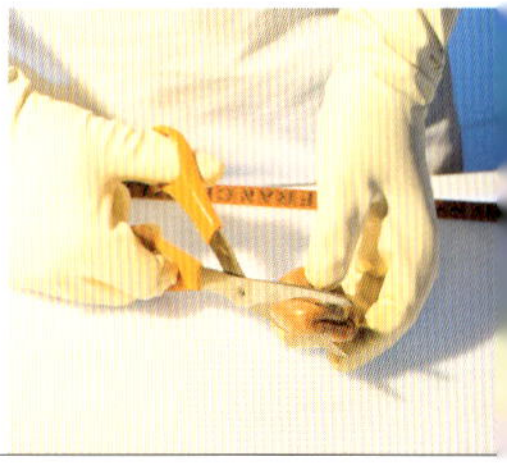

2

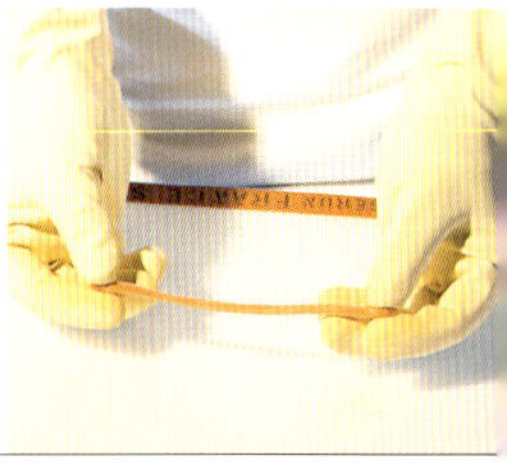

3

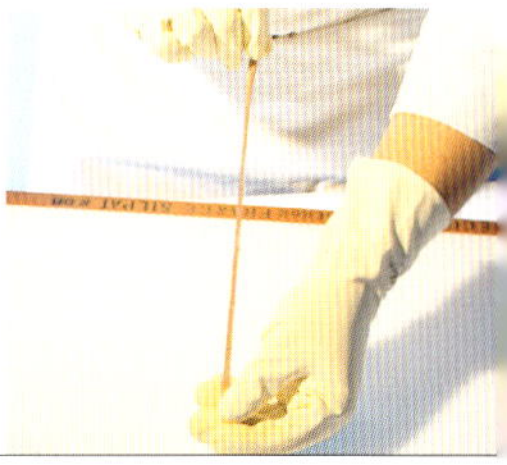

Schokoladensauce

100 g	*Sahne*
150 g	*Milch*
25 g	*Glukose*
	Mark von 1 Vanilleschote
75 g	*Bitterkuvertüre, 66 %*

Sahne, Milch, Glukose und Vanillemark aufkochen. Milchsahne durch ein Sieb gießen und der fein gehackten Bitterkuvertüre zugeben. Die Butter untermixen, dann kalt stellen.

Chocolate sauce

100 g	*cream*
150 g	*milk*
25 g	*glucose*
	pith of 1 vanilla pod
75 g	*dark couverture, 66 %*

Bring the cream, milk, glucose and vanilla pith to boil. Pour the milk and cream through a sieve and then add to the finely chopped dark couverture. Blend in the butter and put in a cool place.

Etwas vom Karamell abschneiden

Cut a piece off the caramel

Gleichmäßig auseinander ziehen

Pull it apart evenly

In die Länge ziehen

Pull it lengthways

4

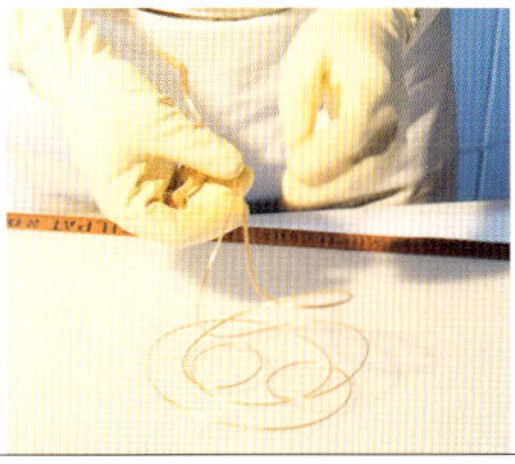

Zuckerfäden ineinander rollen

Roll the sugar threads into each other

5

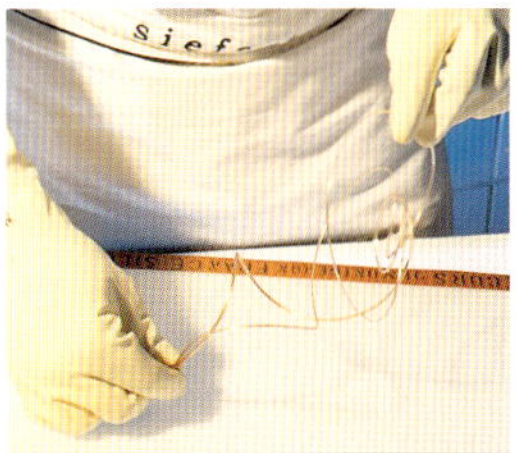

Zuckerfäden auseinander ziehen

Pull the sugar threads apart

Vanilla cream

3	*sheets of gelatine*
20 g	*sugar*
20 g	*corn starch*
50 g	*egg yolk*
200 g	*milk*
	pith of 2 vanilla pods
130 g	*white couverture*
300 g	*whipped cream*

Soak the gelatine in cold water, mix the sugar with the corn starch and egg yolk, boil up the milk with the vanilla pith and let it slowly run into the sugar mixture. Bring to boil and then add the squeezed-out gelatine. Add white, finely chopped couverture and stir into a smooth mixture. Gradually fold in the cream and then leave in a cold place.

Vanillesahne

3	*Blatt Gelatine*
20 g	*Zucker*
20 g	*Cremepulver*
50 g	*Eigelb*
200 g	*Milch*
	Mark von 2 Vanilleschoten
130 g	*weiße Kuvertüre*
300 g	*geschlagene Sahne*

Gelatine in kaltem Wasser einweichen, Zucker mit Cremepulver und Eigelb mischen, Milch mit Vanillemark aufkochen und langsam in den Zuckermix einlaufen lassen. Kurz aufkochen, dann die ausgepresste Gelatine zugeben. Weiße, fein gehackte Kuvertüre zugeben und zu einer glatten Masse verrühren. Die Sahne nach und nach unterziehen, dann kalt stellen.

Rum-Marsala-Rosinen

200 g	*Läuterzucker*
250 g	*Rosinen*
250 g	*Marsala-Dessertwein*
100 g	*brauner Rum*

Läuterzucker mit den Rosinen kurz aufkochen, durch ein Sieb in ein verschließbares Glas geben, Marsala und Rum zugießen, verschließen und mindestens 4 Tage lang ziehen lassen.

Rum Marsala raisins

200 g	*sugar syrup*
250 g	*raisins*
250 g	*Marsala dessert wine*
100 g	*brown rum*

Bring the sugar syrup and the raisins to boil, pass through a sieve into a glass container with a lid, add the Marsala and rum, cover the container and allow to steep for at least 4 days.

Haselnusskrokant

50 g	*Glukose*
250 g	*Zucker*
100 g	*Haselnüsse, gehobelt*

Glukose und Zucker zu einem Karamell kochen. Wenn keine Kristalle mehr zu sehen sind, die Haselnüsse unterarbeiten. Zwischen zwei Backmatten dünn ausrollen und brechen.

Hazelnut brittle

50 g	*glucose*
250 g	*sugar*
100 g	*hazelnuts, shredded*

Boil the glucose and sugar to make caramel. When all crystals have disappeared, work in the hazelnuts. Roll out thinly between two baking mats and break up.

Hazelnut meringue

200 g	*egg white*
100 g	*sugar*
50 g	*hazelnut paste*

Add sugar to the egg white and beat until stiff. Work the egg bit by bit into the hazelnut paste.

Haselnussbaiser

200 g	*Eiweiß*
100 g	*Zucker*
50 g	*Haselnusspaste*

Das Eiweiß mit Zucker zu einem stabilen Schnee schlagen. Den Schnee nach und nach unter die Haselnusspaste arbeiten.

Drink recommendation

1993 Tocaji Aszu 6 Puttonyos Diznókö, Hungary

Getränkeempfehlung

1993 Tocaji Aszu 6 Puttonyos Diznókö, Ungarn

KARIBISCHER SOMMERWIND

CARIBBEAN SUMMER WIND

Eines der leichtesten und erfrischendsten Sommerdesserts, das ich kenne. Es erinnert mich immer an meine Hochzeitsreise in die Karibik.

One of the lightest and most refreshing summer desserts I know. It always reminds me of my honeymoon to the Caribbean.

Ingredients	Zusammensetzung
Coconut tuille	Kokostuille
Coconut granité with white rum	Kokosgranité mit weissem Rum
Passion fruit sauce	Maracujasauce
Strawberry tempura on a vanilla stick	Erdbeertempura auf Vanillestange
Passion fruit espuma	Maracujaespuma
Ingredients for 10 desserts	Zutaten für 10 Desserts

Kokostuille

150 g *Zucker*
2,5 g *Pektin*
100 g *Butter*
50 g *Glukosesirup*
50 g *Kokosmilch*
25 g *Kokosraspel*

Zucker und Pektin mischen, mit Butter und Glukosesirup aufkochen und Kokosmilch und Kokosraspel zugeben. Kühlen, mit einem Plastikspritzsack auf eine Silikonbackmatte aufdressieren. Bei 170 °C backen.

Kokosgranité mit weissem Rum

285 g *Kokosmilch*
55 g *Zucker*
55 g *weißer Rum, 40 Vol.-%*

Kokosmilch mit Zucker aufkochen, dann abkühlen lassen. Rum zugießen, in kleine stabförmige Gummibackformen geben, tiefgefrieren und nach Bedarf mit einer feinen Reibe zu Schnee hobeln.

Maracujasauce

50 g *Zucker*
50 g *Trockenbeeerenauslese*
150 g *Maracujafruchtfleisch*

Zucker leicht karamellisieren, mit der Trockenbeerenauslese ablöschen, dann das Maracujafruchtfleisch zugeben.

Coconut tuille

150 g *sugar*
2.5 g *pectin*
100 g *butter*
50 g *glucose syrup*
50 g *coconut milk*
25 g *grated coconut*

Mix the sugar and pectin, bring to boil with butter and glucose syrup and add the coconut milk and grated coconut. Cool the mixture, then use a plastic piping bag to arrange the mixture onto a silicon baking mat. Bake at 170 °C.

Coconut granité with white rum

285 g *coconut milk*
55 g *sugar*
55 g *white rum, 40 vol. %*

Bring the coconut milk and the sugar to boil and then allow to cool down. Add the rum, pour into small lolly-shaped rubber baking moulds, deep-freeze and use a fine grater to grate some "snow" as required.

Passion fruit sauce

50 g *sugar*
50 g *Trockenbeerenauslese wine*
150 g *Passion fruit pulp*

Lightly caramelise the sugar, douse with the Trockenbeerenauslese and then add the passion fruit pulp.

1

2

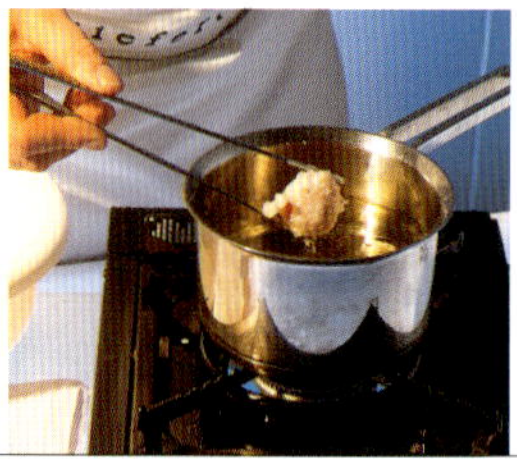
3

4

5

6

Tempurateig herstellen

Make the tempura batter

Erdbeeren in den Tempurteig tauchen, kurz abtropfen lassen …

Dip the strawberries into the tempura batter and allow to drip off briefly …

… frittieren, dann herausnehmen

… deep-fry, then remove …

Auf Küchenkrepp abtropfen lassen

… and place on a paper towel to drain off

Erdbeertempura auf eine Vanillestange stecken

Push the strawberry tempura onto a vanilla stick

Mit Puderzucker bestreuen

Apply a dusting of icing sugar

Strawberry tempura on a vanilla stick

150 g	*tempura flour*
75 g	*water*
300 g	*strawberries*

Stir the water into the tempura flour and then leave to stand. Pull the strawberries through the tempura batter, allow to drain off and then fry in oil. Place them on a paper towel to drain off. Push the strawberry tempura onto a vanilla stick and apply a dusting of icing sugar.

Passion fruit espuma

2	*sheets of gelatine*
375 g	*passion fruit juice*
55 g	*sugar*
125 g	*apricot puree*

Soak the gelatine in cold water. Heat up the passion fruit juice and sugar, add the squeezed-out gelatine and then gradually stir in the apricot puree. Pass everything through a fine sieve into an espuma siphon, insert 2 gas cartridges and put into a very cold place for at least 4 hours.

Drink recommendation

Trockenbeerenauslese 2001, von Renner, Gols, Burgenland, Austria

Erdbeertempura auf Vanillestange

150 g	*Tempuramehl*
75 g	*Wasser*
300 g	*Erdbeeren*

Tempuramehl mit Wasser anrühren und kurz stehen lassen. Die Erdbeeren durch den Tempurateig ziehen, abtropfen lassen, dann in Frittieröl ausbacken. Auf Küchenkrepp abtropfen lassen. Erdbeertempura auf eine Vanillestange stecken und mit Puderzucker bestäuben.

Maracujaespuma

2	*Blatt Gelatine*
375 g	*Maracujasaft*
55 g	*Zucker*
125 g	*Aprikosenpüree*

Gelatine in kaltem Wasser einweichen. Maracujasaft mit Zucker erhitzen, Gelatine ausgepresst zugeben, nach und nach das Aprikosenpüree unterrühren. Alles durch ein Haarsieb in einen Espumasiphon geben, 2 Gaspatronen einschrauben und mindestens 4 Stunden sehr kalt stellen.

Getränkeempfehlung

Trockenbeerenauslese 2001, von Renner, Gols, Burgenland, Österreich

FRENCH CONNECTION

Alles Käse? Vielleicht. Aber ich denke, auch ein Käsegang kann mal etwas anderes sein als nur drei Scheiben Käse mit Trauben und Trockenfrüchten auf einem Teller.

Anybody for cheese? Perhaps. But I think a cheese course can be more imaginative than just three slices of cheddar with grapes and dried fruit on a plate.

Ingredients	Zusammensetzung
Roquefort crème mille-feuille from filo pastry	Roquefortcreme-Millefeuille aus Filoteig
Red wine butter ice-cream	Rotweinbuttereis
Red wine pears	Rotweinbirnen
Red wine reduction	Rotweinreduktion
Walnuts	Walnüsse
Ingredients for 10 desserts	Zutaten für 10 Desserts

1

Gewürze dem Rotwein beigeben

Add the spices to the red wine

2

Birne schälen

Peel the pear

3

In Rotwein legen und kurz aufkochen

Lay into the red wine and bring it to boil

4

Nach einigen Stunden herausnehmen

Remove it after some hours

Millefeuille aus Filoteig

10	*Blatt Filoteig*
30 g	*Vollei*
10 g	*Kümmel*
10 g	*Schwarzkümmel*
40 g	*Leinsamen*
40 g	*Sesam*

Filoteig in Rechtecke schneiden, mit dem Vollei bestreichen und mit einer Mischung aus den verschiedenen Samen bestreuen. Auf eine Backmatte legen und bei 160 °C goldgelb backen. Auskühlen lassen.

Millefeuille from filo pastry

10	*sheets of filo pastry*
30 g	*whole egg*
10 g	*caraway seed*
10 g	*black caraway seeds*
40 g	*linseed*
40 g	*sesame seeds*

Cut the filo pastry into rectangles, brush with the whole egg and sprinkle a mixture of the different seeds over it. Place on a baking mat and bake in the oven at 160 °C to a golden yellow colour. Leave to cool down.

5

Birne halbieren

Halve the pear

6

Mit dem Kugelausstecher das Kerngehäuse entfernen

Remove the core with the corer

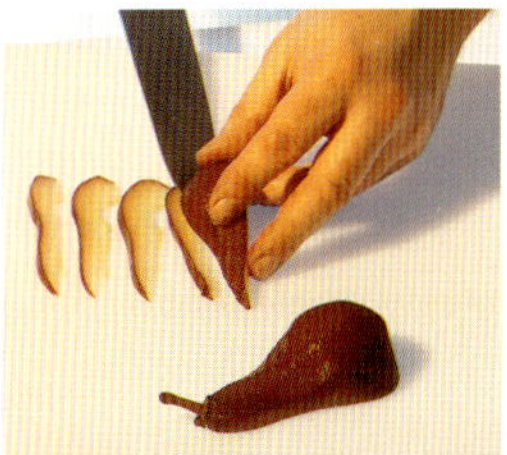

7

Birne in dünne gleichmäßige Spalten schneiden

Cut the pear into thin and even segments

Roquefort Crème

300 g	*Roquefort cheese*
150 g	*curd cheese (quark), 40 %*
150 g	*butter*
	salt
	pepper

First, blend the Roquefort and curd cheese until smooth. Then add the remaining ingredients and whip up to a light crème. Use a piping bag with a round nozzle to arrange the crème between the sheets of filo pastry.

Roquefortcreme

300 g	*Roquefortkäse*
150 g	*Quark, 40 %*
150 g	*Butter*
	Salz
	Pfeffer

Zuerst Roquefort und Quark glatt arbeiten. Dann mit den restlichen Zutaten zu einer leichten Creme aufschlagen. Mit einem Spritzbeutel (Lochtülle) zwischen die Filoteigblätter dressieren.

Rotweinbuttereis

375 g	*Burgunder, Rotwein*
125 g	*Maury-Dessertwein*
20 g	*Cassislikör*
	Mark von 1 Vanilleschote
	Abrieb von 1/4 Orange
25 g	*Blütenhonig*
50 g	*Zucker*
60 g	*Eigelb*
50 g	*Butter*

Burgunder, Maury-Dessertwein sowie Cassislikör mit dem Vanillemark und dem Orangenabrieb auf 250 g Menge einkochen. Honig, Zucker und Eigelb schaumig rühren. Heiße Weinflüssigkeit zugeben und im Wasserbad bei 85 °C pasteurisieren. Masse durch ein Sieb in die Butter gießen und mit einem Mixstab stabil unterarbeiten. Sofort auf 4 °C herunterkühlen, mindestens 4 Stunden reifen lassen und in der Eismaschine abfrieren.

Red wine butter ice-cream

375 g	*red Burgundy wine*
125 g	*Maury dessert wine*
20 g	*Cassis liqueur*
	pith of 1 vanilla pod
	zest of 1/4 orange
25 g	*flower honey*
50 g	*sugar*
60 g	*egg yolk*
50 g	*butter*

Add the Burgundy wine, Maury dessert wine and Cassis liqueur together with the vanilla pith and the orange zest and boil to reduce to 250 g. Beat the honey, sugar and egg yolk until frothy. Add the hot wine liquid and then pasteurise at 85 °C in a bowl in hot water. Pass the mixture through a sieve into the butter and use a hand-held blender to blend it all firmly together. Then immediately cool the mixture down to 4 °C, leave to mature for at least 4 hours and then freeze in the ice-cream machine.

Spicy red wine pears

5	*pears*
500 g	*red wine*
50 g	*sugar*
25 g	*chestnut honey*
1	*twig of thyme*
1	*piece long pepper*
3	*grains of allspice*
1	*bay leaf*

Peel the pears, bring the red wine to boil with the other ingredients, then add the pears and allow these to boil briefly. Let the pears steep until cooked through, then remove from the stove and allow to steep overnight. Core and cut the pears as required.

Rotweingewürzbirnen

5	*Birnen*
500 g	*Rotwein*
50 g	*Zucker*
25 g	*Kastanienhonig*
1	*Thymianzweig*
1	*Stück langer Pfeffer*
3	*Pimentkörner*
1	*Lorbeerblatt*

Birnen schälen, Rotwein mit den anderen Zutaten aufkochen und die Birnen darin kurz aufkochen lassen. Birnen bis zur Garprobe ziehen lassen, dann vom Herd nehmen und über Nacht ziehen lassen. Nach Bedarf entkernen und passend schneiden.

Red wine reduction

Reduce the red wine stock from the pears until it has the consistency of sauce.

Rotweinreduktion

Den Rotweinfond von den Birnen auf Saucenkonsistenz reduzieren.

Drink recommendation

Mas Cornet Banyuls Rimage 2002, Cave de l'Abbé Rous, Vin Doux Naturel, Banyuls, France

Getränkeempfehlung

Mas Cornet Banyuls Rimage 2002, Cave de l'Abbé Rous, Vin Doux Naturel, Banyuls, Frankreich

ZUCKER

SUGAR

ISOMALT

ISOMALT

Grundrezeptur 1

1000 g *Isomalt*
250 g *Wasser*

Isomalt und Wasser auf 170 °C erhitzen.

Diese Grundrezeptur eignet sich besonders gut für große Schaustücke.

Basic recipe 1

1,000 g *Isomalt*
250 g *water*

Heat up Isomalt and water to 170 °C.

This basic recipe is particularly suitable for large exhibits.

Grundrezeptur 2

1000 g *Isomalt*
20 g *Wasser*

Isomalt auf dem Herd oder in der Mikrowelle auflösen und mit dem Wasser die Isomaltmasse ablöschen.

Diese Grundrezeptur ist zum Ziehen gut geeignet.

Basic recipe 2

1,000 g *Isomalt*
20 g *water*

Dissolve Isomalt on the cooker or in the microwave and then douse the Isomalt with water.

This basic recipe lends itself for pulling.

Grundrezeptur 3

1000 g *Isomalt*

Isomalt auf dem Herd oder in der Mikrowelle auflösen.

Diese Grundrezeptur nehme ich zum Gießen kleinerer Figuren oder Bodenplatten.

Basic recipe 3

1,000 g *Isomalt*

Dissolve Isomalt on the cooker or in the microwave.

I use the basic recipe for casting smaller figures or base plates.

ZUCKER

SUGAR

Sugar recipe

1,000 g	*granulated sugar*
500 g	*cold water*
200 g	*glucose syrup*

Boil up the granulated sugar and the cold water. Then add the glucose syrup and boil up again.

If possible leave covered overnight. Then boil this syrup to 156 °C while keeping the inside edge of the pan constantly clean with cold water and a brush so that no syrup splashes can settle at the edge of the pan and crystallise, since that would cause the syrup to die off (crystallise) quicker.

Add 10 drops of tartaric acid and boil everything to 160 °C. Then douse immediately in cold water and pour onto a baking mat over a marble slab. As soon as the edges begin to cool down, work gently from the outside inwards. When the material no longer runs apart, cut it into small pieces and store in an airtight container.

Zuckerrezeptur

1000 g	*Kristallzucker*
500 g	*kaltes Wasser*
200 g	*Glukosesirup*

Den Kristallzucker und das kalte Wasser zusammen aufkochen. Den Glukosesirup zugeben und erneut aufkochen.

Wenn möglich zugedeckt über Nacht stehen lassen. Dann unter ständigem Reinwaschen mit einem Pinsel und kaltem Wasser den Kesselinnenrand sauber halten, so dass sich keine Zuckersirupspritzer am Kesselrand festsetzen und auskristallisieren können, denn das würde die Masse zu einem schnelleren Absterben (Auskristallisieren) bringen. Diesen Sirup auf 156 °C kochen.

10 Tropfen Weinsteinsäure zugeben und alles auf 160 °C kochen. Sofort in kaltem Wasser abschrecken, auf eine Marmorplatte, die mit einer Backmatte belegt ist, aufgießen. Sobald sich die Ränder anfangen auszukühlen, leicht von außen nach innen arbeiten. Wenn die Masse nicht mehr auseinander läuft, in kleine Stücke schneiden und luftdicht aufbewahren.

Hochzeitsschwäne

Wedding Swans

Schwäne sind dankbar und schnell für Hochzeiten realisierbar. Natürlich kann man sie auch weiss gezogen herstellen, aber in klarem Zucker geblasen haben sie eine filigrane Leichtigkeit und passen in ihrer Eleganz zu jeder Torte.

Swans are popular for weddings and can be made quite quickly. You can of course create them in white, but if you blow them in clear sugar they have a delicate appearance and add an elegant decorative touch to any wedding cake.

Techniques

- Basic body: blown
- Wings and leaves: pulled and moulded
- Rose and bent sugar threads: pulled
- Base slab: cast

Techniken

- Grundkörper geblasen
- Flügel und Blätter gezogen und gestempelt
- Rose und gebogene Zuckerfäden gezogen
- Grundplatte gegossen

Making the parts

First blow the basic swan bodies – one standing up and one floating on water. Then pull out the wings from the same unpulled sugar and mould into silicon forms. When the wing cools down, give it the desired posture and when it has completely cooled down, attach it to the body with a torch.

To make the base slab: dissolve some sugar, colour it slightly blue, add metallic powder and pour it into oiled forms on a baking mat. Once it has cooled down, turn out the forms and join the pieces together with liquid sugar.

Make the rose (see page 320) in the colour of your choice. Tip: Ask the customer for the colour of the bride's bouquet – then you can make the rose in that colour. Customers will appreciate your attention to detail.

Pull and mould the sugar to make the leaves (see section for making the wings). To make the pulled and bent sugar threads, colour the sugar in leaf colour and then pull, cut off and bend slightly.

Putting it all together

Warm up sugar pieces and attach to the standing swan. Heat the sugar pieces fully and then place the swan onto the base plate and stabilise it with a cold air fan. Repeat the same process for the floating swan in front. Place and fix the rose to the base plate, then attach the leaves and finally the pulled sugar threads.

1

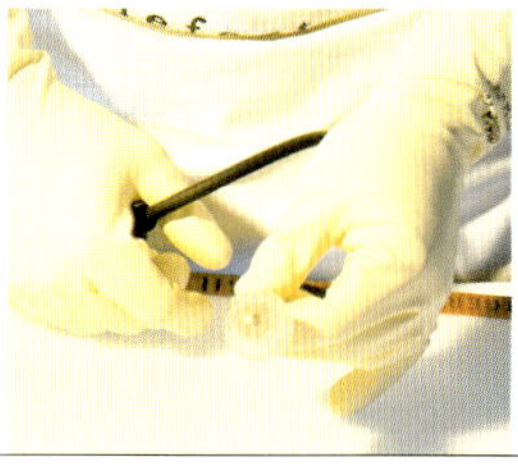

Zucker ansetzen und leicht zur Kugel blasen

Prepare the sugar and blow into a ball shape

2

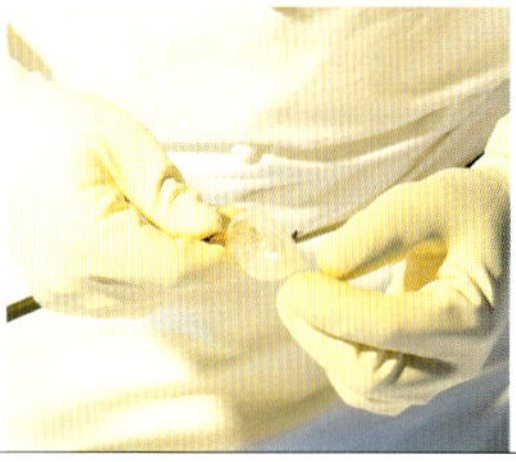

Zuerst den Schnabel modellieren

First form the beak

3

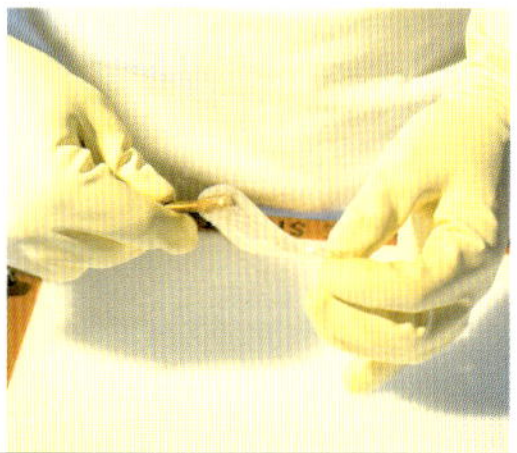

Den Kopf herausmodellieren

Then shape the head

4
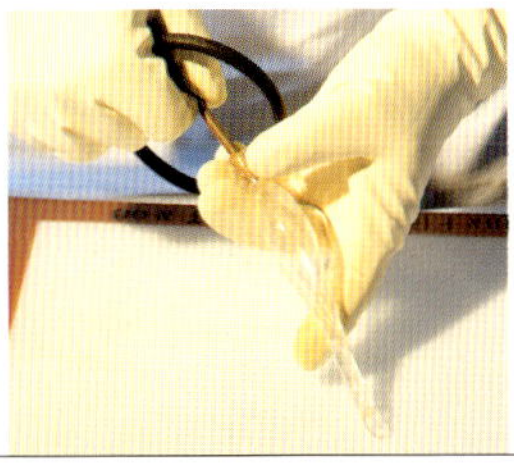
Das Ende herausmodellieren

Now model the rear end

5
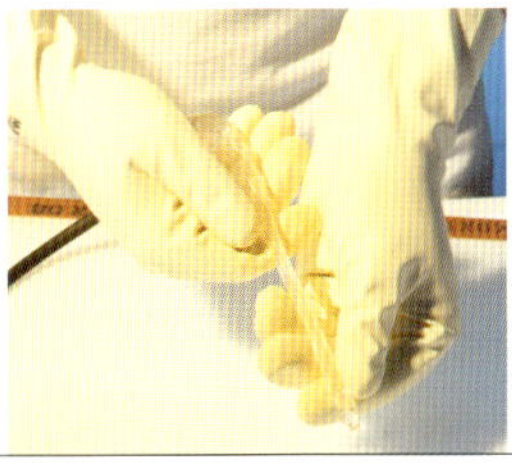
Mit beiden Händen den Hals lang ziehen

Make the long neck using both hands

6
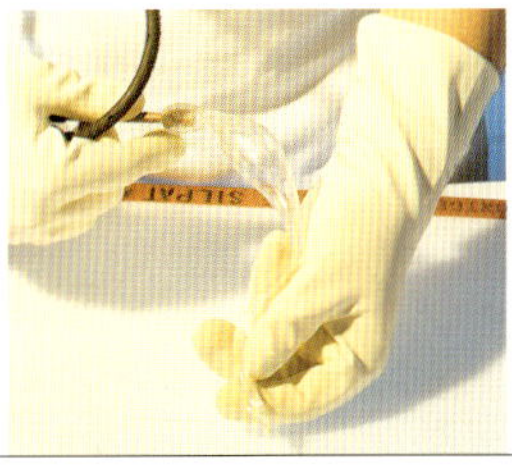
Die gewollte Form geben und den Rumpf leicht aufpumpen

Adjust the overall shape to your liking and pump up the body slightly

7
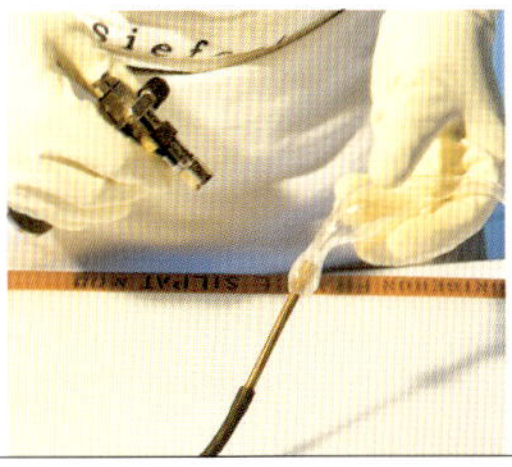
Mit einem Gasbrenner das Schwanzende gleichmäßig erwärmen

Warm the tail end evenly with a torch

8
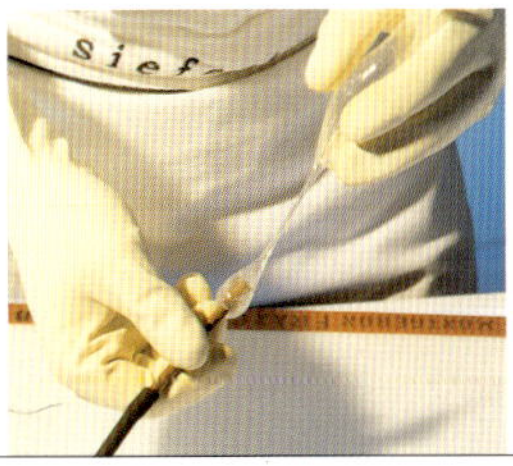
Gleichmäßig abziehen und mit einem Kaltluftföhn stabilisieren

Pull off evenly and stabilise the figure with a cold air fan

9
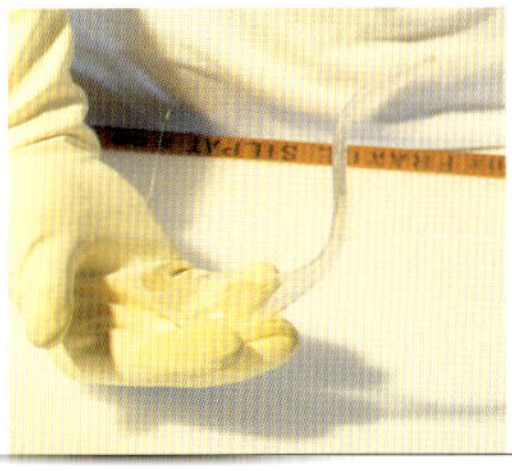
Fertiger Schwanenkörper

The swan is ready

Herstellung

Zuerst die zwei Schwanengrundkörper blasen – einer stehend, einer schwimmend. Dann die Flügel aus dem gleichen ungezogenen Zucker ausziehen und in Silikonformen stempeln. Beim Erkalten dem Flügel die gewünschte Flügelhaltung geben und, sobald erkaltet, mit einem Gasbrenner ansetzen.

Für die Bodenplatte Zucker auflösen, leicht blau einfärben, Metallicpuder zugeben und in geölte Formen auf Backmatte gießen. Nach dem Erkalten ausformen und mit flüssigem Zucker zusammensetzen.

Rose (siehe Seite 320) in gewünschter Farbe herstellen. Tipp: Machen Sie die Rose in der Farbe des Brautstraußes. Kunden freuen sich über diese Aufmerksamkeit.

Blätter gezogen und gestempelt (siehe Herstellung Flügel). Für die ausgezogenen, gebogenen Zuckerfäden Zucker in Blattfarbe ausziehen, abschneiden und leicht biegen.

Zusammensetzung

Zuckerstückchen erwärmen und an den stehenden Schwan anbringen. Zuckerstückchen vollkommen erwärmen und den Schwan auf die Grundplatte setzen und mit einem Kaltluftföhn stabilisieren. Den vorderen, sitzenden Schwan ebenso anbringen. Die Rose auf die Grundplatte ansetzen, danach die Blätter und zum Schluss die ausgezogenen Zuckerfäden anbringen.

OSTERHASE

EASTER BUNNY

Ostern ist in der fröhlichen leichten Jahreszeit, zu der sehr gut bunte, witzige Figuren passen. Mein Lehrer in Sachen Zucker, Willi Pfund, sagte immer: „Wenn du die Kinder ans Schaufenster bringst, hast du die Kunden von morgen vor dir, und die Oma kauft bestimmt ein Schokoladenei!“

Easter is a time of light-hearted anticipation, so now is the time for bright and funny figures. Willi Pfund, who taught me everything about sugar, always said: "If you can get the children to stand in front of your shop window, then you've recruited tomorrow's customers, and Granny is sure to buy a chocolate egg!"

Techniques

- Suit and bows: ribbon technique
- Egg, rabbit body, arms and head: blown
- Base plate and back support: cast
- Mouth, nose and brush: shaped / modelled
- Blossoms and leaves: pulled

Techniken

- Anzug und Schleifen Bändertechnik
- Ei, Hasenkörper, Arme und Kopf geblasen
- Grundplatten und rückseitiger Ständer gegossen
- Mund, Nase und Pinsel modelliert
- Blüten und Blätter gezogen

Herstellung

Zuerst aus klarem, leicht grünlich marmoriertem Zucker die drei Bodenplatten und den ovalen, oben offenen Ständer gießen. Zucker vollständig auskühlen lassen, dann Bodenplatten sowie den Ständer mit etwas flüssigem Zucker zusammensetzen und ebenfalls gut auskühlen lassen.

Für die geblasene Umrandung zwei zweifarbig gedrehte, geblasene Hörner herstellen, welche der Biegung des Ständers angepasst werden. Die Enden nicht schneiden, sondern leicht unregelmäßig abziehen, gut auskühlen lassen und mit den spitzen Enden nach oben ansetzen.

Für den Hasen zuerst den leicht nach vorne gebogenen Körper aus weißem oder gelbem Zucker blasen, dann die Arme (kann man natürlich bei kleineren Figuren auch modellieren) und den Kopf mit den Ohren blasen. Dafür zuerst eine Kugel blasen, diese spitz zulaufend und in der Mitte auseinander modellieren. Sobald das Kopfvolumen erreicht ist, die zugespitzte Seite bis zur Mitte auseinander schneiden und die Form sowie Stellung der Ohren ausmodellieren.

Körper und Kopf des Hasen zusammensetzen, mit dem Airbrush braun schminken und trocknen lassen. Die Arme ebenfalls schminken.

Making the parts

First of all, cast the three base slabs and the oval support, which is open at the top, from clear sugar with slight greenish marbling. Leave the sugar to cool down completely, then assemble the base slabs and the support with a little liquid sugar and again leave to cool thoroughly.

For the blown edging, produce two twisted, blown horns in two colours and adapt them to the curved shape of the support. Do not cut the ends but pull them off slightly irregularly, leave to cool down well and attach with the pointed ends uppermost.

To make the rabbit, first blow the body from white or yellow sugar, making sure that it bends forward slightly, then blow the arms (with smaller models you can also shape these by hand) and the head with the ears. To do that you first blow a ball which you shape to a point at one end and separate in the middle. When the head has reached the right size, cut the pointed end in two up to the middle, and form the shape and position of the ears.

Join the head and body of the rabbit, apply brown colour with the air brush and leave to dry. Also colour the arms.

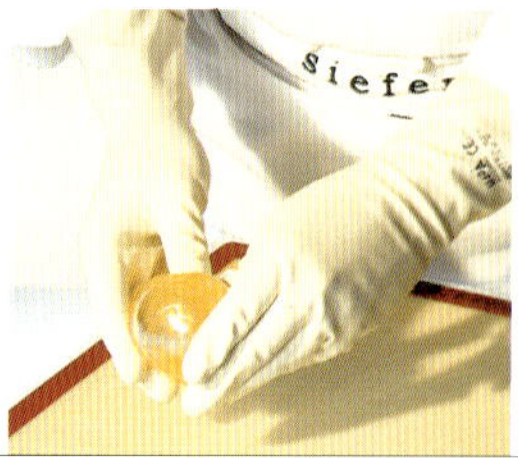
1

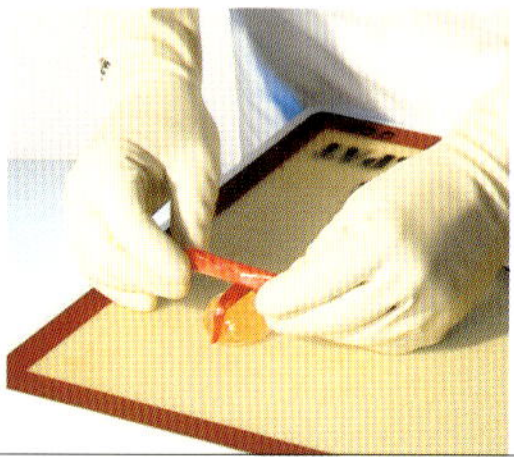
2

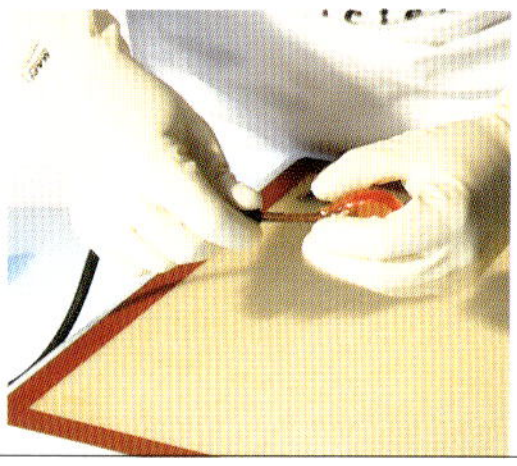
3

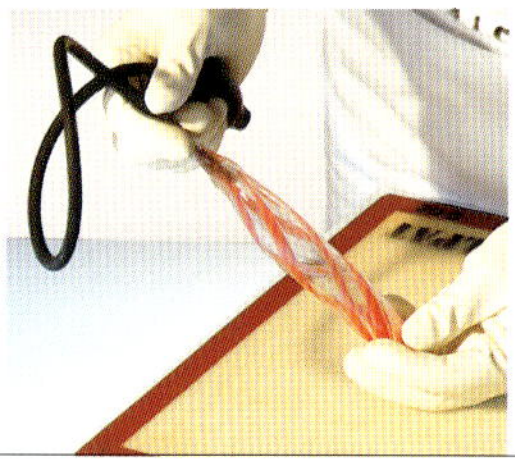
4

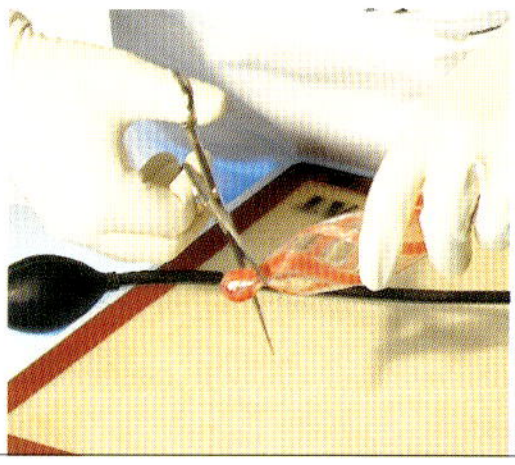
5

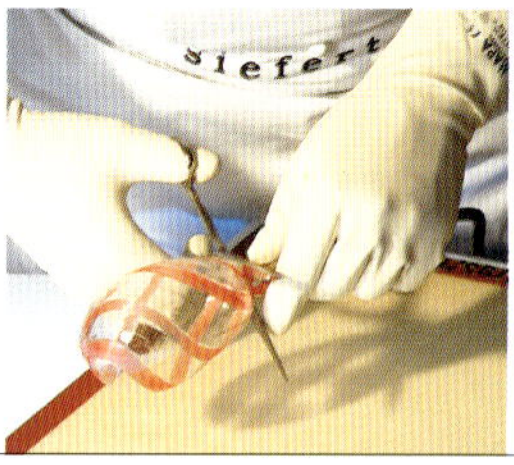
6

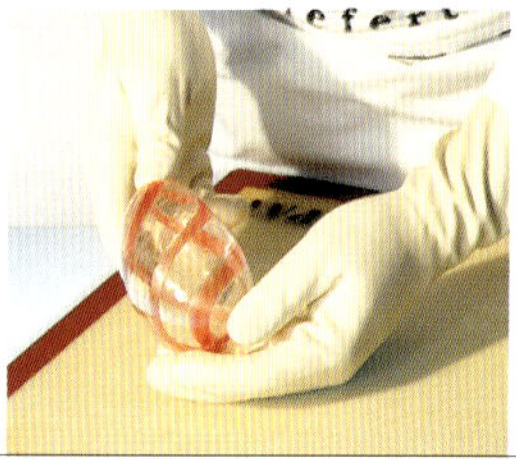
7

Klaren Zucker zur Kugel formen

Form clear sugar into a ball

Gezogenen Zucker über Kreuz auf Zuckerkugel legen

Pull the sugar and fold crosswise, then gather up into a ball

Zuckerkugel an Blasebalg ansetzen

Insert the sugar blowing pump into the sugar ball

Zuckerkugel länglich aufblasen, dabei die Enden in die entgegengesetzte Richtung verdrehen

Blow the sugar ball into an oblong shape, twisting the ends in opposite directions

Unteres Ende rundherum gleichmäßig abschneiden

Cut the lower end off evenly all round

Eiförmig aufblasen, dabei oben mit der Schere abmodellieren

Blow it up into the shape of an egg, flattening it at the top with scissors

Das fertige Ei, mit einem Kaltluftföhn stabil ausgekühlt

Cool down the finished egg with a cold air fan until stable

Then dress the rabbit body and arms in the colour of your choice, using the ribbon technique, and model the remaining parts of the face, such as mouth, nose, moustache and hair.

The eyes are best painted on with a fine brush with the figure lying down.

Pull the daffodils and put them together. Pull the leaves irregularly with ribbon technique, blow the Easter eggs, twisted in two colours, pull the ribbon for the bow; then fold together and attach, and finally form the brush.

Danach den Hasenkörper und Arme in gewünschter Farbe mit Hilfe der Bandtechnik anziehen und die restlichen Teile im Gesicht, wie Mund, Nase, Schnurrbart, Haare, anmodellieren.

Die Augen am besten im Liegen mit einem feinen Pinsel aufmalen.

Die Osterglocken ziehen und zusammensetzen, die Blätter in der Bandtechnik unregelmäßig ziehen, die Ostereier zweifarbig gedreht blasen, das Band für die Schleife ziehen, zusammenlegen und zusammensetzen, den Pinsel modellieren.

Putting it all together

Place the rabbit so that it looks through the arch from behind and attach the arms afterwards in the required position. First position the Easter eggs, then arrange the daffodils and leaves. Finally attach the bow and brush.

Zusammensetzung

Den Hasen von hinten durch den Bogen schauend befestigen, die Arme je nach Stellung nachträglich anbringen. Zuerst die Ostereier ansetzen, dann die Osterglocken und die Blätter anbringen. Zum Schluss die Schleife und den Pinsel befestigen.

Peter Quak, der Piratenfrosch

Peter Croak, the Pirate Frog

Zum Kindergeburtstag muss es was Lustiges sein, und wenn man klassische Märchen untereinander mixt, kommt immer etwas Witziges dabei raus. Wenn man Kopf, Füsse und Farbe wechselt, hat man ruck-zuck eine Katze, einen Löwen ...

For a child's birthday you should do something cheerful. If you mix up classic fairy tales then the result is always amusing. By changing the head, the feet and the colour, you can quickly get a cat, a lion, and so on.

Techniques

- Basic body, legs, head and the ball: blown
- Eyes, feet, hook, eye patch and hand: shaped/modelled
- Raft: plaited
- Scarf, flag and sail: ribbon technique
- The mast is made from a wooden stick with thread wound around it
- The base slab is cast with a marbled pattern onto oiled and crumpled aluminium foil

Techniken

- Grundkörper, Beine, Kopf und Kugel geblasen
- Augen, Füsse, Haken, Augenklappe und Hand modelliert
- Floss in Flechttechnik
- Schal, Flagge und Segel in Bandtechnik
- Umwickelter Holzstab als Mast
- Grundplatte auf geölte, geknüllte Alufolie marmoriert gegossen

Herstellung

Zuerst das Floß herstellen (siehe Stepps). Für den Mast ein Holzstäbchen mit einem Zuckerfaden gleichmäßig umwickeln. Die Fahne und das Segel in Bandtechnik herstellen. Auf die Fahne mit einem Pinsel einen Totenkopf aufzeichnen. Die Enden des Segels mit einem verdrehten Zuckerfaden abschließen. Fahne und Segel an dem Mast anbringen. Mast auf dem Floß fixieren.

Für den Frosch den Grundkörper birnenförmig blasen. Die Beine ebenfalls blasen und noch warm ansetzen. Füße modellieren und anbringen. Arme, Hand und Haken modellieren und ebenfalls ansetzen. Den Kopf blasen, die Augen platzieren. Mit einem Pinsel das Auge und den Mund aufzeichnen. Augenklappe modellieren und anbringen. Den Kopf auf dem Körper befestigen und mit einem dreifarbig gezogenen Schal umlegen. Eine Kugel blasen.

Zusammensetzung

Den Frosch auf dem Floß befestigen. Kugel passend platzieren und das ganze Floß auf die Grundplatte setzen.

Making the parts

First of all, make the raft (see stages). To make the mast, wind a sugar thread evenly around a wooden stick. Make the flag and the sail in ribbon technique. Use a brush to paint a skull and bones on the flag. Finish the ends of the sail with a twisted sugar thread. Attach the flag and the sail to the mast. Fix the mast on the raft.

To make the frog, blow up the basic body in the shape of a pear. Then blow the legs and attach while still warm. Shape the feet and attach. Shape the arms, hand and hook and attach as well. Blow the head and fix on the eyes. Use a brush to paint on the eye and mouth. Shape the eye patch and attach to the head. Attach the head to the body and drape a scarf around it which you have pulled in three colours. Blow a ball.

Putting it all together

Put the frog onto the raft. Place the ball onto a suitable spot and then put the whole raft onto the base plate.

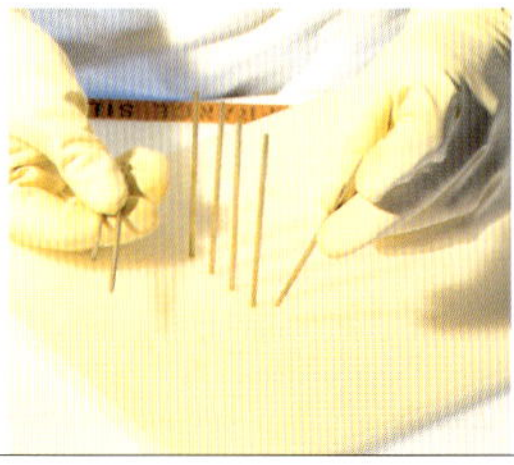

1

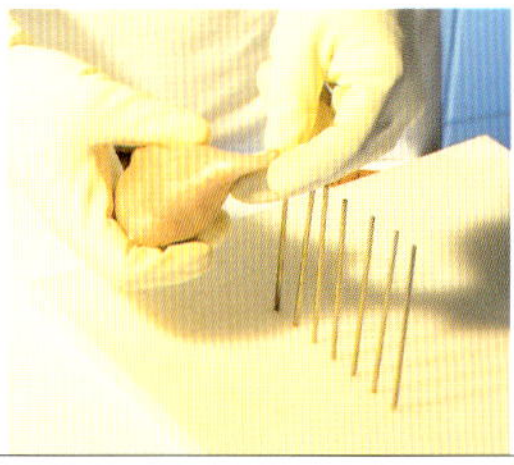

2

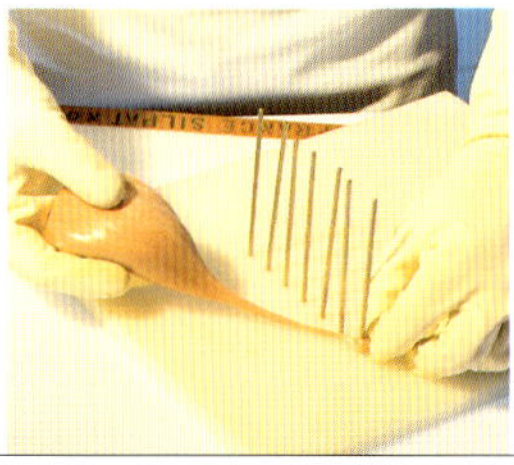

3

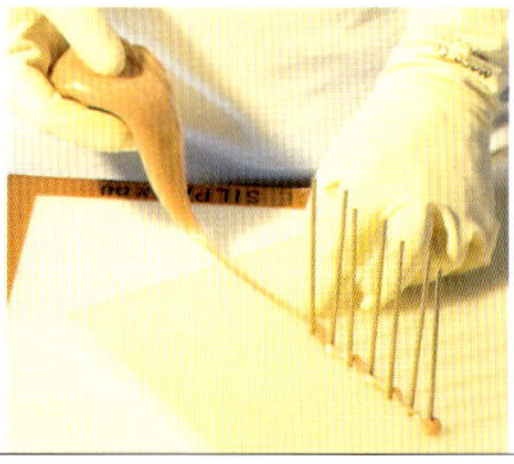

4

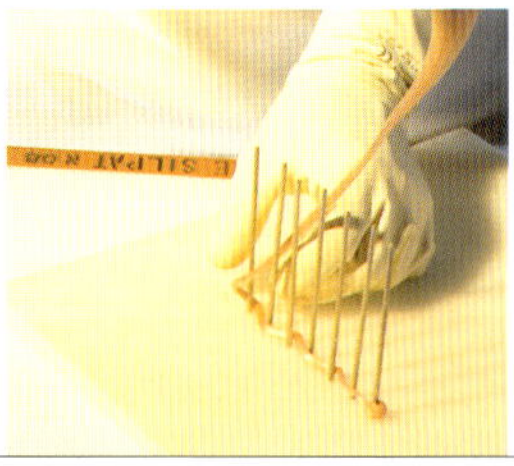

5

6

Stäbe in Flechtbrett stecken

Put sticks into plaiting board

7

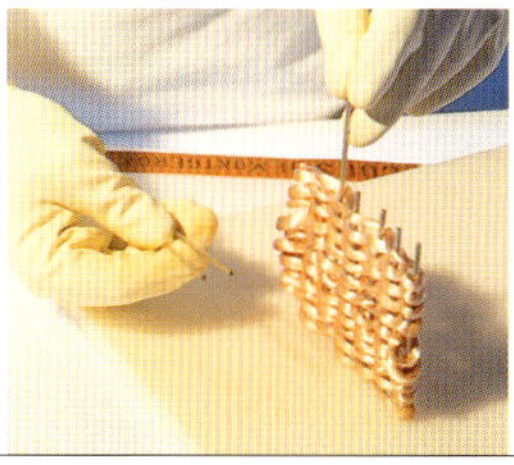

Stäbe herausziehen

Pull out the sticks

Aus einem Zuckerklumpen einen Faden ausziehen

Pull a thread from a sugar lump

8

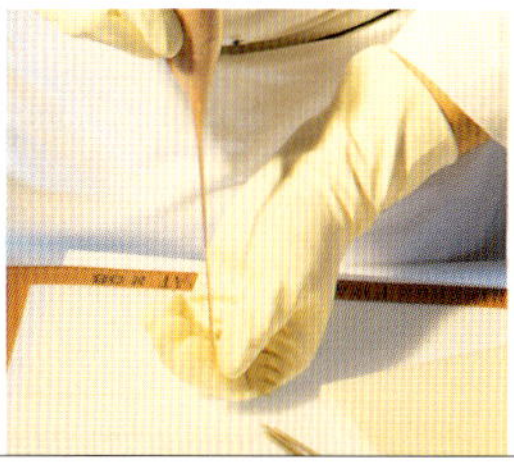

Stäbe aus Zucker ziehen

Pull sticks from sugar

Das Ende des Fadens leicht erwärmen und ansetzen

Slightly warm up the end of the thread and attach

9

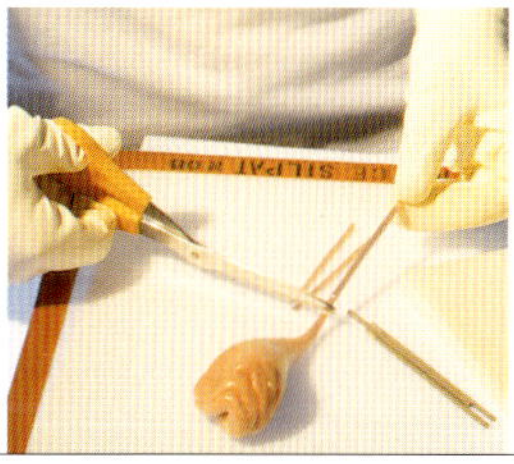

Gewünschte Länge abschneiden

Cut off to the required length

Erste Reihe flechten

Plait the first row

10

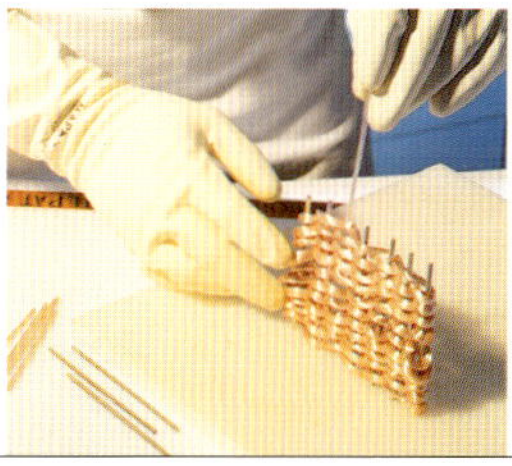

Zuckerstäbe anstatt der Metallstäbe anbringen

Attach the sticks instead of the metal sticks

Nächste Reihe entgegengesetzt draufflechten

Plait the next row in the opposite pattern

11

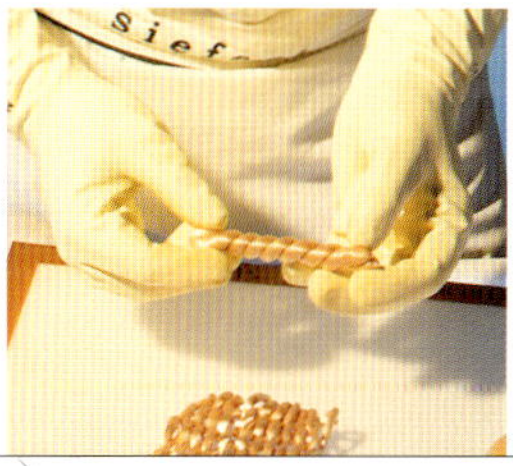

Verdrehte Zuckerstange herstellen

Make a twisted sugar stick

Weiterflechten, bis gewünschte Größe erreicht ist

Keep on plaiting until you have reached the desired size

12

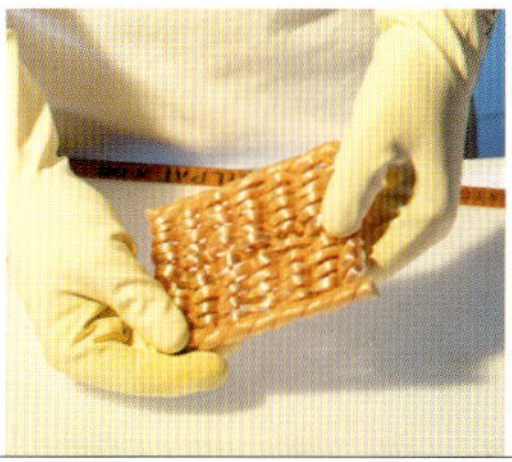

Als Seitenstabilisierung ans Floß anbringen

Attach to the raft in order to stabilise the side

El Papagayo

Papagayo the Parrot

Im Sommer ist jeder im Urlaub. Und auch hier, bei uns, muss man die Urlauber ans Fenster locken. So ein bunter exotischer Vogel weckt in jedem Urlaubserinnerungen. Die Orchidee ist eine schnell herzustellende, dekorative Blume, die sogar eine Rose auf einer Hochzeitstorte ersetzen kann.

Everyone goes on holiday in the summer. Here at home, we also have to entice holidaymakers to our shop window. A colourful exotic bird like this brings back holiday images. The orchid is a decorative flower which is quick to make and can even be used instead of a rose on a wedding cake.

Techniques

- Basic body of the parrot and the beak: blown
- Feathers and leaves: pulled and moulded
- Base structure: cast
- The branches are made from pulled sugar interlaced with granulated sugar
- Orchid: pulled

Techniken

- Papageigrundkörper und Schnabel geblasen
- Federn und Blätter gezogen und gestempelt
- Grundaufbau gegossen
- Äste aus gezogenem Zucker, der mit Kristallzucker durchwirkt wurde
- Orchidee gezogen

Herstellung

Zuerst grüne Bodenplatten und grünen Stab gießen. Die zwei kleineren Bodenplatten wieder gleichmäßig erwärmen und halbrund biegen. Den grünen Stab nochmals mit Silikonstangen umlegen und in klarem Zucker eingießen. Sobald der Stab vollkommen ausgekühlt ist, ausformen und mit einem Gasbrenner klar schmelzen. Den Stab auf der Bodenplatte statisch sinnvoll befestigen.

Für den Ast schwarzen Zucker mit Kristallzucker durchwirken, flach ausziehen und durch mehrmaliges hohles Zusammenlegen bis kurz vor dem Erstarrungspunkt einen kräftigen Zweig für den Papagei und dünnere für die Orchidee herstellen.

Herstellung der Orchidee siehe Stepps. Ein großes grünes Blatt mit einem Silikonstempel herstellen.

Für den Papagei einen Grundkörper aus rotem Zucker blasen. Aus weißem Zucker die Maske ziehen und noch warm anmodellieren. Schnabel aus weißem und schwarzem Zucker blasen, zusammen- und ansetzen.

Flügel blasen und an den Grundkörper ansetzen. Die Federn für die Flügel einzeln ziehen und mit einem Silikonstempel Federstruktur geben.

Making the parts

First of all, cast the green base slabs and the green stick. Warm the two smaller base slabs up again evenly and bend them to a semi-circular shape. Place silicon sticks around the green stick and cast in clear sugar. As soon as the stick has cooled down completely, take it out of the form and then use a torch to melt it clear. Fix the stick on the base slab so it fits in with the structure of the model.

To make the branch, interlace black sugar with granulated sugar, pull out flat and then make a strong branch for the parrot and thinner ones for the orchid by folding over hollow several times until they are close to setting.

See above stages for making the orchid. Make a large green leaf with a silicon mould.

To make the parrot blow the basic body from red sugar. Pull the mask using white sugar and attach while still warm. Blow the beak out of white and black sugar, put together and attach.

Blow the wings and attach them to the basic body. Pull the feathers individually for the wings and use a silicon mould to give them a typical feather texture.

1

2

3

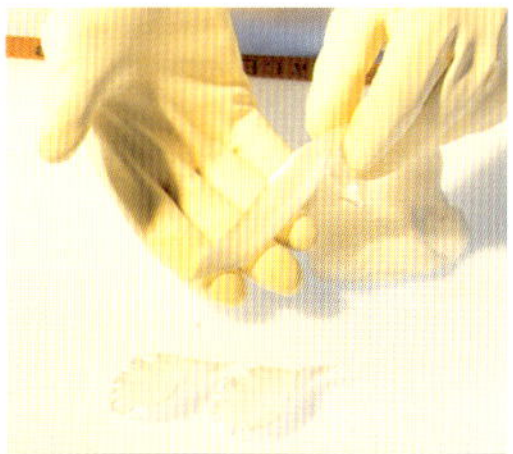

4

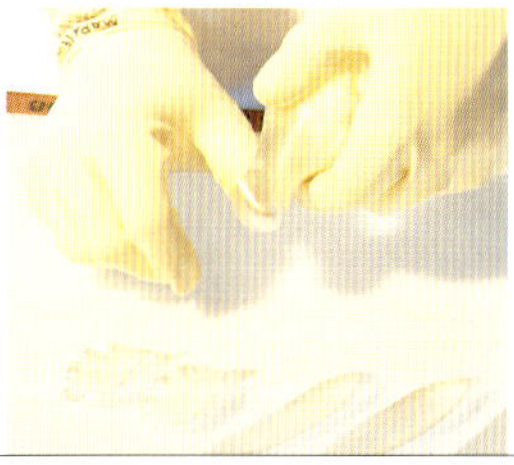

5

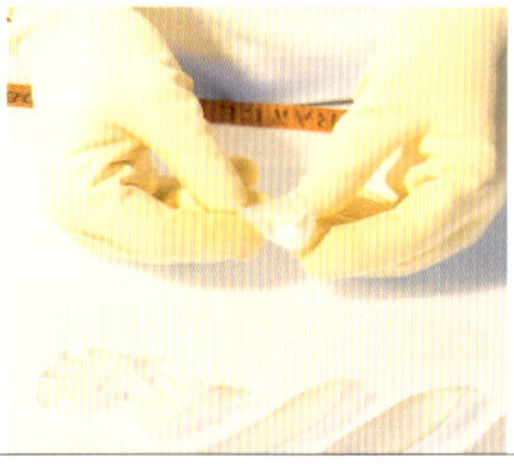

6

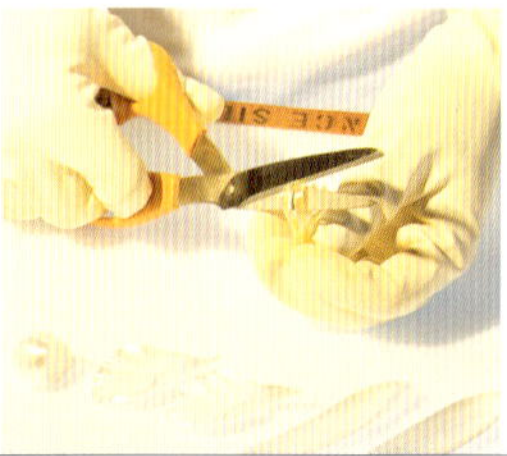

7

Blatt aus Zucker herausziehen

Pull a leaf out of sugar

Mit einem Silikonstempel Blatt stempeln

Mould the leaf with a silicon mould

Langes Orchideenblatt herausziehen

Pull out a long leaf for the orchid

Fertiges langes Orchideenblatt

The completed long orchid leaf

Mit dem Daumen Orchideenkelch herausmodellieren

Use your thumb to model the cup shape of the orchid

Fertiger Orchideenkelch

The completed orchid cup

Blütenstempel ziehen und mit einer Schere zurechtschneiden

Pull the blossom stamen and use scissors to trim the stamen into shape

Putting it all together

Attach the prepared branch to the stick. Put on the basic parrot body. Pull the tail feathers in red and blue, mould and attach to the body while still warm. Then pull and mould the wing feathers from blue through to yellow and red and then attach to the wings while still warm. Use a brush to paint a face onto the white mask.

Place the semi-circular plates and the orchid with leaf onto the base slab.

Zusammensetzung

Den vorbereiteten Ast am Stab befestigen und den Papageigrundkörper aufsetzen. Schwanzfedern in Rot und Blau ziehen, stempeln und noch warm am Papagei ansetzen. Danach die Flügelfedern von blau über gelb nach rot ziehen und stempeln und jeweils noch warm auf den Flügeln anmodellieren. Gesicht mit einem Pinsel auf die weiße Maske aufmalen.

Halbbögen und Orchidee mit Blatt auf der Grundplatte ansetzen.

8

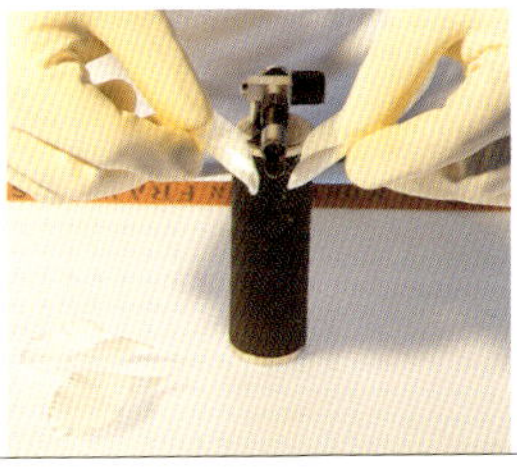

Wenn alle Bestandteile vorbereitet sind, Orchidee mit Hilfe eines Gasbrenners zusammensetzen

When you have prepared all the parts, put the orchid together with the help of a torch

9

Zuerst die drei langen Blätter zusammensetzen, dann die kurzen Blätter

First put together the three long leaves, then the short leaves

10

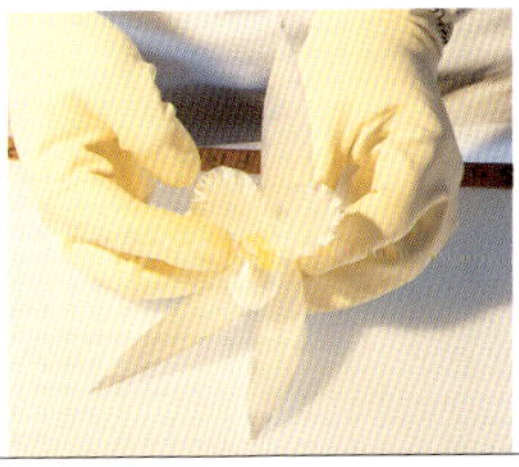

Blütenstempel und Orchideenkelch anbringen

Then attach the stamen and the orchid cup

11

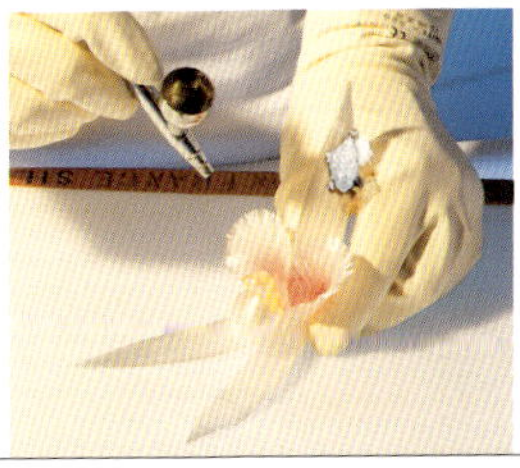

Orchidee mit dem Airbrush schminken

Colour the orchid with the airbrush

INFOPOINT ORANGE

ORANGE DISPLAY

In letzter Zeit habe ich ein Faible für in Zucker gegossene, getrocknete Zutaten. Hier ist eine Variante davon – eine Werbeskulptur für Orangentrüffel. Sie ist in maximal 60 Minuten herstellbar. Einfach schlicht und effizient wirbt sie für das Produkt, das auf die drei vorderen Zuckerpunkte platziert wird.

I have recently developed a liking for dried ingredients cast in sugar. Here is a variation – a promotional sculpture for orange truffles. It takes no more than 60 minutes to create this promotional piece. It advertises our product simply and plainly, but effectively. Just place the chocolates on the three sugarpoints.

Techniques

- Cocoa beans and dried oranges: pulled through liquid sugar
- Base slab: cast
- Orange: blown
- Rings: ribbon technique
- Yellow-green ribbon: blown in ribbon technique

Techniken

- Kakaobohnen und getrocknete Orangen durch flüssigen Zucker gezogen
- Grundplatten gegossen
- Orange geblasen
- Ringe in Bändertechnik
- Gelbgrünes Band geblasen in Bandtechnik

Herstellung

Zuerst die Stand- und Bodenplatten gießen, den restlichen Zucker mit Kornblumen mischen und in vorbereitete Silikonformen gießen.

Getrocknete Orangenscheiben und Kakaobohnen durch klaren Zucker ziehen und auf Backmatte erstarren lassen.

Weiße Ringe in Bandtechnik ziehen. Für das grüne Band zuerst den Zucker mit einem Blasebalg leicht aufblasen, länglich ziehen und dann in Bandtechnik in gewünschte Form bringen und mit einem heißen Messer zurechtschneiden.

Für die Orange mit Kristallzucker durchwirktem gezogenem Zucker orangenförmig blasen. Stiel modellieren, Blatt ziehen und stempeln.

Making the parts

First of all, cast the base and holding plates, mix the remaining sugar with cornflowers and cast into prepared silicon forms.

Pull the dried orange slices and cocoa beans through the clear sugar and leave to set on the baking mat.

Pull the white rings in ribbon technique. To make the green ribbon, first slightly inflate the sugar with the sugar pump, pull into a longish shape and then use the ribbon technique to obtain the desired form. Next use a hot knife to trim into shape.

To make the orange, use sugar that has been pulled and interlaced with granulated sugar and blow it up to the shape of an orange. Model the stalk, pull and mould the leaf.

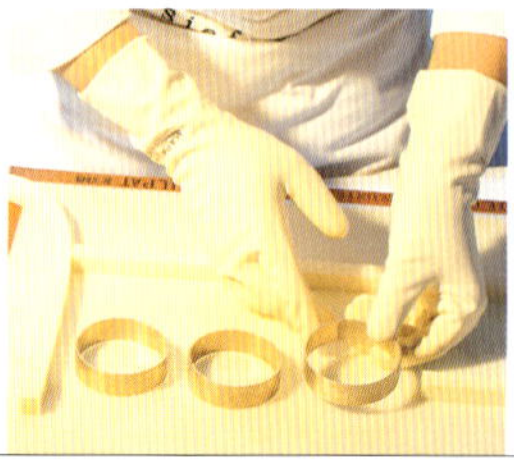

1

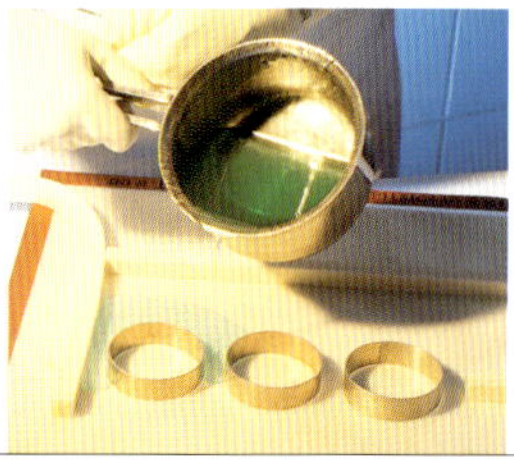

2

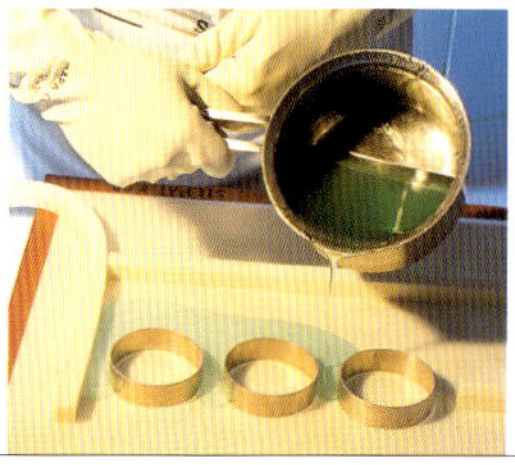

3

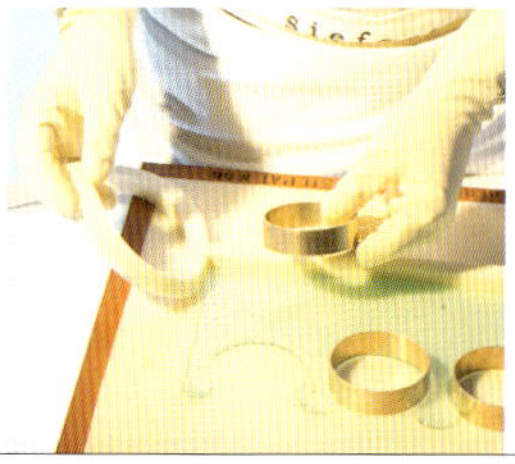

4

5

Zuerst Silikonstangen legen. Ringe leicht ölen und dann mit Abstand auf Backmatte legen

First place the silicon sticks. Oil the rings slightly and then place on the baking mat with a gap between them

Transparent glasfarbenen Zucker gleichmäßig in die Zwischenräume gießen, dass sich Tropfen bilden können

Evenly cast glass-coloured transparent sugar into the gaps so that drops can form

Gesamte Fläche gleichmäßig ausgießen

Fill the whole surface by casting sugar evenly

Nach dem Erkalten vorsichtig ausformen

Once it has cooled down remove the forms carefully

Fertig gegossene Standplatte

The completed holding plate

Putting it all together

First of all, melt the cornflower ribbon and circle onto the holding plate. Then place it all onto the base slab and attach the second base slab. Put the three cornflower circles into place.

Place the orange slices between the drops and attach the cocoa beans with a torch.

Fix the white rings in front of the holding plate. Position the green band and the orange so that they look attractive.

Zusammensetzung

Zuerst den Kornblumenstreifen und den -kreis auf die Standplatte aufschmelzen. Dann auf der Bodenplatte anbringen und die zweite Bodenplatte ansetzen. Die drei Kornblumenkreise aufsetzen.

Die Orangenscheiben zwischen die Tropfen setzen, die Kakaobohnen dazwischen mit einem Gasbrenner anbringen.

Die weißen Ringe vor der Standplatte befestigen. Das grüne Band und die Orange ansprechend platzieren.

Tip

Present the truffles on the small cornflower circles.

Tipp

Die Trüffel auf den kleinen Kornblumenkreisen präsentieren.

Chinesischer Neujahrsdrache

Chinese New Year Dragon

Natürlich fällt mir zu Neujahr als Deutscher zuerst der Schornsteinfeger und das Glücksschwein ein. Aber, da ich oft in Asien bin, habe ich ein besonderes Faible für dieses Fabelwesen – den Neujahrsdrachen. Und ein Feuerwerk vertreibt sowohl in Asien als auch bei uns die bösen Geister.

As a German the first thing I think of on New Year's Eve is the chimney sweep and the lucky pig. But since I often travel to Asia I have taken a shine to this mystic animal – the New Year's Dragon. There is also the fact that fireworks are meant to chase away evil spirits, both here and in Asia.

Techniques

- Base slabs: marbled casting
- The balls are blown in white and clear, up to bursting point
- Make the colour explosions
- The two middle sticks: blown and twisted in two colours
- Basic body and head of the dragon: blown
- Wings, back mane, horns, tongue, teeth and eyes: modelled
- Head mane: ribbon technique

Techniken

- Bodenplatten marmoriert gegossen
- Kugeln weiss und klar geblasen und zum Platzen gebracht
- Farbexplosionen hergestellt
- Zwei Mittelstäbe zweifarbig gedreht geblasen
- Grundkörper und Kopf des Drachen geblasen
- Flügel, Rückenmähne, Hörner, Zunge, Zähne und Augen modelliert
- Kopfmähne in Bandtechnik hergestellt

Herstellung

Bodenplatten in den Farben Schwarz, Rot und Gold-Metallic gießen.

Die Mittelstäbe zweifarbig verdreht blasen und mit einem Kaltluftföhn stabilisieren. Die Farbexplosionen in den entsprechenden Farben und verschiedenen Größen herstellen (siehe Stepps).

Die Kugeln aus gezogenem und ungezogenem weißem Zucker blasen, bis sie platzen. Man kann z. B. mit einer Schere nachhelfen.

Den Drachengrundkörper aus rotem Zucker blasen und über einem Rollholz spiralförmig fest werden lassen. Der Kopf wird geblasen, wobei das Maul mit einer Schere aufgeschnitten und modelliert wird. Die Flügel, Rückenmähne, Hörner, Zunge, Zähne und Augen modellieren und jeweils direkt anmodellieren. Die Kopfmähnen in Bandtechnik herausziehen, abschneiden und mit der breiten Seite weg vom Kopf anbringen.

Making the parts

Cast the base slabs in the colours black, red and metallic gold.

Blow the middle sticks twisted in two colours and stabilise with a cold air fan. Produce the colour explosions in the different colours and sizes (see stages).

Blow the balls from pulled and unpulled white sugar until they burst. To help things along one can use a pair of scissors to make them burst.

Blow the basic body of the Dragon from red sugar and leave to set in spirals draped around a rolling pin. Use the blowing technique to blow the head, then use scissors to cut open and model the mouth. Model the wings, back mane, horns, tongue, teeth and eyes and attach them as soon as they have been made. Pull out the head manes in ribbon technique, cut off and attach with the wider side away from the head.

1

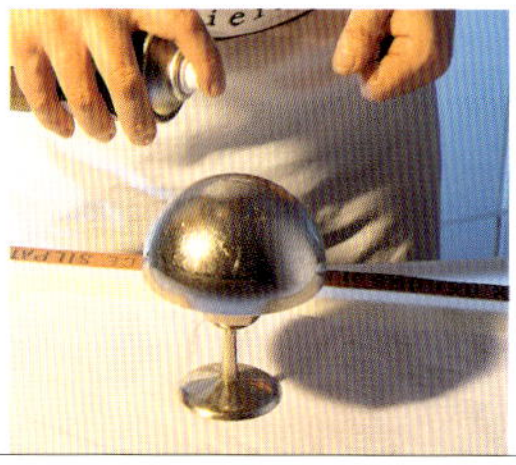

2

3

4

Putting it all together

Place the base plates on top of each other, first the large one, then the small one and then the medium sized one, using liquid sugar.

Push the middle sticks through the spiral-shaped body of the dragon and attach to the base plate. Fix the dragon body at several points on the sticks and the base plate. Attach the head.

Arrange the exploded balls as part of the colour explosions and fix to the middle sticks.

Zusammensetzung

Bodenplatten, zuerst die große, dann die kleine und darauf die mittlere, mit flüssigem Zucker aufeinander setzen.

Die Mittelstäbe durch den spiralförmigen Körper des Drachen schieben und auf der Bodenplatte befestigen. Den Drachenkörper an mehreren Punkten an den Stäben und der Bodenplatte befestigen. Kopf anbringen.

Die explodierten Kugeln in die Farbexplosionen einfügen und an den Mittelstäben arrangieren und befestigen.

Metallhalbkugel auf ein Podest setzen

Put a metallic hemisphere onto a pedestal

Mit Trennspray leicht besprühen

Slightly spray with separating spray

Aufgelösten zähflüssigen Zucker über die Mitte in alle Richtungen spinnen

Spin the dissolved and viscous sugar across the middle in all directions

Sobald der Zucker stabil ist, vorsichtig abformen

As soon as the sugar is stable, carefully remove from the forms

Onkel Edgars Fische

Uncle Edgar's Fishes

Schon als kleines Kind haben mich die Fische meines Onkels Edgar fasziniert. Daher kommt wohl auch meine Liebe zum Tauchen. Und deshalb müssen Fische einfach sein! Sie sind relativ schnell herzustellen, wenn man auf die Schuppen verzichtet. Man sollte immer versuchen, so viel wie möglich zu stilisieren, dann kommen wir auch nach und nach von dem Kitschimage der Konditoren weg.

Uncle Edgar's fishes always fascinated me, even when I was a small child. Perhaps that's why I like scuba diving so much. And that's why fishes should be easy to make! It's easy to make fish quickly if you leave out the scales. We should always try to stylise them as much as possible. This also helps us to get away from the 'kitsch' image that is sometimes associated with confectionery.

Techniques

- Basic body: blown
- Fins: pulled in ribbon technique
- Basic shape: cast
- Bubble sugar
- Sugar threads: pulled
- Eyes: dropped

Techniken

- Grundkörper geblasen
- Flossen in Bandtechnik gezogen
- Grundform gegossen
- Blasenzucker
- Zuckerfäden gezogen
- Augen getropft

1

Metallröhrchen mit Blasebalg erwärmen

Warm up the metal tube of the sugar pump

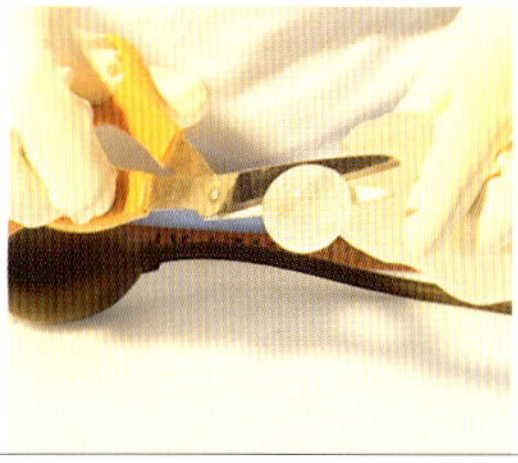

2

Gleichmäßig temperierten Zucker kugelförmig abschneiden

Cut off the evenly tempered sugar in the shape of a ball

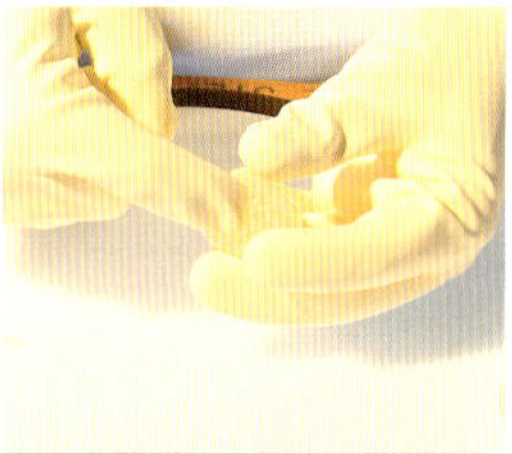

3

Kleine Vertiefung in die Kugel modellieren

Make a small indentation in the ball

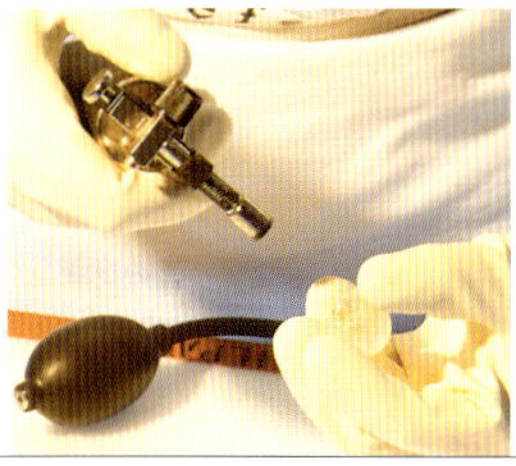

4

Vertiefung erwärmen

Warm up the indentation

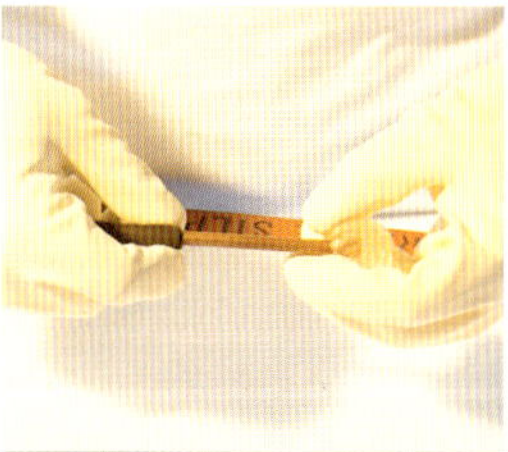

5

Zuckerkugel an das Metallröhrchen ansetzen

Place the sugar ball at the end of the metal tube

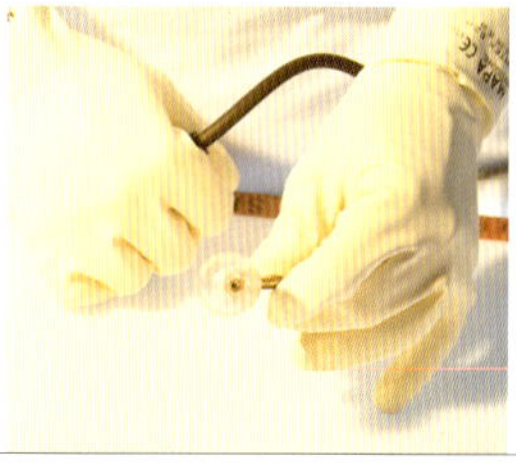

6

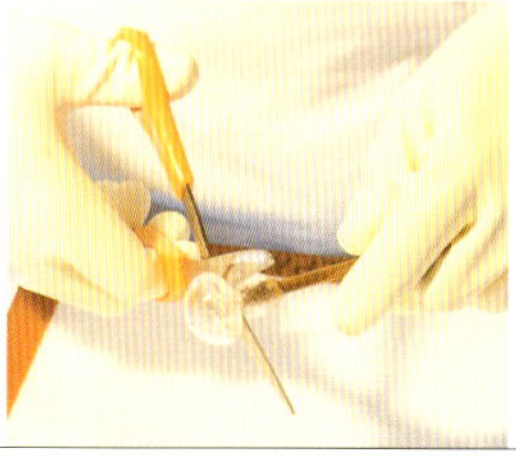

7

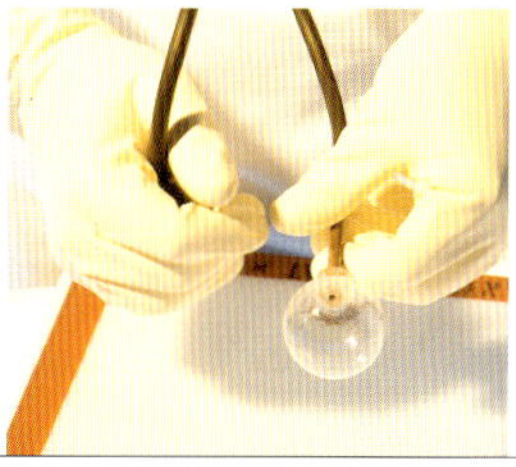

8

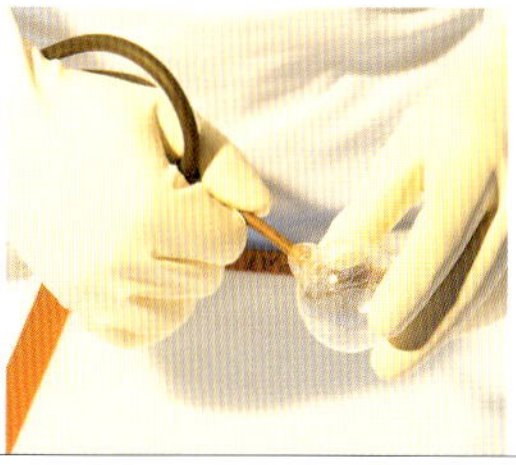

9

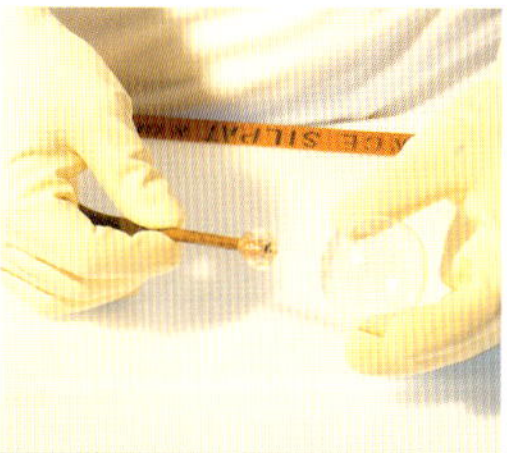

10

Zucker leicht aufblasen

Slightly blow up the sugar

Sollbruchstelle mit einer Schere am Ende des Röhrchens vormodellieren

Use scissors to score the ball at the end of the tube

Der Kugel Volumen geben

Blow the ball up to the right volume

Bei gewünschter Größe mit Kaltluftföhn abkühlen

When it reaches the right size, cool it down with a cold air fan

Sobald erkaltet, an der Sollbruchstelle abbrechen

Once it has cooled down, break it off at the line of scoring

Making the parts

Cast the base slab as a square on crumpled aluminium foil. Cast the middle stick between silicon rods. First cast a thin gold-coloured frame, then put a wider frame completely around it while leaving a square in the middle. Fill this square with green sugar. When the frame has set, heat up evenly, bend into the shape of waves and leave to set.

Blow sugar balls of various sizes (see stages). Make bubble sugar (see stages on page 252) and spin sugar threads.

Blow the two basic fish bodies. Pull out the fins in ribbon technique and cut to shape. Model the mouth and the bump over the eyes and attach to the basic body while still warm. Then use an airbrush to colour it like a Koy carp. To make the eyes, first let some blue sugar drop onto the baking mat and then apply a small black drop on the middle of the eye drop. When the eyes have set, attach them underneath the bumps.

Herstellung

Grundplatten auf geknüllter Alufolie quadratisch gießen. Den Mittelstab zwischen Silikonstangen gießen. Zuerst einen dünnen goldfarbenen Rahmen gießen, dann diesen mit einem breiteren Rahmen vollständig umlegen und in der Mitte ein Quadrat aussparen. Mit grünem Zucker ausgießen. Wenn der Rahmen erkaltet ist, gleichmäßig erwärmen, wellenförmig biegen und erstarren lassen.

Zuckerkugeln in verschiedenen Größen blasen (siehe Stepps). Blasenzucker herstellen (Stepps Seite 252) und Zuckerfäden spinnen.

Die zwei Fischgrundkörper blasen. Flossen in Bandtechnik ausziehen und teilweise zurechtschneiden. Mund und Augenwülste modellieren und im noch warmen Zustand am Grundkörper anbringen. Dann mit dem Airbrush wie einen Koikarpfen schminken. Die Augen zuerst klar blau auf Backmatte auftropfen und auf die Mitte einen schwarzen Punkt auftropfen. Wenn erkaltet, unter die Augenwülste setzen.

Putting it all together

Join the base plates together and fix the stick in the middle. Firmly attach the frame below in front of the stick and above behind the stick. Position the fishes at various points of the basic model. Then arrange the bubble sugar, the balls and the sugar threads.

Zusammensetzung

Grundplatten zusammensetzen und den Stab in der Mitte fixieren. Den Rahmen unten vor dem Stab und oben hinter dem Stab stabil anbringen. Die Fische an verschiedenen Punkten des Grundaufbaus befestigen. Dann den Blasenzucker, die Kugeln und den Zuckerfaden arrangieren.

Zirkusclown

Circus Clown

Zirkus, Karneval oder Kindergeburtstag, ein Clown verspricht immer viel Freude. Hier ist eine kleine Hommage an einen grossen Clown und den grössten Kaffeehaus-Sammler, den ich kenne – Bernhard Paul vom Zirkus Roncalli.

Clowns are always a good laugh, whether at the circus, a carnival celebration or a children's birthday party. Here is a small homage to a famous clown and the greatest collector of café interiors I know – Bernhard Paul from the Roncalli circus.

Techniques

- Basic body, head, arms, legs and the balloons: blown
- Base plates and the half moon: made in marbled casting
- Sugar threads: pulled
- Eyes, mouth, hat, hands, nose and shoes: modelled
- Hair: pulled
- Sugar threads: pulled and bent
- Blossom: pulled; heart: blown
- Sugar sticks: blown and twisted in three colours
- Trousers, tie, jacket and bow: made in ribbon technique

Techniken

- Grundkörper, Kopf, Arme, Beine und Luftballons geblasen
- Bodenplatten und Halbmond marmoriert gegossen
- Zuckerfäden gezogen
- Augen, Mund, Hut, Hände, Nase und Schuhe modelliert
- Haare gezogen
- Zuckerfäden ausgezogen und gebogen
- Blüte gezogen, Herz geblasen
- Zuckerstangen dreifarbig gedreht geblasen
- Hose, Krawatte, Jacke und Schleife in Bandtechnik

Herstellung

Grundplatten und Halbmond marmoriert gießen (siehe Stepps). Die dreifarbig gedreht geblasenen Zuckerstangen herstellen und in gewünschter Form auskühlen lassen.

Die Luftballons blasen und mit dem Airbrush schminken. Die schwarzen Luftballonschnüre ziehen und beim Auskühlen leicht verdrehen. Schleife in Bandtechnik ziehen und zur Schleife modellieren.

Für die Blüte zuerst eine klare, leicht spitze Kugel blasen. Dann klare kleinere Blütenblätter modellieren. In zweiter Reihe glänzend gezogene weiße Blütenblätter und in dritter Reihe mit Titanoxid weiß gefärbte Blütenblätter herstellen.

Körper, Arme und Beine blasen. Die Beine in Bändertechnik mit schwarz-weiß gestreiftem Zucker umlegen. Den Körper an die Beine aufsetzen, den Mantel aus kupferfarbenem Zucker in Bandtechnik herausziehen und um den Körper legen. Die Arme in der gleichen Farbe und Technik bekleiden und ansetzen. Schuhe und Hände modellieren und anbringen.

Für den Kopf rosa Zucker eiförmig blasen. Dabei schon die Grundstruktur des Gesichts festlegen und Haare, Nase, Mund sowie Augen modellieren und anbringen. Das Hütchen aus schwarzem und weißem Zucker modellieren und aufsetzen. Das Gesicht mit einem Pinsel aufmalen. Kopf auf den Grundkörper aufsetzen. Krawatte und Schulterklappen in Bandtechnik zweifarbig fertigen und ansetzen.

Making the parts

Cast the base slabs and the half moon with a marbled effect (see stages). Make the twisted, blown sugar sticks with three colours and let them cool down in the desired shape.

Blow the balloons and colour them. Pull the black strings for the balloons and slightly twist them while they are cooling down. Use the ribbon technique to pull the ribbon and drape it to make the bow.

To make the blossom, first blow a clear, slightly pointed ball. Then model clear smaller blossom leaves. Make up the second row of glossy pulled white blossom leaves and a third row of blossom leaves with titanium oxide white colouring.

Blow the body, legs and arms. Wind a black and white striped sugar ribbon around the legs. Attach the body to the legs, then pull the coat in copper-coloured sugar with ribbon technique and place it around the body. Use the same technique to dress the arms in the same colour and attach them to the body. Now model the shoes and hands and attach them.

To make the head, blow some pink sugar in the shape of an egg. In the meantime prepare the basic structure of the face and model the hair, nose, mouth and eyes. Model the little hat from black and white sugar and put it on the head. Use a brush to paint on the face. Place the head onto the basic body. Use the ribbon technique to make the tie and epaulettes and put them on the figure.

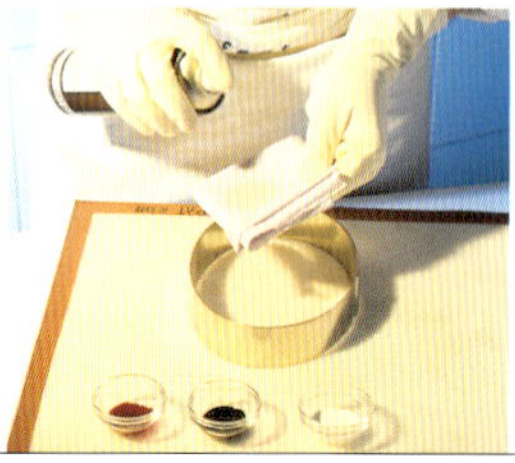

1

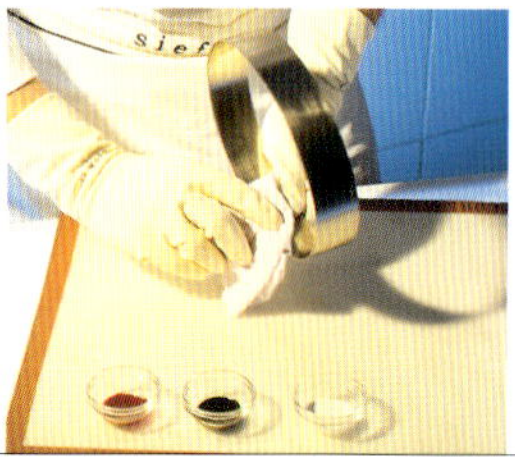

2

3

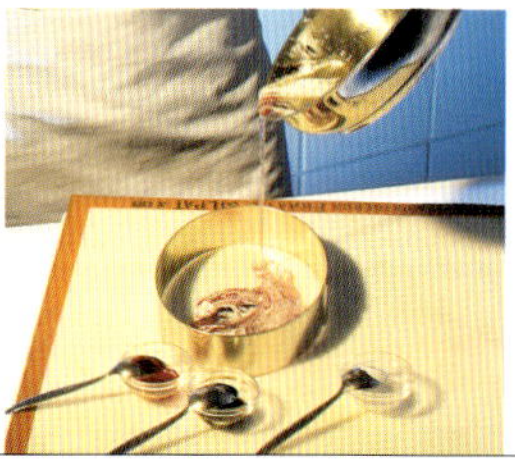

4

5

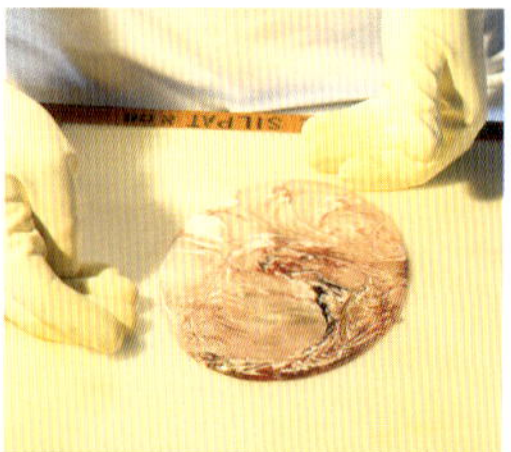

6

Papiertuch fetten

Grease a paper towel

Ring damit auswischen

Use it to wipe out the ring

Aufgelösten Zucker mit Weiß, Rot und Schwarz besprenkeln

Sprinkle white, red and black colouring onto the dissolved sugar

In die gefettete Form gießen, so dass sich automatisch eine Marmorierung ergibt

Pour the material into the greased form so that there is automatically a marbling effect

Erkalten lassen

Leave to cool down

Ausformen

Remove the forms

Putting it all together

Put the base slabs together with spacers. Place the half moon upright on the base and fix it firmly. Arrange the blown sugar sticks. Place the clown into the moon and attach it at several points. Attach the balloons to the basic structure and the strings to the balloons at one end and hand at the other end. Finish off with the bow into the hand. Finally, put together the blossom and fix it to the base plates using the bent sugar threads.

Zusammensetzung

Grundplatten mit Abstandshaltern zusammensetzen. Halbmond stehend aufsetzen und stabil fixieren. Die geblasenen Zuckerstangen anbringen. Den Clown in den Mond setzen und an mehreren Punkten festmachen. Die Luftballons am Grundaufbau befestigen und die Schnüre jeweils zwischen Hand und Luftballon anbringen. Die Schleife als Abschluss in die Hand geben. Zu guter Letzt die Blüte zusammensetzen und mit den gebogenen Zuckerfäden auf der Grundplatte fixieren.

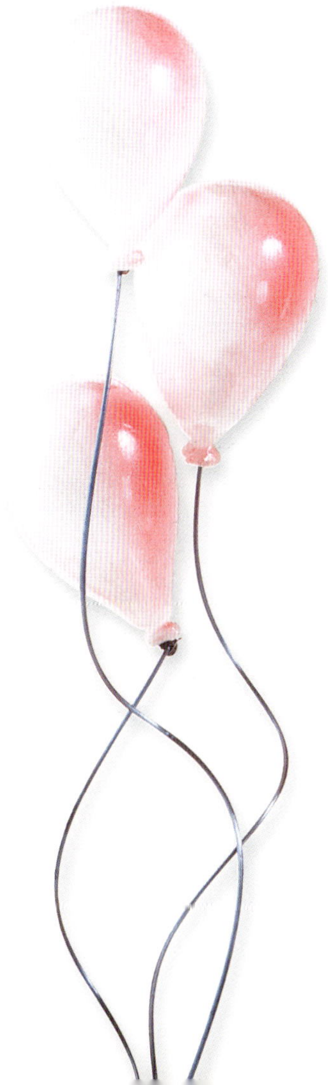

Kolibri

Hummingbird

Die Phantasieblüte auf diesem Schaustück ist meine Lieblingsblume. Und der zweifarbig geblasene Kolibri ist eine schöne Erinnerung an meine ersten Gehversuche mit dieser heissen, klebrigen Masse, die die Welt versüsst.

My favourite flower just happens to be the fantasy flower on this showpiece. And this two-coloured, blown hummingbird reminds me of my first attempts to work with this hot sweet material.

Techniques

- Basic structure: cast onto oiled and crumpled aluminium foil
- Sugar bowl of the blossom: spinning technique
- Blossom leaves: pulled
- Basic form of the hummingbird: blown in two colours
- Wings: pulled
- Tail feathers: pulled in three colours
- Sugar threads: pulled and bent
- Head decoration: pulled in ribbon technique
- Beak: modelled

Techniken

- Grundaufbau auf geölte, geknüllte Alufolie gegossen
- Zuckerkugel der Blüte gesponnen
- Blütenblätter gezogen
- Grundform des Kolibris zweifarbig geblasen
- Flügel gezogen
- Schwanzfedern dreifarbig gezogen
- Gebogene Zuckerfäden gezogen
- Kopfschmuck in Band-technik gezogen
- Schnabel modelliert

Herstellung

Grundaufbauten herstellen (siehe Stepps). Die Spinnzuckerkugel herstellen, dann die Blütenblätter ziehen und in gewünschte Form biegen.

Den Kolibri zweifarbig blasen. Für die Flügel von weiß nach blau verlaufende Federn ziehen. Für die Schwanzfedern dreifarbig gezogene Zuckerfedern herstellen, in Form bringen und die gebogenen Zuckerfäden in dunklerem Blau fertigen. Den Schnabel modellieren und den Kopfschmuck in zweifarbiger Bandtechnik herstellen.

Making the parts

Make up the basic structure (see stages). Make the spin sugar ball, then pull the blossom leaves and bend into the required shape.

Blow the hummingbird in two colours. Pull feathers for the wings, graduating the colour from white to blue. To make the tail feathers, pull three-coloured sugar into the shape of feathers and make the bent sugar threads in a deeper blue. Model the beak and make the headdress in two colours, using ribbon technique.

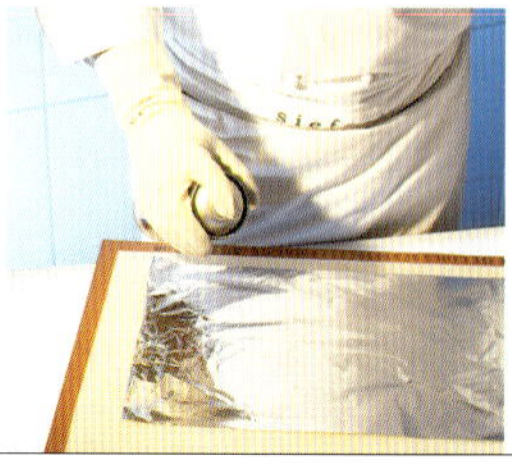

1

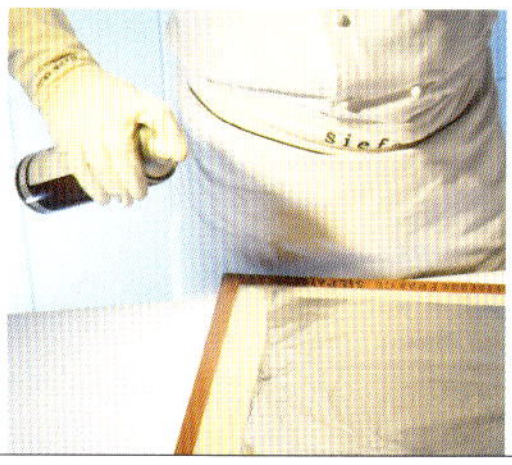

2

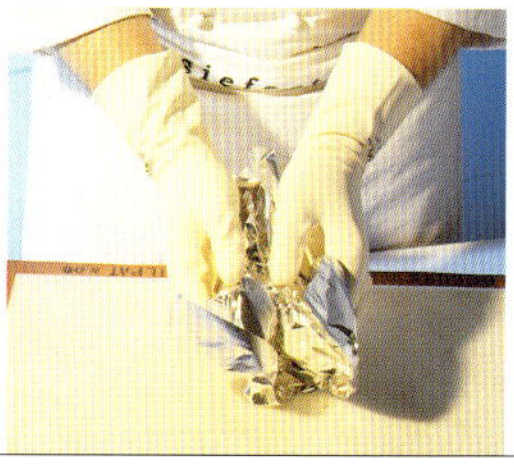

3

Alufolie auf Backmatte legen

Place aluminium foil on the baking mat

4

Zucker zwischen vorbereitete Silikonstangen und geölte Metallringe gießen

Cast sugar between the prepared silicon rods and oiled metal rings

Mit Trennspray einfetten

Apply a coat of separating spray

5

Nach dem Erstarren vorsichtig ausformen

Once it has set carefully remove the forms

Alufolie knüllen

Crumple up the aluminium foil

6

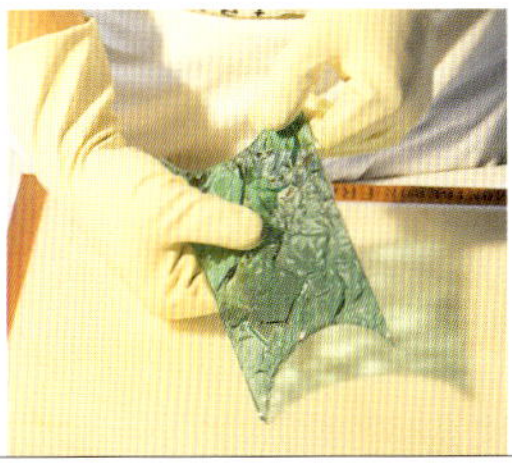

Alufolie abziehen

Pull off the aluminium foil

Putting it all together

Put the base slab together from the four parts, making sure that it is stable. Build up the hummingbird and paint on the eyes. Put the hummingbird into place. Make up the blossom from the blossom leaves and arrange it decoratively on the base slab.

Zusammensetzung

Die Grundplatte aus den vier Teilen statisch stabil zusammensetzen. Den Kolibri herstellen und die Augen aufmalen. Kolibri anbringen. Die Blüte aus den Blütenblättern fertigen und dekorativ auf der Grundplatte montieren.

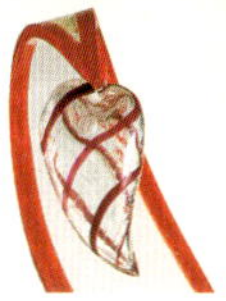

HERZENSSACHE

FOR MY SWEETHEART

Egal ob zum Muttertag oder zum Valentinstag – dieses Schaustück lässt die Herzen höher schlagen. Natürlich kann man auch viele Elemente für eine Hochzeitsdeko benutzen.

Whether it is Mother's Day or Valentine's Day – this showpiece makes an exciting present. Obviously, many of the decorative elements can also be used for wedding decorations.

Techniques	Techniken
Sugar hearts: made in spinning technique	Zuckerherzen gesponnen
Base structure: cast onto greased, crumpled aluminium foil	Aufbau auf gefettetem, geknülltem Alupapier gegossen
Pointed ribbon: bent, after casting in two colours	Zweifarbig gegossenes spitz zulaufendes Band, gebogen
Hearts: blown in two colours	Zweifarbig geblasene Herzen
Sugar spirals and sugar flowers: pulled	Zuckerspiralen und Zuckerblumen gezogen
Sugar leaves: pulled and moulded	Zuckerblätter gezogen und gestempelt

Herstellung

Für den Grundaufbau farblosen Zucker auf gefettetem, geknülltem Alupapier in Form gießen. Sobald der Zucker erkaltet ist, Alupapier abziehen. Bodenplatten zusammensetzen und die zwei Podestteile stabil zusammensetzen. Für das zweifarbig gegossene Band zuerst den inneren Teil gießen, danach die äußere rote Umrandung angießen und, nachdem es erkaltet ist, wieder gleichmäßig erwärmen und in gewünschte Form biegen. Dann mit einem Kaltluftföhn stabilisieren. Für die zweifarbig geblasenen Herzen klaren und bordeauxfarbenen Zucker verwenden (Herstellung siehe Osterei). Die gesponnenen Herzen herstellen (siehe Stepps). Zuckerspiralen aus bordeauxfarbenem Zucker herstellen. Blätter aus transparentem, weißem und bordeauxfarbenem Zucker ziehen und stempeln. Für die abstrakte Rose Zuckerblütenblätter ziehen und zusammensetzen.

Making the parts

To make the basic structure, cast colourless sugar in forms onto greased and crumpled aluminium foil. As soon as the sugar has cooled down pull off the aluminium foil. Place the base plates together and firmly put the two parts of the pedestal together. To make the two-coloured ribbon: first cast the inner part and then the outer red edging. Once it has cooled down, warm it up again evenly and bend into the required shape. Then stabilise it by cooling with a cold air fan. To make the blown two-coloured hearts, use clear and burgundy-coloured sugar (for instructions how to make, see Easter egg). Then make the spun hearts (see stages). Make the sugar spirals from burgundy-coloured sugar. Pull and mould the leaves from transparent, white and burgundy-coloured sugar. To make the abstract rose, pull the sugar blossom leaves and put them together.

1

2

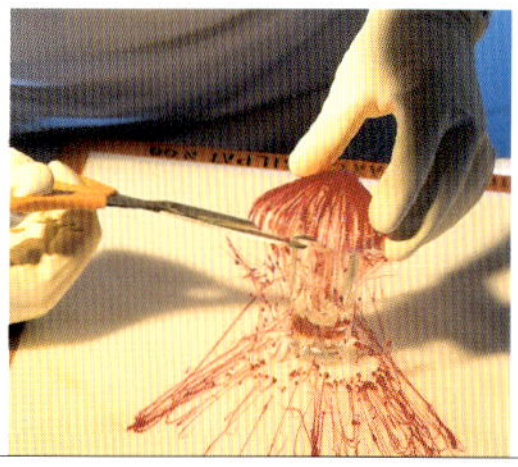

3

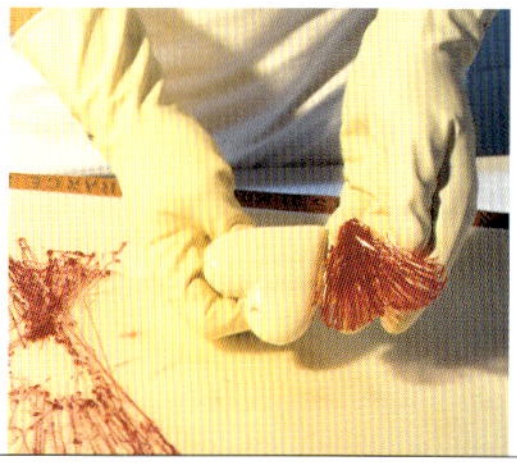

4

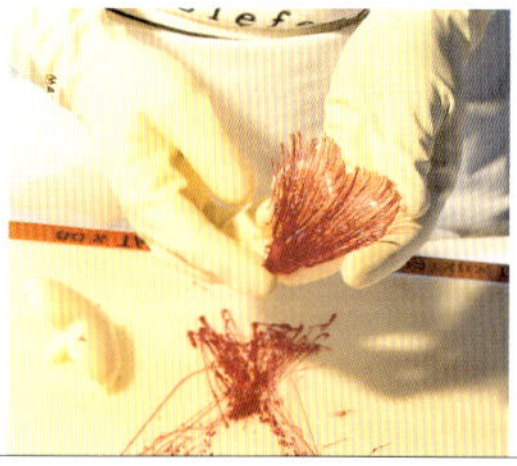

5

Silikonstempel erhöht platzieren. Mit rotem Zucker von der Spitze ausgehend bespinnen

Place the silicon mould higher up. Spin around the mould with red sugar, starting from the point

Dies so lange wiederholen, bis eine stabile Oberfläche entstanden ist

Continue doing this until you have created a stable surface

Mit einer Schere in Form schneiden

Use a pair of scissors to cut the shape

Den Stempel vorsichtig ablösen

Carefully detach the mould

Fertiges filigranes Zuckerherz

The completed filigree sugar heart

Putting it together

Join up the basic structure and the pedestal with liquid sugar. Then add the two-coloured cast ribbon. Place the spun sugar hearts where they look most decorative. Arrange and fix the leaves, flowers and spirals. Finally fix the blown hearts.

Zusammensetzung

Den Grundaufbau und das Podest mit flüssigem Zucker zusammensetzen. Das zweifarbig gegossene Band aufsetzen. Die gesponnenen Zuckerherzen dekorativ anbringen. Blätter, Blüten und Spiralen arrangieren und fixieren. Zuletzt die geblasenen Herzen anbringen.

KALIF STORCH

KING STORK

Mein ganzer Stolz – mein Sohn und natürlich dieses Schaustück. Dieser Storch, so filigran und zerbrechlich wie ein Märchen aus Tausendundeiner Nacht. Die Taufe ist ja eher etwas für die Erwachsenen. Da kann es sehr gut ein stark stilisierter Storch sein.

My pride and joy: my son and, of course, this showpiece. This stork is so delicate and fragile, like a fairy tale from the 1001 Night. Christening celebrations are more a theme for the adults, so this highly stylised stork fits very well.

Techniques

- Basic body and wings: blown
- Beak: modelled
- Two-coloured rose: pulled
- Sugar threads: made in spinning technique
- Base plates: cast in relief
- The spacers are filled out in granulated sugar with a marbled effect
- The sugar threads are pulled and then bent

Techniken

- Grundkörper und Flügel geblasen
- Schnabel modelliert
- Zweifarbige Rose gezogen
- Zuckerfäden gesponnen
- Grundplatten in Relief gegossen
- Abstandshalter in Kristallzucker marmoriert ausgegossen
- Gebogene Zuckerfäden ausgezogen

Herstellung

Drei kleiner werdende Grundplatten auf eine Silikonreliefmatte gießen. Zuckerfäden spinnen. Für die Abstandshalter weiß marmorierten Zucker in leicht vertiefte Kristallzuckerform gießen, wenn er zu erstarren beginnt, leicht ineinander verdrehen und schnell in gewünschter Form auskühlen lassen. Zuckerrose herstellen (siehe Stepps). Sie kann natürlich auch einfarbig hergestellt werden. Zuckerfäden ausziehen und leicht aufrollen.

Für den Storch den gesamten Körper aus einem Stück blasen und die Flügel separat dazu blasen. Den Schnabel modellieren.

Making the parts

Cast three base slabs onto the silicone relief mat, each smaller than the one below. Spin the sugar threads. For the spacers cast white marbled sugar into slightly recessed granulated sugar forms. When they start to set, turn them slightly into each other and leave to cool down quickly in the required shape. Make the sugar rose (see stages). You can, of course, also make the rose in a single colour. Pull out the sugar threads and roll up loosely.

To make the stork, blow the body from one piece and blow the wings separately. Make the beak by modelling.

1

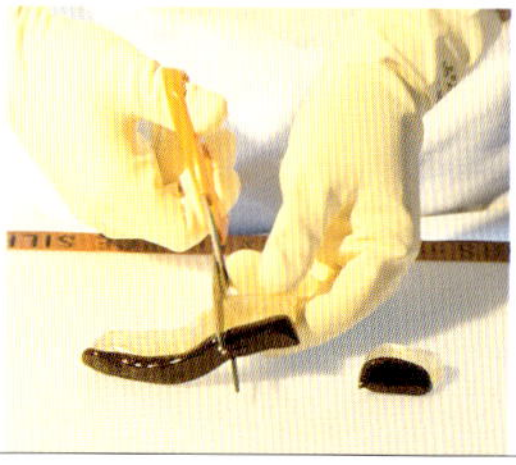

2

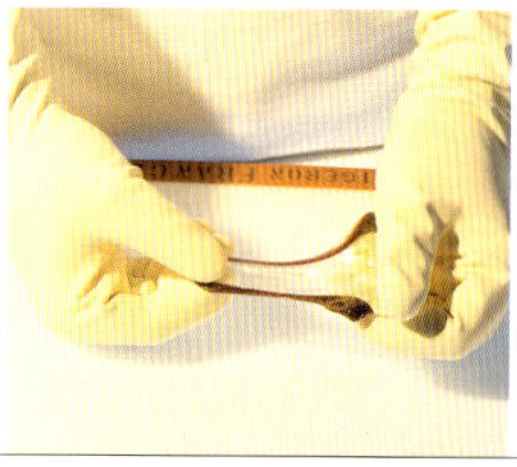

3

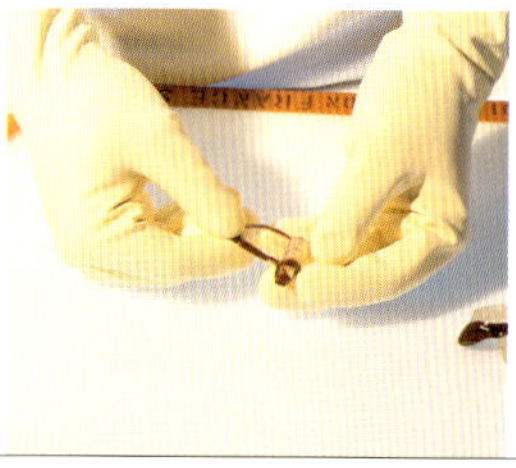

4

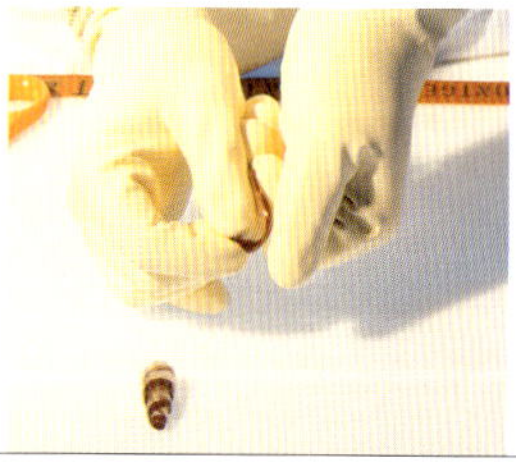

5

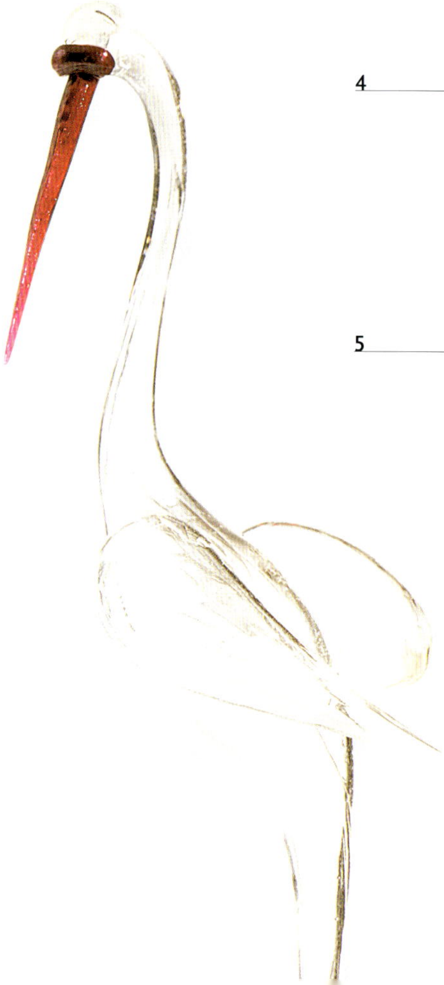

Bordeauxfarbenen und klaren Zucker aneinander setzen

Place the burgundy-coloured and clear sugar next to each other

6

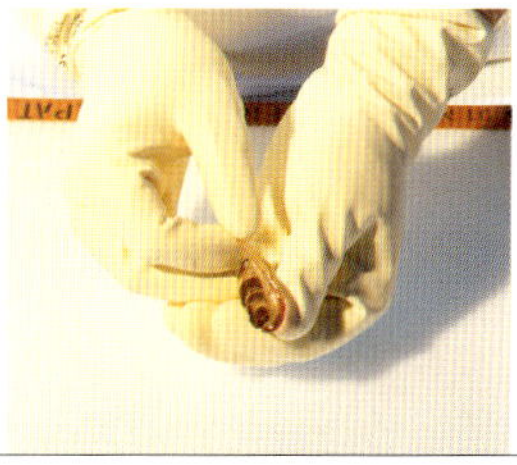

An das aufgerollte Blatt anmodellieren

Model them onto the rolled leaf

In kurze Stücke schneiden

Cut into short pieces

7

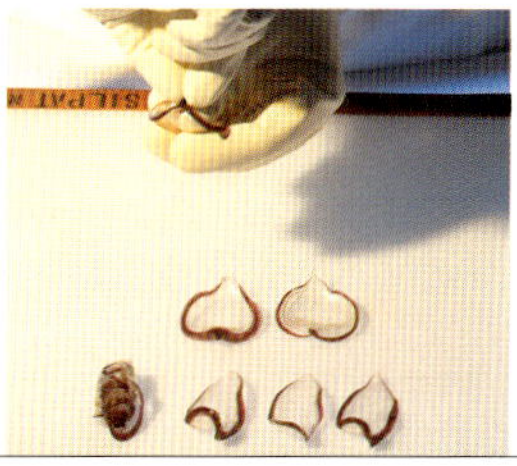

Blütenblätter formen

Shape the blossom leaves

Zuerst ein langes Blatt ziehen

First pull a long leaf

8

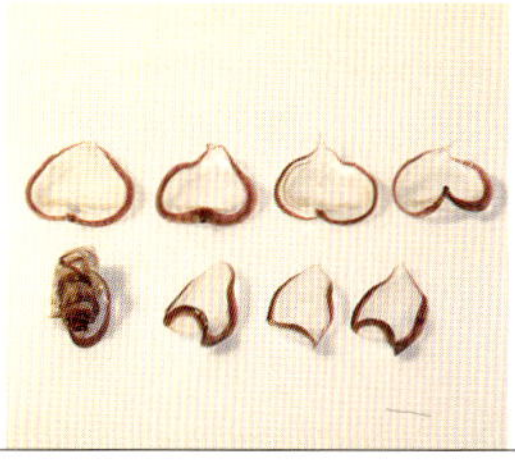

Für die gesamte Rose werden drei einfach gedrehte Blätter und fünf zweifach gedrehte Blätter benötigt

To make the whole rose you will need three leaves with a single twist and five leaves with a double twist

---

Blatt schneckenförmig zusammenrollen

Roll the leaf together in the shape of a snail

9

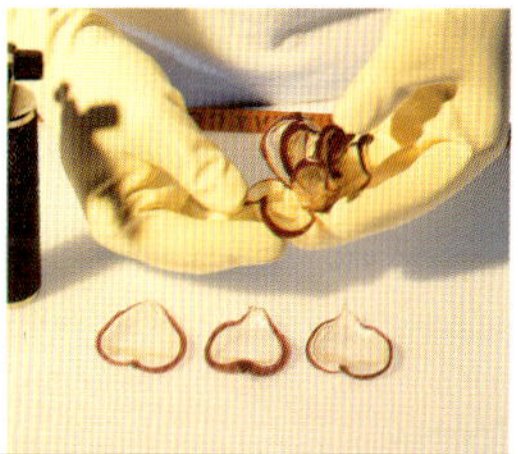

Rose mit einem Gasbrenner zusammensetzen

Put the rose together with the help of a torch

Zwei längliche Blätter ziehen

Pull two oblong leaves

10

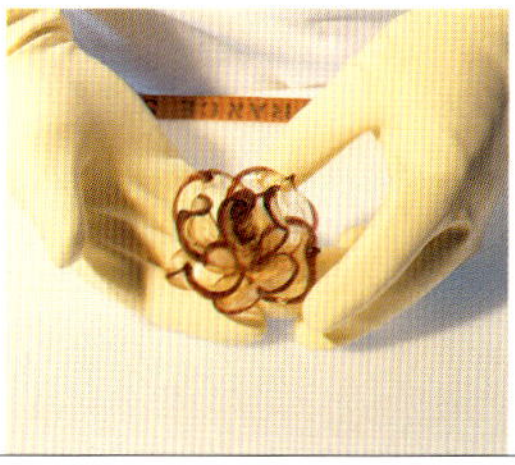

Fertige Rose

The completed rose

Putting it all together

Put the base slabs together, alternating with the spacers, and drape the spin sugar around them. Attach the body of the stork onto the top slab. Attach the wings and beak. Arrange the rose and rolled-up sugar threads at the foot of the stork.

Zusammensetzung

Grundplatten abwechselnd mit den Abstandshaltern zusammensetzen und mit dem Spinnzucker umlegen. Den Körper des Storchs auf der obersten Platte anbringen. Flügel und Schnabel ansetzen. Rose und aufgerollte Zuckerfäden am Fuß des Storchs anbringen.

Hochzeit in Venedig

Wedding in Venice

Ich bin oft in Italien und gebe Seminare. Wenn es die Zeit erlaubt, schaue ich bei den Glasbläsern in Murano vorbei. Ich lerne dort viel über Glaskunst. Die Zuckerkunst, die der Glaskunst ähnelt, hat ihre Stärke in der stilisierten Darstellung von Skulpturen.

I often go to Italy and give seminars there from time to time. When I have enough time I always like to pay a visit to the glassblowers in Murano. I learn a lot from them, especially how to make my sculptures simpler and more stylised. I see this as a way of giving the art of sugar decoration a new lease of life and a secure future.

Techniques

- Basic body, heads, arms, top hat and ball: blown
- Basic structure: made in marbled pulling technique
- Veil and white ribbon: pulled in ribbon technique

Techniken

- Grundkörper, Köpfe, Arme, Zylinder und Kugel geblasen
- Grundform marmoriert gezogen
- Schleier und weisses Band in Bändertechnik gezogen

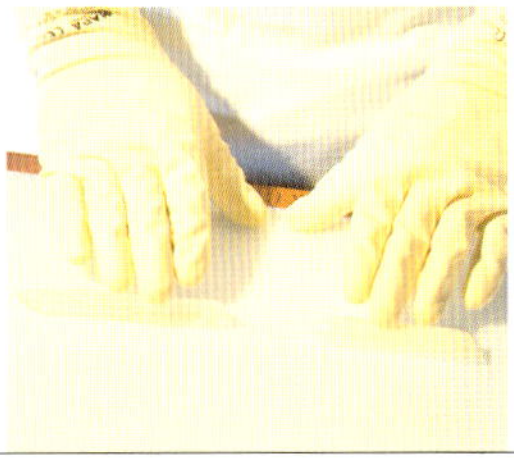

Aus weißem und klarem Zucker gleichmäßige Wülste modellieren

Model even shapes from white and clear sugar

1

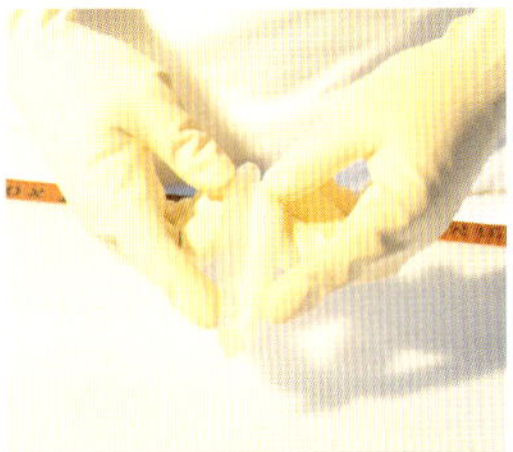

Zusammensetzen

Put them together

2

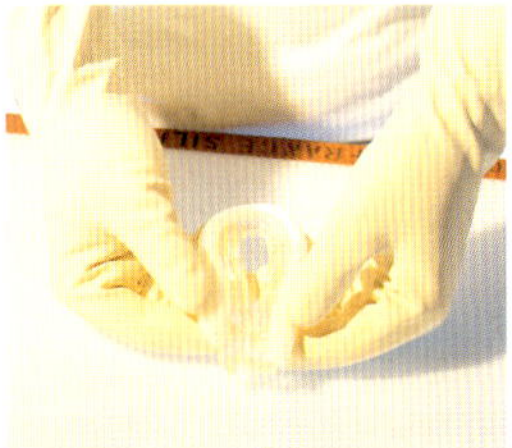

Ziehen und zusammenlegen

Pull and fold together

3

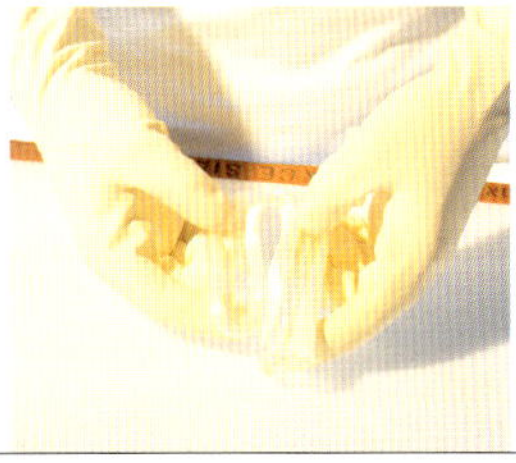

Den Vorgang wiederholen ...

Repeat this process ...

4

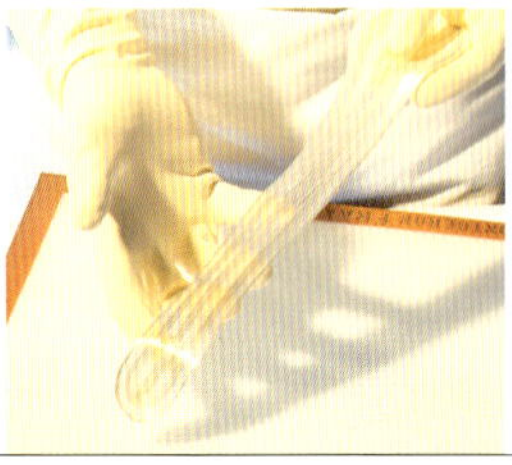

5

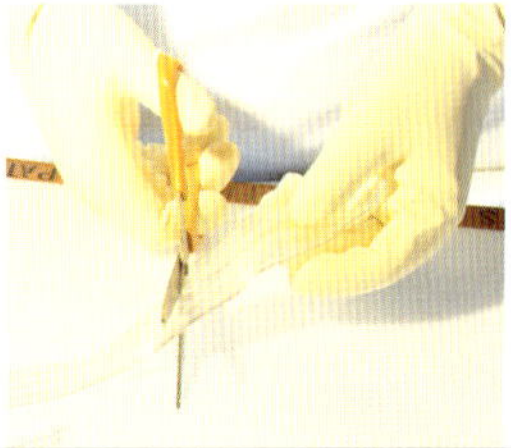

5

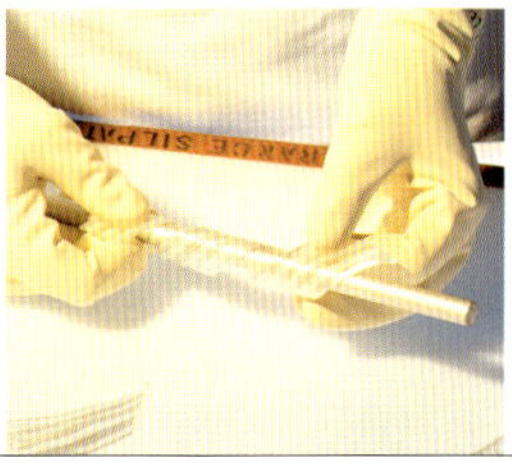

7

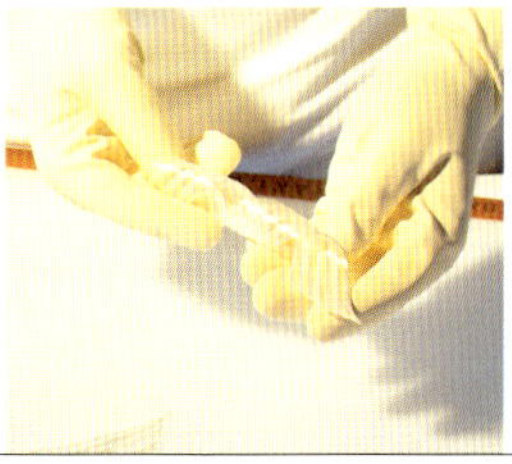

8

... bis ein dünnes Band entsteht

... until you have a thin ribbon

Mit einer Schere auf die gewünschte Länge schneiden

Use a pair of scissors to cut it to the required length

Locker über Stab wickeln

Loosely wind it around the stick

Fertiges Band

The completed ribbon

Making the parts

First of all, roughly pull the base slab from blue and clear sugar mixed with metallic silver powder and then leave to cool down.

Blow the ball in two colours, making it quite stable; then blow the basic body for the couple, the two heads and the arms. Blow the top hat from black sugar and model the rim around it.

Use ribbon technique to make the veil and the ribbon (see stages).

Herstellung

Zuerst die Grundplatte aus blauem und klarem Zucker, welcher mit Silbermetallicpulver vermischt wurde, grob ziehen und erkalten lassen.

Die zweifarbig geblasene stabile Kugel herstellen, dann den Grundkörper für das Paar, die zwei Köpfe und die Arme blasen. Den Zylinder aus schwarzem Zucker blasen und die Krempe modellieren.

Den Schleier und das Band in Bandtechnik herstellen (siehe Stepps).

Putting it all together

Start by placing the ball onto the base slab, then attach the body of the couple to the ball and attach the heads and arms to the body so they look like two people.

Now fix the veil and top hat to the heads and finally the ribbon on the base plate.

Zusammensetzung

Zuerst die Kugel auf der Grundplatte anbringen, danach den Körper des Paars auf der Kugel befestigen und dann die Köpfe und Arme so auf dem Körper platzieren, dass aus dem einen Körper zwei Personen werden.

Schleier und Zylinder auf den Köpfen anbringen und zu guter Letzt das Band auf der Grundplatte befestigen.

Goldener Herbst

Golden Autumn

Hier ist es die Kastanie, auf die ich besonders stolz bin. Sie war ein Element meines Schaustücks zum Vorentscheid zur Weltmeisterschaft gewesen. Der Fasan ist für mich eines der herbstlichen Tiere im Walde.

Here's an old chestnut of which I am particularly proud. It was an element in my showpiece for the preliminary selection in the run up to the world championship. For me, pheasants are wood animals which I associate with autumn.

Techniques

Basic body and chestnut: blown

Base slab: cast in relief with bronze powder

Rock sugar

Leaves: pulled and moulded

Branch: pulled

For colouring use an airbrush and gold dust

Techniken

Grundkörper und Kastanie geblasen

Grundplatte reliefartig gegossen mit Bronzepulver

Felsenzucker

Blätter gezogen und gestempelt

Ast gezogen

Geschminkt mit Airbrush und Goldstaub

Herstellung

Grundplatten und Aufbau herstellen (siehe Stepps).

Ast aus braunem Zucker ziehen. Blätter aus gelbem Zucker ziehen und stempeln. Grün airbrushen.

Für die Kastanie zuerst eine kleine weiße Kugel blasen und braun schminken, so dass ein weißer Fleck in der Mitte bleibt. Eine zweite, etwas größere gelbe Kugel blasen, in der Mitte mit einem heißen Messer zerteilen, die Stacheln aufbringen und grün und braun gesprenkelt schminken.

Felsenzucker herstellen und in passende Größen zerteilen.

Für den Fasan den Grundkörper aus gelbem Zucker blasen und rot schminken. Die Halsfedern in Schwarz und Gelb ziehen, den Bart auftupfen und dabei dünne Fäden herausziehen. Bart rot airbrushen. Augen in Blau ziehen und schwarz aufmalen.

Schnabel in Orange modellieren. Die Kopffedern des Goldfasans aus Spinnzucker ansetzen.

Die Flügel in Bändertechnik herausziehen, passend modellieren und rot färben. Federn aus gelbem, blauem, braunem und schwarzem Zucker ziehen. Die Ränder der blauen Federn mit einer Schere einschneiden. Wenn der Fasan auf seinem Ast sitzt, Federn direkt ansetzen.

Making the parts

Make the base slabs and basic structure (see stages).

Pull the branch using brown sugar. Pull and mould the leaves from yellow sugar. Apply green colour by airbrush.

To make the chestnut, first blow a small white ball and colour it brown, but leaving a white patch in the middle. Then blow a second yellow ball, which should be slightly larger, separate it in the middle with a hot knife, apply the spikes and then colour in green and brown speckles.

Make Rock sugar and cut it down to appropriately sized bits.

To make the pheasant, blow the basic body from yellow sugar and airbrush it red. Pull the feathers around the neck in black and yellow, dab on the beard and pull out thin threads. Colour the beard red using the airbrush. Pull the eyes from blue sugar and paint on the black markings.

Model the beak in orange sugar. Attach the pheasant's head feathers, which are made from spin sugar.

Use ribbon technique to pull the wings, model the right shape and apply red colour. Pull the feathers from yellow, blue, brown and black sugar. Use a pair of scissors to make cuts into the edges of the blue feathers. After you have placed the pheasant onto its branch you can attach the feathers directly.

1

2

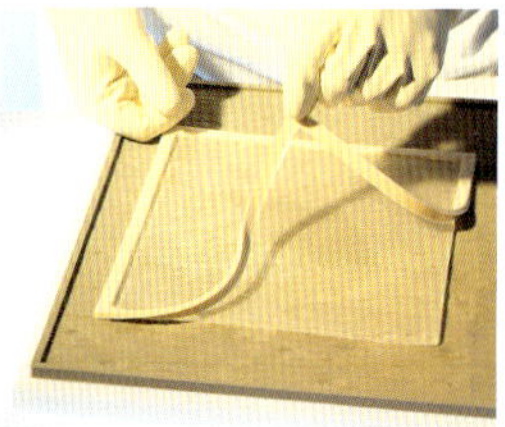

3

4

Silikonrahmen auf Reliefmatte auflegen

Place the silicon frame onto the relief mat

5

Platte mit einem Heißluftföhn gleichmäßig erwärmen

Heat up the slab evenly with a hot air fan

Zucker in Silikonrahmen einfüllen

Fill the sugar into the silicon frames

6

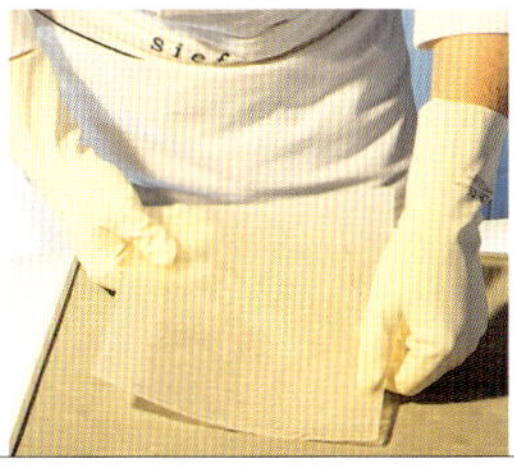

Platte biegen

Bend the slab

Sobald erkaltet, ausformen

When it has set, take it out of the forms

7

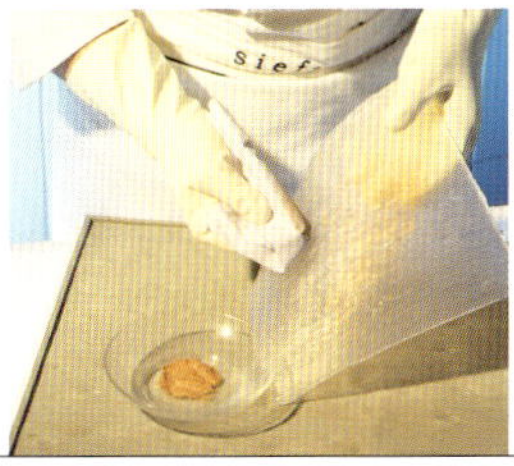

Mit Bronzepulver abreiben

Colour it by rubbing bronze powder into it

Gegossene Platte

The cast slab

8

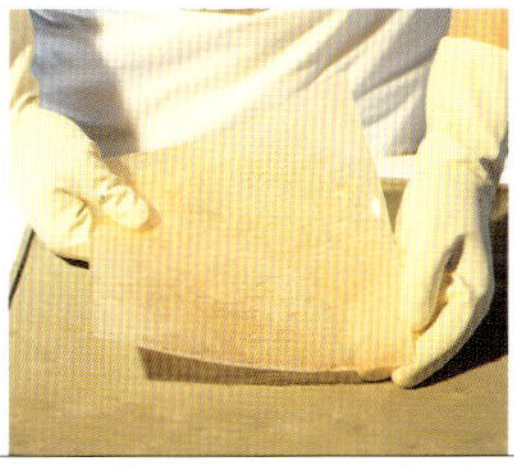

Fertige Grundplatte

The completed base slab

Putting it all together

Join the base slabs together. Attach the branch and place the pheasant on it. Fix the wings to the pheasant; set the chestnut in its shell and join the chestnut leaf together. Decorate everything, including the rock sugar.

Zusammensetzung

Grundplatten zusammenbauen. Ast ansetzen. Fasan aufsetzen. Flügel am Fasan anbringen. Kastanie in die Schale setzen und das Kastanienblatt zusammensetzen. Alles, auch den Felsenzucker, dekorativ anbringen.

Michelstädter Weihnachtsmarkt

Christmas Market of Michelstadt

Ohne Weihnachten könnten wir Konditoren nicht überleben, und für unsere wichtigste Jahreszeit sollte man auch ein Schaustück in petto haben um zu zeigen, dass sich hinter diesem Schaufenster ein kunsthandwerklich produzierendes Gewerbe befindet.

Without Christmas, we confectioners would not survive, and for this most important time of the year we should always have a showpiece ready in order to demonstrate that there is an artistic profession going on behind those shop windows.

Techniques

- Trees and base plates and pedestal: cast
- Ribbons: pulling technique
- Blossom: pulled and moulded
- Balls and icicles: blown
- Candles: blown in three colours and twisted
- Fill in the spacers in granulated sugar with a marbled effect
- Make the ice flowers by dipping
- Use pulling and cutting to make the stamens of the flowers
- Flames of the candles: pulled in two colours
- Wicks for the candles: modelled

Techniken

- Bäume und Grundplatten und Podest gegossen
- Bänder gezogen
- Blüte gezogen und gestempelt
- Kugeln und Eiszapfen geblasen
- Kerzen dreifarbig gedreht geblasen
- Abstandshalter in Kristallzucker marmoriert ausgegossen
- Eisblumen getaucht
- Blütenstempel gezogen und geschnitten
- Flamme der Kerzen zweifarbig gezogen
- Kerzendochte modelliert

Herstellung

Grundplatten, Abstandshalter und Tannenbäume grün und gold-metallic marmoriert gießen. Zum Auflockern der Bodenplatte grün marmorierten Zucker in Kristallzucker ausgießen, wenn er anfängt stabil zu werden, leicht zusammenknüllen und schnell in gewünschter Form abkühlen. Mehrere pastell lilafarbene Kugeln blasen. Die Eisblumen in verschiedenen Größen herstellen (siehe Stepps). Das Band dunkellila, pastelllila und gelb ziehen und Schleifen formen. Für die Blüte Blätter ziehen und stempeln. Den Blütenstempel aus ausgezogenem gelbem Zucker ziehen und schneiden. Direkt in Form bringen.

Die Eiszapfen aus klarem Zucker blasen. Die Kerzen aus dreifarbig verdrehtem Zucker blasen. Die Kerzendochte modellieren, die Flammen der Kerzen aus gelb-rotem Zucker ziehen und in sich verdrehen.

Making the parts

Cast the base slabs, spacers and Christmas trees in green and metallic gold, with a marbled effect. In order to add extra interest to the base slab, cast green marbled sugar in granulated sugar and when it starts to set, crunch it together a little and quickly cool down in the required shape. Blow several balls in a pastel purple colour. Make the ice flowers in different sizes (see stages). Pull the ribbon in dark purple, pastel purple and yellow and form the bows. To make the blossom, pull and mould the leaves. Pull the stamens from pulled-out yellow sugar and cut into shape. Apply directly to the flower.

Blow the icicles from clear sugar. Blow the candles from twisted sugar in three colours. Model the wicks for the candles, pull the flames of the candles from yellow-red sugar and twist them inwards.

1

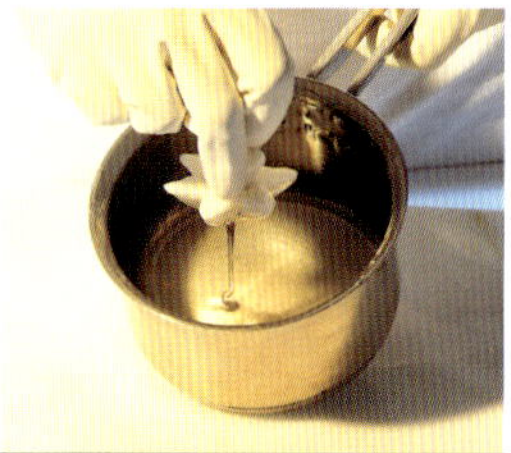
2

3

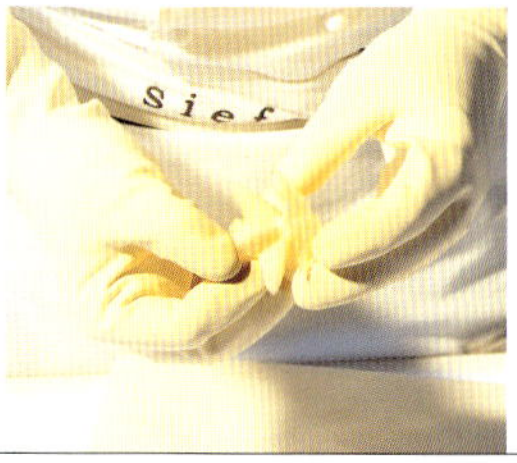
4

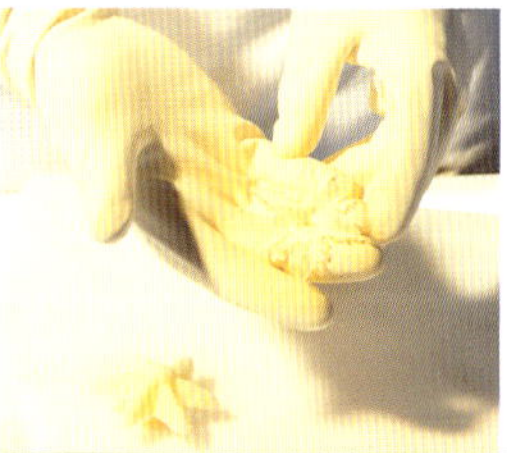
5

Silikonstempel in aufgelösten Zucker tauchen

Dip the silicon mould into dissolved sugar

Etwas abtropfen lassen

Allow any excess to drip off

Mit Kältespray stabilisieren

Use a cooling spray to stabilise

Vorsichtig abmodellieren

Carefully model into shape

Fertig gestempelte Zuckerblüte

The complete moulded sugar blossom

Putting it all together

Join the base plate with the spacer. Place the Christmas trees on the top slab with the candles in front. Attach the icicles. Make up the blossom from the stamens and leaves and fix in front of the candles. Attach the bow. Place the green abstract sculpture on the lower base slab. Arrange the balls and ice flowers decoratively over the entire showpiece. Finally, attach the wicks and flames to the candles.

Zusammensetzung

Grundplatte mit dem Abstandshalter zusammensetzen. Die Tannenbäume auf die obere Platte setzen. Kerzen davorstellen. Eiszapfen anbringen. Die Blüte mit Stempel und Blütenblättern zusammensetzen und vor den Kerzen fixieren. Die Schleife ansetzen. Grüne abstrakte Skulptur unten auf die Bodenplatte ansetzen. Die Kugeln und die Eisblumen dekorativ auf dem gesamten Schaustück arrangieren. Zum Schluss die Dochte und die Flammen auf die Kerzen ansetzen.

ACKNOWLEDGEMENTS

What would a book be without all the people involved in the process?

Many thanks for the warm words of appreciation from my very dear colleagues in the catering industry from all over the world. I am very proud to be honoured with such friends.

Special thanks go to Matthias Hoffmann, the photographer of the book. Without his wonderful pictures, it would have just been a collection of recipes. His creative approach and unerring judgement helped me along the way quite a few times, even when he just encouraged me to try again the next day. His patience in standing by while I develop new creativity is admirable.

Many thanks also to Bruni Fetscher, my contact at the Matthaes Verlag publishers.

And now I would like to express a big thank you to my family, without whom all this would not have been possible. Thank you Astrid, Isabel, Karin, Leon and Wilhelm for your help (in alphabetical order).

My sister Astrid, who is my partner in my parents' business, has always supported me with advice and help, but also with her uncompromising criticism.

My wife Isabel, who won the title Pastry Cook of the Year 2003, naturally contributed her professional expertise. More important for me than her professional competence was her ability to renew my enthusiasm.

My mother Karin, without whom I would not be what I am today and who built up our patisserie shop together with my father.

My son Leon has left his own special imprint on the book. Some of the work would certainly have had a different outcome if he had not been in my thoughts. Thank you for your smile.

My father Wilhelm, who perhaps left the deepest imprints on me. He has always given me enough space and thereby has awakened my creativity and love for this profession – which is surprising because I had never wanted to become a pastry cook. But that's how I became what my father is – a pastry cook.

I would also like to mention my grandmother Cäcilie, who unfortunately has passed away. She was one of the most important persons in my life. I am sure that I have my love and devotion from her.

There are many other people who accompany me on my path. I would like to name but a few: one is Monsieur Biecher, a Frenchman, whom I met by chance in our Café and who later took me on a guided tour around Paris. In doing so, he awakened my love for France. Without him, I am sure I would not have had the courage to apply to the best houses in France and to work there.

I also like to mention Mr. Pfund, the expert in working with sugar. This field of patisserie is definitely the reason why today I am a pastry cook through and through.

An important companion on the path was Manfred Bacher. He persuaded me to take part in the World Championship again.

And last but not least, I would like to mention Francis Cardin, without whom the German patisserie craft would not be where it is today.

Many thanks also to all the others I have not mentioned by name. Everybody who helped me along the path is important.

DANK DES AUTORS

Was wäre ein Buch ohne die Menschen, die es begleiten

Vielen Dank für die lieben Grußworte meiner hoch geschätzten Kollegen aus Küche und Keller, die in der ganzen Welt zu Hause sind. Ich bin sehr stolz darauf, solche Freunde zu haben.

Ein besonderer Dank gilt Matthias Hoffmann, dem Fotografen des Buchs. Ohne seine wunderschönen Bilder wäre es nur eine Sammlung von Rezepten geworden. Seine Kreativität und sein unumstößlicher Blick zeigten mir so manches Mal den richtigen Weg. Und sei es nur, dass er mich ermutigte, es am nächsten Tag nochmals zu probieren. Seine Geduld, wenn ich während der Arbeit neue Kreativität entwickle, ist bewundernswert.

Mein Dank gilt natürlich auch Bruni Fetscher, meiner Ansprechpartnerin beim Matthaes Verlag.

So, nun möchte ich mich aber bei meiner Familie bedanken, ohne die alles nicht möglich gewesen wäre. Danke Astrid, Isabel, Karin, Leon und Wilhelm für eure Hilfe (in alphabetischer Reihenfolge).

Meine Schwester Astrid, meine Partnerin im Betrieb, hat mir immer mit Rat und Tat, aber auch als Kritikerin zur Seite gestanden.

Meine Frau Isabel, „Konditorin des Jahres 2003", hat sich natürlich auch fachlich eingebracht. Viel bedeutender als ihre Fachkompetenz ist für mich aber, dass ich bei ihr meine Batterie immer wieder aufladen konnte.

Meine Mutter Karin, ohne die ich nicht das wäre, was ich heute bin, und die mit meinem Vater zusammen unsere Konditorei aufgebaut hat.

Mein Sohn Leon hat das Buch in ganz besonderer Art geprägt. Manche Arbeit wäre sicherlich anders ausgefallen, wenn er nicht in meinen Gedanken gewesen wäre. Danke für dein Lächeln.

Mein Vater Wilhelm hat mich vielleicht am meisten geprägt. Er gab mir stets genügend Freiraum und hat so meine Kreativität und Liebe zum Beruf geweckt, denn eigentlich wollte ich nie Konditor werden. Aber so wurde ich das, was auch mein Vater ist – Konditor.

Erwähnen möchte ich auch meine Großmutter Cäcilie, die leider nicht mehr lebt. Sie war eine der wichtigsten Personen meines Lebens. Von ihr habe ich viel Liebe und Hingabe erfahren.

Es gibt viele weitere Menschen, die meinen Weg begleiteten. Einige möchte ich hier stellvertretend nennen: Da ist zum Beispiel Herr Biecher, ein Franzose, den ich zufällig bei uns im Café kennen lernte und der mich später in Paris herumführte. Er weckte so meine Liebe zu Frankreich. Ohne ihn hätte mir bestimmt der Mut gefehlt, mich in Frankreichs besten Häusern zu bewerben und dort auch zu arbeiten.

Gerne erwähne ich auch Herrn Pfund, den Fachmann in Sachen Zuckerarbeiten. Dieses Gebiet der Konditorei war definitiv der Grund, warum ich heute mit Leib und Seele Konditor bin.

Ein wichtiger Wegbegleiter war Manfred Bacher für mich. Er hat mich damals dazu überredet, nochmals an der Weltmeisterschaft teilzunehmen.

Last, not least möchte ich Françis Cardin nennen, ohne den die deutsche Konditorei nicht so weit gekommen wäre, wie sie es heute ist.

Danke auch an all die, die ich nicht erwähnt habe. Jeder, der meinem Weg begleitete, ist wichtig.

BERND SIEFERT ...

... und seine Familie

... and his family

Bernd Siefert, Jahrgang 67, ist Konditor und Patissier aus Passion. Viele seiner süßen Versuchungen wurden mit „Gold" gekürt, Titel wie „Deutscher Meister", „Vize-Weltcup-Sieger" sowie „Weltmeister der Konditoren" sind dem Weltenbummler mit Wurzeln im Odenwald verliehen worden. Wenn Filmstars, Modezaren oder Scheichs exquisite Desserts wünschen, ist Bernd Siefert gefragt. Aber auch Rundfunk und Fernsehen klopfen regelmäßig an. Berater für exklusive Marken der süßen Branche, Referent an Fachschulen, Foodstylist sowie Betreiber des familieneigenen Cafés sind nur ein kleiner Auszug seiner vielfältigen Betätigungen.

Born in 1967, Bernd Siefert is a pastry chef and confectioner by passion. Many of his sweet temptations have gained gold awards. This globetrotter, with his rootes in the Odenwald region of Germany, has won titles such as German Champion, World Cup Vice-Champion, as well as World Pastry Champion. When film stars, fashion gurus and sheikhs call for exquisite desserts, they often ask for Bernd Siefert. Other regular callers are broadcasting and television companies. Consultant for exclusive brands in the sweets industry, lecturer at Further Education colleges, food stylist, as well as manager of his own family-owned café: these are just a few of his many attributes.

Matthias Hoffmann

Die Arbeiten von Matthias Hoffmann, Food-Fotograf mit langjähriger Erfahrung, wurde vielfach ausgezeichnet. Neben Industrie und Werbung arbeitet er regelmäßig für Zeitschriften- und Buchverlage.

Matthias Hoffmann, a food photographer with many years of experience, was awarded several prizes for his work. Besides industry and advertising agencies, he is working for book and magazine publishers on a regular basis.

Impressum

ISBN 3-87515-101-1

Übersetzung: DDDienst, Gerlingen
Fotografie: Matthias Hoffmann, Delmenhorst
Grafische Gestaltung und Satz: Atelier Krohmer, Dettingen/Erms

Imprint

ISBN 3-87515-101-1

Translation: DDDienst, Gerlingen
Photography: Matthias Hoffmann, Delmenhorst
Graphic Design and Typography: Atelier Krohmer, Dettingen/Erms